Also By M. William Phelps

HIGHEST PRAISE FOR M. WILLIAM PHELPS

"M. William Phelps dares to tread where few others will: into the mind of a killer."
—**TV Rage**

THE KILLING KIND

"In this true crime book, Phelps focuses on unrepentant killer Danny Hembree . . . [who] seizes the chance to take center stage with lurid confessions of a decades-long career of violent robbery, assault, rape, and murder. . . . Fans of the author's Discovery TV series, *Dark Minds*, will be rewarded."
—**Publishers Weekly**

OBSESSED

"True-crime junkies will be sated by the latest thriller from Phelps, which focuses on a fatal love triangle that definitely proved to be stranger than fiction. The police work undertaken to solve the case is recounted with the right amount of detail, and readers will be rewarded with shocking television-worthy twists in a story with inherent drama."
—**Publishers Weekly**

BAD GIRLS

"Fascinating, gripping . . . Phelps's sharp investigative skills and questioning mind resonate. Whether or not you agree with the author's suspicions that an innocent is behind bars, you won't regret going along for the ride with such an accomplished reporter."
—**Sue Russell**

NEVER SEE THEM AGAIN

"This riveting book examines one of the most horrific murders in recent American history."
—**New York Post**

"Phelps clearly shows how the ugliest crimes can take place in the quietest of suburbs."
—**Library Journal**

"Thoroughly reported . . . the book is primarily a police procedural, but it is also a tribute to the four murder victims."
—**Kirkus Reviews**

"M. William Phelps is the rising star of the nonfiction crime genre, and his true tales of murder are scary-as-hell thrill rides into the dark heart of the inhuman condition."
—**Douglas Clegg**

LETHAL GUARDIAN

"An intense roller-coaster of a crime story . . . complex, with twists and turns worthy of any great detective mystery . . . reads more like a novel than your standard non-fiction crime book."
—**Steve Jackson**

PERFECT POISON

"True crime at its best—compelling, gripping, an edge-of-the-seat thriller. Phelps packs wallops of delight with his skillful ability to narrate a suspenseful story."
—**Harvey Rachlin**

"A compelling account of terror . . . the author dedicates himself to unmasking the psychopath with facts, insight and the other proven methods of journalistic leg work."
—**Lowell Cauffiel**

TO LOVE
AND
TO KILL

M. WILLIAM
PHELPS

PINNACLE BOOKS
Kensington Publishing Corp.
http://www.kensingtonbooks.com

PINNACLE BOOKS are published by

Kensington Publishing Corp.
119 West 40th Street
New York, NY 10018

Copyright © 2015 by M. William Phelps

All Kensington Titles, Imprints, and Distributed Lines are available at special quantity discounts for bulk purchases for sales promotions, premiums, fund-raising, and educational or institutional use. Special book excerpts or customized printings can also be created to fit specific needs. For details, write or phone the office of the Kensington special sales manager: Kensington Publishing Corp., 119 West 40th Street, New York, NY 10018, attn: Special Sales Department, Phone: 1-800-221-2647.

Pinnacle and the P logo Reg. U.S. Pat. & TM Off.

ISBN-13: 978-0-7860-3499-4
ISBN-10: 0-7860-3499-8
First Kensington Mass Market Edition: September 2015

eISBN-13: 978-0-7860-3500-7
eISBN-10: 0-7860-3500-5
First Kensington Electronic Edition: September 2015

10 9 8 7 6 5 4

Printed in the United States of America

For Little Mark, Mark Jr. and Brittany Phelps—
Big Mark would be so proud of you.

*Death is someone you see very clearly
with eyes in the center of your heart:
eyes that see not by reacting to light,
but by reacting to a kind of a chill from
within the marrow of your own life.*

—Thomas Merton,
The Seven Storey Mountain

CHAPTER 1

FOOTSTEPS. THE SOFT, spongy slap of rubber work shoes against the scratched, unwaxed, filthy surface of a tile floor.

One after the other.

Pitter-patter.

Squeak, squeak, squeak.

Waitresses take perhaps thousands of steps during a shift. Always coming and going, while certain obnoxious patrons bark orders, make crass comments and groundless, tasteless judgments, before getting up and leaving squat for a tip.

The South is full of roadside diners serving up high cholesterol and diabetes—all you have to do is walk in, sit down in a booth sporting ripped, waxy seats and grimy checkered tablecloths, and the journey into the greasy-spoon experience has begun.

Heather Strong had been a waitress at one of these places for nearly ten years, though she mainly worked the register as a cashier these days. She took to the job because it suited her character—outgoing, loud, always on the move—and put food on the table for her children. In February 2009, Heather, a beautiful, blue-eyed, brown-haired, twenty-six-year-old mother and soon-to-be divorcée, was working at the Petro Truck Stop out on Highway 318 in Reddick, Florida. The

Iron Skillet restaurant inside the Petro was a busy joint. It was one of those just-off-the-freeway pit stops filled with tired, hungry, dirty, foul-mouthed, penny-pinching, smelly men coming in off the road, filing out of their musty Mack trucks, looking for cheap fast-food meals saturated in grease. Heather drew the eyes of most of these men because she was so stunningly gorgeous in a simple American-girl kind of way. She had the figure of a swimsuit model, sure; but that exterior beauty was juxtaposed against an inner abundance of innocence and purity, a warm heart. Still, for anyone who knew Heather, there was no mistaking the fact that this young woman could take care of herself if necessary.

There was also a hidden vulnerability there within Heather's forced smile: You could tell she had struggled in life somewhat. But with the right man by her side (whom she had found just the previous year, but had let go of after getting back with her husband), Heather could find that picket-fence happiness all young women in her shoes longed for.

"What's a hot little thang like you doing in a place like this?" was a common remark Heather endured more times than she could count. She hated it every time. Paid no mind to men who spoke to her disrespectfully like that. She had a job to do. Kids to feed. She was making ends meet. It didn't mean she had to take insults and sexually aggressive comments.

"Give me your check and let's get y'all cashed out?" Heather would snap back. "I ain't got all day."

Heather seemed tired on this day. She'd been having a rough go of things lately, to say the least. Most of those problems stemmed from the relationship with her children's father, her husband, twenty-seven-year-old Joshua "Josh" Fulgham, a rather complicated and volatile man with a past she had recently separated from. Since the breakup, Heather had been living with another man, more out of convenience than love. But that leash Josh had around his wife had not been severed completely. Josh wanted his kids and was afraid Heather would one day take off with them; he promised a nasty custody battle coming down the road. He was also enraged at the fact that Heather was living with a man Josh saw as a danger to his children.

"You seen Heather around?" Heather's boss asked a coworker a day after Valentine's Day, February 15, 2009. It had been a normal day at the Petro: regulars, new customers, broken coffee machine, same dirty dishes coming from the kitchen, stains on the silverware. 'Bout the only thing different was that Heather had not come to work. It was so unlike her not to show up. If there was one thing about Heather Strong, work was first and foremost. She needed the money to support her kids—and that darn husband of hers, he rarely gave her anything to help out, yet always seemed to have the cash to buy "party goods" or go out and have a good time.

"She always called," Heather's boss later explained.

"I haven't seen her," Heather's coworker said.

"Huh," Heather's boss responded. "If you do, tell her to call me."

Heather generally worked the morning shift, although she did sometimes take on a double. On most days, she'd come in and set up the salad bar and then go about her ordinary duties.

She should have been in by now, thought Heather's boss, looking at the clock in her small office, trying to shake a bad feeling that something was terribly wrong.

CHAPTER 2

HEATHER'S FIRST COUSIN, Misty Strong, was at home in Columbus, Mississippi, where Heather grew up and had lived most of her life. Misty, equally as beautiful as Heather, could pass for Heather's identical twin—the two girls looked so much alike.

"Heather was like a sister to me," Misty later said.

A few weeks had gone by and Misty had not heard from her cousin. This was odd. Heather and Misty kept in touch. However streetwise Heather had become over the years, especially while living in Florida, she was green in many ways of the world, Misty knew. It seemed that Heather had only one man most of her life and he had taken her to Florida: Joshua Fulgham. Josh and Heather met in Starkville, Mississippi. Heather was sixteen, waitressing after school at a local restaurant; Joshua, one year older, was a customer. Josh was that tough, rugged, overprotective and overly jealous type. He was well known in the Mississippi town where he grew up as a bruiser and tough, troubled kid. Josh was five feet eight inches tall and weighed about 175 pounds—one of those physiques people might say he was born with, a guy who could eat anything and never gain an ounce. Josh generally wore his hair shortly cropped, but had turned to an entirely shaved head later in life. For Heather, Josh fit the image of a badass she liked so much. Heather felt comfortable around Josh. She felt protected. The two of them hit it off right away on that day inside the restaurant.

From the start, Misty Strong later observed, Josh and Heather had issues. He was rough with her. He liked to manhandle Heather a lot when he wanted his way. The cops were often involved. After meeting, dating and then living together as teens, Heather having a child, with another on the way, Mississippi didn't seem to entice them as it once had. So Josh and Heather made the decision to move to Florida. It was 2004. Josh had potential job prospects in Florida—or so he said. He had family down there. The move felt like a step up. Heather wasn't thrilled at going, moving away from her family in Mississippi, but she thought what the hell, why not give it a try. They could always move back if things didn't work out.

Misty knew with Heather moving away, there was little she could do. Once Heather was gone, in fact, Misty had lost touch with her for a time, and Misty believed it was Josh holding her down, keeping Heather from contacting her family. One more way for Josh to govern over Heather and keep her tied down.

"He was just too controlling," Misty explained. "He didn't want her around any family or anybody that cared about her."

Heather didn't even have her own cell phone or computer back then, during their early days in Florida. She had been totally cut off from everyone back home.

Just the way Josh liked it.

Then, in early 2008, after nearly four years of living with Josh, raising two kids and going through hell and back, Heather showed up in Columbus one day.

"I've finally left him," she told Misty.

"Thank God."

Misty and Heather's grandmother was sick at the time.

She was actually dying. So they bonded over that family crisis. The two women picked up their "sister" relationship from back in the day and stayed in touch daily. Misty kept telling her cousin it was all going to be okay. There was no need to worry about anything. She'd help with the kids. She'd help Heather start over. The key to it was for Heather to stay the hell away from Josh, who was still in Florida. If Heather could do that, she had a chance. Everyone in her family believed this.

There was one day when Misty went to see their grandmother, who was on her last days. When Misty returned, Heather was gone.

And so were her bags.

Damn.

"Josh had . . . brought her back to Florida," Misty later recalled. No one knew it, but he snuck into town, convinced Heather she needed him and drove her back.

Heather had gone willingly, apparently. She wanted to work things out for the kids' sake. That was Heather—always yearning to find that pristine image of the American family unit on the other side of a dark rainbow. What mother, after all, doesn't want her children's father to be a part of their lives? Maybe Josh was changing. He was angry and sometimes violent; but when he was good, he was a nice guy. They got along and loved each other.

Or was Heather locked in that same fantasy that many abused women see in their dreams?

I'll give him just one more chance. He'll change. You'll see.

Things didn't work out for Heather. Josh *didn't* change. So Heather moved out and found someone else to live with in Florida, thinking it would be better for the kids if she stayed in the state this time. The place she found had a computer. Heather now had a cell phone. She and Misty were in contact just about every day, sometimes several times a day.

"Myspace, cell phone, e-mail," Misty said.

But then, suddenly, it stopped. *Boom!* One day Heather

wasn't communicating anymore. Misty and Heather had been talking for months. Heather was saying that Josh had a girlfriend now. He was letting go. Heather had someone new, too. There had been some issues between Heather and Josh's new girlfriend, and Josh sometimes seemed to want to reconcile with Heather, but Heather was saying things were beginning to settle down. They finally had figured out that maybe they just weren't meant to be together. Josh seemed to accept this.

Now Misty was concerned, however. It was late in the day on February 25, 2009, and she had not heard from Heather in well over a week. Misty knew damn well that something was up. It was so unlike Heather not to call or e-mail for this long a period.

So Misty called Heather's brother, Jacob, and asked if he had heard from her.

"No," Jacob said.

"Any idea where she is?"

Jacob responded, "I got a call from [Heather's friend]. She was concerned."

"Concerned? How so?"

"Well, Heather had all her belongings over there at her friend's. Now all of her stuff is gone and she is missing."

"Missing?" Misty answered. She felt her stomach turn. Her body now felt numb. Then that life-will-never-be-the-same-after-today feeling came on all at once. Misty felt it.

"Missing"—the word that no one wants to hear. It sounded so final.

So dangerous.

So deadly.

CHAPTER 3

MISTY KNEW HER cousin well enough. If Heather had gone off on her own, she would have called Misty, sent her a text or e-mail. She would have said where she was going. Even if Heather wanted to skip away under the radar, she would have told Misty.

But maybe not? Perhaps Heather was embarrassed, or she just wanted some downtime, alone?

Misty thought about another possible scenario. Heather had probably gone back to Josh. She didn't want to admit it. She was ashamed. All this breaking up and getting back together. It went back a decade between them. Heather was locked in that revolving-door cycle with the father of her kids. She and Josh, despite fighting and threatening each other, having each other arrested, seemed to always find their way back into the same bed.

Misty thought: *I better call her work.*

Maybe someone there knew something.

Within a few minutes, Misty got Heather's boss on the phone.

"Have you seen her?"

"No."

"How long?"

"Over a week . . . and I'm deeply concerned."

Misty now went back to being seriously worried. That's how these things go. The emotional seesaw effect: Your gut tells you the worst has happened. Your heart tells you to hang on—there's a simple explanation for it all. You go back and forth.

"Go ahead and call the sheriff's department," Heather's boss suggested. It was time someone got law enforcement involved.

"Yeah . . . ," Misty agreed.

Officer Beth Billings from the Marion County Sheriff's Office (MCSO) responded on February 24, 2009, calling Misty in Mississippi. Billings explained she had gotten a report of a missing person and was following up.

"Since February fifteenth," Misty explained to Billings, after the sheriff's deputy asked when the last time she had heard from Heather actually was. "It's unusual not to hear from her. We were keeping in touch daily."

They spoke about Josh next. Misty said Josh had been arrested in January 2009 for threatening Heather and her then-boyfriend. But they'd reconciled, Misty believed. What neither of them knew then was that Heather had apparently dropped the charges against Josh.

"They actually just got married [in December 2008], but had separated," Misty explained, trying to give Billings a bit of background regarding how complicated the relationship had been.

Billings said the MCSO would look into Heather's whereabouts. Yet, she warned Misty that this would not be an easy mystery to solve. Missing person cases involving adults are tough to investigate. Nine times out of ten times, the adult chooses to go missing. She takes off, doesn't tell anyone, moves to another town and starts over. Running is often an easier choice than dealing with the stressors life can sometimes bring. There have been cases of wives returning home from work, husbands doing the same, only to find their spouses gone. Vanished. Nothing afoul. Nothing even missing. But the spouse wanted to start another life, in another town, with another partner, and did not have the guts to say it.

Although Misty and Heather's boss felt different here, Heather was her own person. She had dreams. Goals. No one knew her completely. She kept things to herself.

MCSO SHERIFF'S DEPUTY Beth Billings drove to Lane Road in Reddick, just opposite Orange Lake, where Heather had been shacking up, the sheriff's deputy had been told, with a guy named James[1] Acome, whom Billings described in her report as Heather's "live-in boyfriend."

James had met Heather some years prior, when Heather and Josh first moved into town. They were all friends at one time. James and a junior high school friend of his, Emilia Yera, had actually been part of a group of friends that hung out with Josh and Heather. James had dated Emilia for "a number of years," he later said, "on and off." Emilia was young and attractive: thick, curly, shiny dark black hair, bolstering her Latino heritage against perfectly clear olive skin. Emilia was at one time considering a modeling career. Responsibility caught up to her and she abandoned that plan after she and James had a child together.

The four of them—James, Emilia, Heather and Josh—were tight for a while. They drank. Partied. Watched TV. Went to the movies. Then it was over. Each sort of went his or her separate way, but they still saw each other once in a great while.

---

[1] James Acome went by the name "Jamie." Just about everyone involved in this case called him that. Because there is another man named Jamie in this case, and his name comes up often, I have chosen to use James instead of Jamie when referring to James Acome, even when certain players were quoted as saying "Jamie," I changed it to "James" for clarity.

James was at the house he lived in with Heather when Deputy Billings arrived. After being prompted, he explained that back on February 15, Heather came home from work in a frantic state. It was near 3:30 P.M. Her shift that day wasn't supposed to end until eleven. She was working a double.

"What was wrong with Miss Strong, Mr. Acome?" Billings asked, sizing up James Acome and the inside of the home he and Heather rented. This area of Florida was populated with locals. There were no snowbirds around these parts, the men and women from the North who flew down for the winter. Mostly, the area was run-down trailers, houses in need of makeovers and repairs, swampland, locals looking for work, which was never going to be available, and young kids hanging out, moving from one part of life to the next. People drank around here. They fished in the lake. Hunted frogs and gators. Sat on their porches bullshitting about their neighbors.

"Don't really know for sure," James explained. He had a wiry look to him. Blazing blue eyes, dark brown—nearly black—hair (tightly cropped), James was about five feet ten inches, but thin at 150 pounds. He sweated a lot. He'd had his share of trouble with the law. "She came home and said that she had received an 'emergency telephone call' from Josh while she was at work." James explained to Billings who Joshua Fulgham was and his relationship with Heather.

Deputy Billings felt James knew a bit more about the call, but he was holding back for some reason.

"She didn't say why? Or what Mr. Fulgham wanted?"

"Well . . . she did. She said Josh called to tell her he was taking possession of their two kids because of me."

"You, sir?"

"Yeah. Josh told Heather he was pissed off that I'd had a relationship with a sixteen-year-old girl."

"Okay, well, what did Heather do?"

"I'm not sure. I left right after she came home. I had to

go somewhere. I assumed she'd be here when I got home. We only have one vehicle. There was no way for her to leave." James said that when he got home, he searched the house and noticed some of Heather's belongings, along with the kids', were gone.

"Just a few of the kids' things, and nothing else looked suspicious," James added.

"That's all?"

"No. A few days went by. I didn't hear anything. Then Josh called."

"What did Mr. Fulgham say?" Billings asked.

"He told me to pack my shit and get out of the house. That him and Heather were back together. He was moving back in. He told me not to try and contact Heather *ever* again."

"Did you leave?"

"I waited a day and moved out. I have not returned since today. The electric bill was in my name, so I needed to come back and get that disconnected."

"Anything else?" Billings wanted to know.

That was all James Acome said he could offer.

CHAPTER 4

JOSHUA FULGHAM WAS the first to admit that he was not John Q. Public, briefcase in hand, kissing his wife and children on the cheek every weekday morning, before he headed out the door with a steaming cup of coffee in hand, hopping into his Taurus and heading toward another day at the office. Josh was anything but, actually. Joshua Fulgham was a criminal for years: fraud and larceny and assault on the top of his rap sheet. Yet, as he grew up in the down-home country life of Mississippi, it was a time that was mostly devoid of him getting into serious trouble, he explained to me. This was more or less a period of survival for him as his mother raised his sister and him "on her own" and then unwittingly, and unknowingly, brought a monster into their household.

"For some reason, he liked to beat me," Josh said of his mother's boyfriend. "I don't know why he felt he had to do so, but he did it on a regular basis."

Josh pointed out that he was not talking about your average "spanking," which was maybe popular in other households back then.

"No," Josh said, "that son of a bitch would beat me with his fists like I was a grown man. But I was seven years old."

Josh reckoned this was one reason why "I turned out so tough and mean myself."

Before long, Josh, his mother and sister moved from the Columbus area (where Josh had spent his early youth) to Clarkson, Mississippi. Clarkson had a population then of about three hundred, Josh recalled. It was there that Josh's mother dropped the abuser and met a man who would soon become Josh's stepfather. Josh had fond memories of this man, who took him fishing and taught him how to hunt.

"They had a little girl when I was nine years old," Josh remembered.

The family stayed in Clarkson until 2000. Josh had turned nineteen. It was some years before that, Josh explained, when he "gave up on life." Something happened and, as Josh later put it, he told himself to "fuck it." He then dropped any dreams he had as a child, thus lacking any motivation to move on toward a better life. His grandmother had died suddenly one day. Josh had been "very close" to his "mamau," as he called her. "I just gave up hope for everything," Josh remembered, after losing her. On top of that list was school. Then he started getting into trouble. By the time he was fifteen, Josh recalled, he was already facing an arson charge and had been sent off to a reformatory, the Oakley Training School, in Raymond, Mississippi, a place with a military-style regimen for what the school said was mostly "nonviolent offenders."

That first time in, they sent Josh home after eight weeks because of overcrowding. He wasn't acting up. He had done what he was told. They gave him a chance.

Home, however, without much discipline and no one looking over his shoulder, Josh found more trouble. He had heard from local kids that a house in the neighborhood had a lot of guns. So Josh decided to kick the door open one night and steal the weapons so he could sell them for "drug money." By then, Josh was already caught for booze and dope and was not yet old enough to drive a car.

Needless to say, Josh was sent back to Oakley to complete his program. This time, they said there would be no trouble finding Josh a bed, and overcrowding wouldn't be a problem for him. He had been given an opportunity to prove he could be rehabilitated and had failed. Josh was now facing hard time.

He got out just before turning sixteen. It was on that night of his birthday when Josh and a friend went out to a local restaurant in Mathiston, Mississippi, that Josh sat down and looked up from his meal to see a gorgeous, knockout waitress walking by his table.

Josh took one look. She was perfect in every way. There was chemistry immediately, he recalled.

"Heather," the waitress said her name.

"Hi, Heather . . . I'm Josh."

The boy lit up as though he had never seen a female before.

At the time, Heather wore her hair blond, which contrasted nicely against her striking blue eyes and porcelain skin. She was young, naive, not yet ready to take on a boy with the life experiences Josh had accumulated.

Josh was taken. He couldn't eat.

"I knew I had to have her," Josh remembered. "She was such a pretty girl."

They started dating and it got serious right away. Josh had a girlfriend at the time, whom he was "just crazy about," he said. He'd known her since they were ten years old. "[She] was the love of my life," Josh claimed. But still, there was something about Heather. It was as if they connected on a deeper level—from the first moment, the energy, Josh felt, could not be denied. He had to act on it.

Not long after this, Josh was out drinking one night with friends and happened to get into a fight with a local cop, whom Josh made a point to say later, he "pummeled." That alleged ass-whupping Josh had given to the cop got him tossed back into Oakley, where he stayed for quite some time. With Heather alone on the outside, Josh told her she could always count on his family if she ever needed anything while he was locked up. In fact, according to Josh, Heather took him up on that offer one night when she arrived at Josh's mother's house with her bags. She claimed to have been sexually assaulted by someone she knew and wanted a safe place to stay.

"Of course," Josh's mother said.

Josh was happy about it because it meant he knew where she was. He didn't have to worry about Heather stepping out.

After getting out of Oakley for a third and fourth time, Josh said he realized the way he viewed life was not getting him anywhere. He needed to make changes. He'd gone through a tough time, according to him, leaving that girl-friend he had before Heather, and felt he was giving up the love of his life for the lust he felt for Heather. (Incidentally, this would be a recurring theme in the life and times of Joshua Fulgham. The grass was *always* greener from where Josh saw it.) But when he returned home, with Heather now living at his house, he felt as though he was lucky to have her. Heather was good-hearted; she had a tender soul. They got along great. A year and a half went by, Josh had gotten a job building and setting up trailer homes while Heather—both of them now considered adults, eighteen years old and over—was now pregnant with their first child.

Another problem entered their lives, however. As Heather was about to give birth to a daughter, whom they would call Carol-Lynn (pseudonym), Josh said he was then introduced to what become the second love of his life.

Crystal meth.

"From the very first time I did it," Josh said years later, "that is all I cared about and worked for."

Even after Carol-Lynn was born, a time when Josh tried desperately to stop doing the drug, he continued.

Afterward, though, Josh got a job working on a riverboat, "making good money." He and Heather were still living at his mom's. Soon Josh was able to purchase a home and he had even stayed away from the meth.

This fleeting moment of normalcy, however, didn't last. Within a short period, he was back not only doing the drug, but hanging out with people who were cooking it. Now Josh's addiction went from zero to one thousand. He was so strung out, Josh took some time off to try and purify his body by going cold turkey. That week turned into two weeks. He was fired from his job. He and Heather now had nothing.

So Josh decided to go into his own business.

Yet, instead of buying meth and then selling it for a profit, Josh Fulgham decided he was going into the business of cooking up batches of the drug himself.

CHAPTER 5

DEPUTY BETH BILLINGS needed to track down Josh Fulgham and see what that supposed last call between him and Heather at her work was all about. If it had sparked some sort of reaction from Heather to the point where she packed her bags and took off, it must have been pretty heavy. In addition, maybe Josh knew where she had run off to.

Josh was at a friend's house, where he had been staying. Billings found him and asked if he didn't mind answering a few questions about his wife, Heather.

"Not at all," Josh said. He seemed sincerely interested in what was going on. Cops don't show up every day asking about your soon-to-be ex-spouse.

"When did you last speak to Miss Strong?"

Josh had difficulty recalling the exact date and time, but he decided it must have been back on February 15. "Yeah, I know it was now . . . she called *me*. She wanted me to meet her at Petro, where she works out on the 318."

"Did you go to meet her?"

"I did. I did, yes. It was, oh, I don't know, somewhere around nine, nine-fifteen that night."

"What did she want?"

Josh explained that Heather appeared flustered. There

was something going on with her that she would not talk about. "She told me she 'needed time to clear her head' . . . and asked if I could take our children." Josh further added, "She had two suitcases with her. She was going somewhere, but she wouldn't share where with me."

"Did she say anything else?"

"I'm not sure when she was set to return, because she wouldn't tell me."

"Any idea where she is now?"

Josh scratched his bald head. He took a breath. "I do. I think she's with this older dude. I only know him as Wayne. He's helped her with money in the past." Josh said he had no idea where Wayne lived or how to get hold of him.

Billings told Josh to call the MCSO if he remembered anything else, or if he heard from Heather.

He said no problem.

LITTLE JOE'S TRAILER Park was a sparsely spread-out mobile home community on the 13200 block of Jacksonville Road in Citra. From outward appearances, it looked as though the office to Joe's—with a mud-stained and rusted steel mailbox out front, a small wicker bench seat, discolored from dirt and wear, a nearly unreadable sign hanging from a rotting wooden pole—had been abandoned long ago. The beige paint on the building itself was faded, the rust red trim cracking and in need of lots of TLC. In back of that office were mobile homes, those, too, a bit shoddily kept, brush and trees overgrown and camouflaging nearly all of the homes.

Beth Billings found the landlord and had a conversation about one particular trailer, where Heather had lived recently. Billings wanted to know about any movement or people at the mobile home recently. Had the landlord seen anyone?

"Nope," she said. "I ain't seen nobody there since two

weeks ago now. But about four or five days ago, Mr. Fulgham, he called me and, after stating he was Miss Strong's 'ex-husband,' asked if he could get into Miss Strong's trailer."

"Did he say why?"

"Yup. Said he wanted to get the children's clothes and things."

"What'd you tell him?"

"I told him no."

Beyond that, the landlord said she knew nothing more.

And so Beth Billings went on her way to the only other place she knew might provide some information about where Heather had run off to, perhaps.

CHAPTER 6

THE FIRST BIT of information raising the eyebrows of Beth Billings as she searched for Heather Strong—a true missing person case or a woman who had taken off on her own accord—came from a visit to Heather's workplace, the Iron Skillet restaurant inside the Petro center. Billings found the assistant manager and pulled her aside, hoping to clear up a gut instinct the deputy had that Heather had not gone off on her own—that there was more to her disappearance than a woman scared of something, running from her problems.

"She took an 'emergency phone call' on February fifteenth," the Iron Skillet manager explained to Billings. "I knew it was from Joshua Fulgham, her ex, because she told me. It was short. When she got off the phone, Heather was visibly upset."

But Mr. Fulgham said Heather had called him*?* Beth Billings knew.

"Did she say what Mr. Fulgham said to her?"

"No, she didn't."

As they talked, Billings got the impression that this type of stressful phone call was not at all out of the norm for Heather Strong.

"She's had ongoing problems with him," the manager

explained. "It was not unusual for her to get a phone call and for her to be upset after speaking with him."

The manager went on to describe how the last time she saw Heather was at 3:00 P.M. that day, when Heather's shift ended. This made sense with what James Acome had reported: Heather had shown up at the house at three-thirty, although James had it wrong that Heather was working a double; she was not. "She was supposed to return at eight A.M. the following morning, but never showed up and never called. That is very unusual for Heather. She generally shows up, or if not, she *always* calls in."

"Anything else you can think of, ma'am?"

"Here's the thing," the manager said, "Heather never picked up her paycheck."

So she left town, as Joshua Fulgham thought, without any money?

This scenario didn't make much sense to the deputy. Heather would surely want as much money as possible with her if she had run away.

"Is there any other way for her to get that money?"

"Well, yes, now that I think of it. She could still access the money from her bank without actually having the paper check. Our bookkeeper would be the only one who could tell you whether she withdrew that money or not."

Employees had special debit cards given to them by the company so they could withdraw their paycheck at any time after it was deposited into their account.

"Can I talk to her?"

"She'll be here tomorrow morning at eight."

Beth Billings headed back to the sheriff's office in Ocala to file her report and issue a BOLO (be on the lookout) order. Then she called Misty Strong to report back what she had found out. It was Misty, after all, who had initiated the search.

"Call us if you have any additional concerns," Billings

told Misty after the deputy explained to Heather's cousin all she could. "Right now, there's not much more we can do."

By March 2, 2009, the MCSO was growing increasingly concerned about the well-being of Heather Strong. Heather's family kept up the pressure on the sheriff's office. They were firm in their belief that Heather had not left town by her own volition. When an investigator contacted the bookkeeper from the Iron Skillet on that following morning, additional unease emerged as the MCSO learned that Heather's account had been accessed back on February 19, but not at any time after that date. Her most recent paycheck funds had not been withdrawn. Heather had never gone back to the restaurant to pick up her last paycheck and did not withdraw those funds from the bank. Like a lot of people, Heather lived paycheck to paycheck. There was no way, family members told the MCSO, that she would have left town and not contacted family or friends, and not cashed or accessed her last paycheck. But beyond all of that, Heather would have never left town without her children.

Her children were her life.

With all of that, Heather's case went from missing to "missing and endangered."

It was a simple move by several curious and experienced cops that would change this entire investigation.

CHAPTER 7

AFTER A FEW additional weeks of not hearing anything from Heather, MCSO deputy Beth Billings took another ride over to the Iron Skillet, on March 18, after hearing that the Petro manager had more information regarding that final conversation she'd had with Heather.

Brenda Smith, Heather's boss, was concerned about her friend, coworker and employee as she thought about the circumstances surrounding Heather's disappearance back on February 15. Heather had taken two calls on that day, Brenda told Billings. She was very upset. When the second call came in, Brenda went out into the restaurant and found Heather.

"Come back into the office. You have a call . . . sounds urgent." Brenda had no idea who was calling, but only knew that it was a male's voice she did not recognize.

When Heather and Brenda returned to the office, the line was dead.

"What's going on, Heather?" Brenda asked. "Do you think something is wrong with the kids?"

"Well, I'm going to call."

Brenda waited. She heard Heather call Joshua Fulgham and ask, "Are the kids okay?" Then Brenda walked out of the office to give Heather some privacy.

Heather finished her phone conversation and soon went

back to her station, where she was prepping the salad bar. Brenda walked over to see if things were okay.

She noticed Heather was crying.

"Heather . . . are the kids okay?"

"It's Josh," Heather said through tears.

Brenda left it there. It was the last time she spoke to Heather—because Heather had left work shortly after that conversation and never came back.

CHAPTER 8

SCARS—EMOTIONAL OR otherwise—were something Heather Strong had a lot of experience with, especially after Josh Fulgham came into the picture. Their relationship, almost from the time they met as teenagers, was punctuated with problems, mainly beset by Josh's inability to contain his violent tendencies.

"It was a big party at my house every day," Josh explained to me. He had lost his job on that riverboat for not showing up. Meth had become Josh's number one priority in life.

"I got Heather started using the drug," Josh claimed. "That was when things started really going downhill for us."

You think!

Josh said after they began using methamphetamine together, "I became abusive." He also confessed to stepping out on Heather. Life had not so much turned into one big party than it had gone from two unfettered kids, not realizing what they were getting themselves into, to two jaded adults, now trying to figure out life. One of them had a savage addiction to a drug that showed no mercy—all with kids now depending on them.

Meth does not discriminate or care who it brings down; it is a drug that has such a strong withdrawal that doing it is seemingly the only remedy for the user. As the cliché claims, it is a vicious cycle once the addict is caught up within it. We've all seen those before-and-after photos of meth addicts aging decades inside of a few years of chronic use.

Using meth—even once—can easily be considered a death sentence.

Not long after Heather gave birth to their first child, they agreed it would be best for Heather to go live with her grandmother. Josh and Heather were toxic together; maybe they (and their child) had a chance if apart.

"But I was still going over to her grandmother's, visiting and bringing drugs," Josh explained.

The drugs kept them together and also having sex. Soon Heather was pregnant with their second child.

"I am not sure," Josh said years later, "that one is mine." (Josh's proof is only that, according to how he feels, the child does not look like him.)

While Heather was pregnant this second time, Josh's mother, Judy Chandler, moved to Florida. Josh said it was around then that he "became a bum," although it's hard to argue that before then he was anything else.

What Josh meant was that he had no place to call his own at that time. He was simply bouncing around, all doped up, staying with friends and an occasional night sleepover with Heather, when she decided to put up with him.

"I hooked up with this guy who was in the meth game and started staying with him, inside an old school bus."

According to only to Josh, Heather continued to use meth, this after they started not seeing each other regularly. Josh soon met another woman, he said, which was "more lust, not love." The woman was thirty-two, and Josh twenty-one at the time. She loved him, he claimed, but he had no feelings for her other than as a bed and meth-smoking partner.

There was one day when his new girlfriend took off for work. Josh stayed in bed, but managed to get up at one point and walk into the bathroom.

"I had been up for almost two weeks," he claimed. It was

a meth binge like he had never been on before. The drug had taken over. Josh had no more control of his life.

After going to the bathroom, Josh happened to stop and look at himself in the mirror. The creature he saw looking back was not a man he had recognized. It scared him. He showered and shaved, figuring that would help.

Problem was that Josh couldn't wash off the addiction he had to meth.

"I looked like a zombie from some horror movie. . . ."

Josh had seen enough, he said. He was tired of ripping and running.

"Mom," Josh said a few minutes later on the phone. He was desperate and in tears. "I cannot do this anymore. I cannot live this life any longer. I have to get my life together. I have children."

Josh's mother had been speaking to Heather once a week because of the kids. Although she had moved to Florida, Josh's mother stayed in contact with everyone she could back home. According to Josh's later recollection, his mother told him that Heather had said recently that she still loved him and wanted to get back together and be a family for once in their lives. It was something Heather, like all new mothers, dreamed about: a good man, jobs, a house, cook-outs, neighbors, school functions, birthday parties for the kids with family. Simple dreams any young girl might have. The drugs had gotten in the way of it all. But Heather—and apparently, Josh—was ready to give up the street life and make a go of it.

Heather, alone and young, gave up that baby for adoption, Josh explained. As she dealt with that loss, he spent months getting his act together. Soon they were reunited in Florida.

"I got myself back in good health and was working every day, doing like I was supposed to do, taking care of my family."

They found a home in Citra. Heather got herself that job at Petro. Life was not necessarily a citadel of happiness and all things good and healthy, but it was okay. They weren't rolling in money, but they were living somewhat normal lives. They were getting up and trying to do the right thing every day.

It was 2006 when Heather got pregnant again. It was a welcomed blessing this time around. Josh was running a lawn care crew of a few men. He had his life together as best he could.

"We were a happy, little family," Josh told me. "But there was something missing there. We had a poor sex life—and that caused us to argue a lot."

It was around this time that Josh fell in with a new group of people he had met in town. One of them was Emilia "Lily" Yera, who was dating a guy Josh knew. Josh's buddy, Adam Stover, told him how hot the sex was with Emilia. She was a firecracker in bed, like nothing the guy had ever experienced. Josh seemed interested. Due to an abusive childhood, he had serious issues with sex, which would be revealed much later. For Josh, sex was something he needed to control, especially the time and place. Inside his own home, he wasn't getting anything like that sex Emilia was giving his friend. He often wondered what it was like to have such an experimental, sadomasochistic life in the bedroom. He didn't know it then, but Josh's psyche was craving a certain type of sex because of what he had been through as a child.

One night, Adam made a suggestion to Josh. He said, "Josh, you want to make a porn film with us?" The friend was speaking of himself and Emilia.

Josh was stunned by this, but the prospect seemed intriguing. According to what Josh said many years later, at the time he didn't think Emilia, the way she looked then, was all that attractive, but he believed "she had potential."

"Yeah," Josh said. "Okay. What the hell!" He was reluctant, but it sounded like a good time. It would be Josh, Emilia, and Adam in the movie. Emilia was all for it, Josh was told. She was entirely into it.

When the specific night for the tryst and filmmaking came, Josh backed out. It just seemed too crazy and unlike anything he had ever done.

Josh and this guy, however, became close friends.

Soon they were best friends.

"I'm moving to Tennessee," Adam told him one day. "Me and Emilia."

"Wow, really?"

Josh knew that it was a good move for his friend, but he'd miss him like the dickens. They were really tight.

"Truly, they were like brothers," Emilia told me later, describing the friendship between Josh and Adam Stover.

Adam moved to Tennessee with Emilia, and Josh went back to his life with Heather and the kids. He missed his friend. They kept in touch via phone, text, and saw each other on occasion, but Josh longed for that daily interaction. He couldn't shake missing the close companionship and the way they had shared everything between them. They had relied on each other for life advice and support.

Some time went by, and then that call no one wants came into Josh's home. He and Heather were still together, but this second time around, it wasn't that bright and new relationship it had started off as. They were falling into old habits and fighting again. They had moments, but Josh was not the easiest man to get along with. He was demanding and often flew off the handle for no reason. He'd strike Heather from time to time. She'd hit him back, according to several reports. And there was always that on-edge feeling being around Josh—as though, Heather knew, the guy could snap at any moment and either come home blazed on meth, running around like a wild man, drunk and stumbling and mumbling, or simply pissed off and in a rage because life had not been what Josh expected it to be.

"Accident?" Josh said, responding to the phone call. His best buddy had gotten into a car accident in Tennessee.

"I'm sorry," Josh was told, "he's dead."

After he hung up, Josh didn't want to believe it. "I'm going to Tennessee," he told Heather a day later. "I need to speak with Emilia." Josh wanted to talk to someone who was close to Adam during his last days. He needed to hear from Emilia how his friend was before he died, what he was talking about, what was going on in his life.

There was no "connection" there between Josh and Emilia; they were friends because of the mutual love they shared for the guy who had died. They sat and talked, sharing stories about their relationship with Adam. It was good, Josh said, to sit and speak to someone who knew his friend as Josh had. He needed that.

"Remember when he thought we could make porn?" Josh said to Emilia.

They laughed about it.

The more Josh got to talking to Emilia, the more he saw beyond his lack of attraction to her physically. They were connecting on a much deeper level. There was this sudden, shocking tragedy between them, in a way bringing them closer together.

"Here's my cell number," Josh said to Emilia as he got ready to leave. She had come into town to be there in this time of need. "If you ever need to talk, call me."

They hugged and said their good-byes. Josh went back to his life in Florida with Heather and the kids.

CHAPTER 9

DEPUTY BETH BILLINGS felt there was something in what Brenda Smith had said regarding those two calls Heather had received that day she went missing. Call it a cop's instinct, or that little voice every cop has on his or her shoulder, whispering, *"Follow this lead. Listen more intuitively to this witness. Don't believe him."*

"Heather would confide in me regarding her relationship with Josh," Brenda explained to Billings on March 18. Billings had brought along Officer David McClain. The investigation was widening, expanding in scope and sensitivity. The MCSO was growing more curious (and suspicious) as each day passed and Heather had not returned or been heard from. With several detectives now involved, it was about gathering as much information as possible from all the parties, tallying it up and making a decision where to take the investigation next. Obviously, something was wrong here. It had been nearly a month and Heather had not called or come back to check on her kids—not once. She had simply vanished.

"What would she say about her and Mr. Fulgham?" Billings asked Brenda.

Brenda skipped that question and moved right into the heart of the matter, at least from her point of view: "I'm scared. I fear for Heather's life. . . . He (Josh) was continually harassing her and threatening to do her harm in some way. . . ."

CHAPTER 10

BARTOW, FLORIDA, IS nearly smack in the middle of the state. East of Tampa, southeast of Orlando, Bartow is one of those areas of Florida that is close to the flashy tourism the "Sunshine State" so much depends on: Disney World, Universal Studios, Busch Gardens and so on. Emilia Yera was born on August 4, 1984, and grew up in Bartow, but soon her family moved to McIntosh, a little over two hours north, where Emilia would spend the rest of her life. It was the birth of her little sister, Milagro, "born with thirteen birth defects," Emilia told me, when the family decided to move north into the Orange Lake region of McIntosh.

"My childhood was a freakin' nightmare," Emilia said, adding how she "endured years of abuse, regardless of the form." She claimed two immediate family members, her father and grandfather, "sexually abused" her from the time she was four until the age of fifteen. "I finally came forward when I found out my sister was to be next." Emilia couldn't allow that to happen. She had to do something to protect Milagro.

Both parties were charged, and Emilia and family members would later testify about the abuse in court. Emilia later withdrew the charges of sexual abuse.

"Before his trial," Emilia said of her father, "my dad tried to have me, my mom and grandma killed so we couldn't testify." Her father was later convicted of attempting to solicit the murders of family members and given a four-year prison sentence.

"My childhood consisted of responsibility, secrets and sexual perversion," Emilia told a newspaper reporter during an interview.

She described a typical night from her childhood as sitting in bed while experiencing terrifying anxiety over hearing the floorboards in front of her door creak. It was because Emilia knew that if those floorboards made that creepy sound in the middle of the night, it was her father coming into her bedroom to sexually assault her.

"You'd hear that floorboard creak and you'd think, 'It is going to be tonight,'" Emilia told that same interviewer.

It was a noxious and abusive upbringing, Emilia concluded, with the lack of a healthy male role model in her life. That absence set her up for future failures as she grew into her teen years and adulthood—not to mention all of the abuse she claimed to have survived.

Emilia said she dropped out of high school as a teen. From there, she was a frequent guest in foster homes. People "whispered" about her, she felt, wherever she went. Emilia was "that girl"—the one who'd been through hell and back and had been touched mentally by it all. She was the talk of the town. For her, small-town life in the South, Emilia said, was not an episode of *The Andy Griffith Show,* featuring a red-haired boy, fishing pole slung over his back, whistling as he walked down a dirt road. Hers was a form of torture, Emilia explained, a living hell she could not escape from.

"I got pregnant with my first son at the age of seventeen," Emilia said. "I married his dad to keep the man from going to prison courtesy of the age difference."

It was all of this, Emilia said, that made her emotionally

unavailable to people in her life as she grew into adulthood. Emilia had no traditional family structure or parental guidance to fall back on. She had to learn how to live and survive, essentially, on her own.

With a son, Emilia realized she needed to work in order to care for him properly—she certainly couldn't rely on her husband. Theirs was a relationship that was doomed from how it had started. It wasn't supposed to work. After that relationship ended, Emilia jumped right into another. She constantly needed to have a man in her life. This was a subconscious need for her always to be on the lookout for that one person who would rescue her, take care of her, tell her everything was going to be okay, the suffering was all over: *"I'll now be your protector."*

"I dated because I was 'supposed to be' with men," she said. "Yeah, you gotta love the South!"

Emilia said she grew up figuring out that it was best not to let the people around her "know everything" about her. Keeping secrets became a way of life. Hold on to personal things and never reveal the truth about you. Develop a shield from your emotions, not allowing anyone to get too close. Keep people at arm's length. This was how Emilia walked through life.

All that ever mattered to Emilia were her kids. As time moved forward, Emilia got her GED and became a certified massage therapist, giving herself a chance for a life. She was determined to break the cycle, get out of poverty and abusive relationships and find peace and happiness.

Through one new relationship, as Emilia dated James Acome (before Heather got him), she said she'd see Josh "around town" once in a while. "Josh and Adam Stover," Emilia said, "were like joined at the hip. James had always tried to get close," Emilia added, "but James could hang out with them, but couldn't come close to being what those two were."

It was James, Emilia said, "who was my first when I was fifteen." Emilia was "with James," she said, when Josh went off to Tennessee to visit Adam from time to time. It was James who came "flying into my mother's front yard" that day, Emilia said, announcing (in tears) that "Adam was killed in a car wreck. . . ."—which then sent Emilia running up to Tennessee to be near him.

"Has anyone told Josh?" Emilia asked James. She knew how close Josh and Adam were.

"I couldn't. . . . I just couldn't," James had said.

It was Emilia who ended up telling Josh over the phone that night before she headed out herself for a quick visit to Tennessee to be Adam's friend.

CHAPTER 11

THE IDEA THAT Heather Strong took off on her own seemed less likely as the middle of March came. The focus of the MCSO's investigation had taken a turn toward Josh Fulgham and his rather unpredictable and volatile relationship with Heather. Thus far, everyone the MCSO had spoken to regarding Josh and Heather had nothing positive to say about Josh and Heather's marriage. The two of them were like oil and water—where the oil (Josh) was always on fire.

Based on police reports alone, however, another angle emerged—one that didn't quite fit into the MCSO's attention on Josh and his violent tendencies. Back in September 2008, the MCSO had been called out to Josh's home at 3rd Terrace in Citra. Josh and Heather had split up by then and Josh had been hanging out with Emilia for quite some time. It was near 7:15 P.M. when Josh called into the sheriff's department to report a domestic dispute. He said Heather had come by the trailer to drop off their children and attacked him.

"You get [the child] out of the car, Josh," Heather had said, according to that report.

As Josh leaned in to pick up the kid, he later told police, Heather came up from behind and "struck him with her hand on the left side of his head." Josh was Kojak bald, with one of those heads as shiny as a cue ball. The officer noted in his report that Josh's head and ear were "red in color." This was "consistent with being struck by a hand."

"You need to leave," Josh told Heather.

Heather took off.

Emilia was with Josh at the trailer when the incident had occurred. She witnessed it all. She told the officer it happened the way Josh had described it.

"I saw it!"

The officer drove over to Heather's and had a chat with her.

"I did drop off our child[ren]," Heather explained, "but I never struck him. That's bullcrap."

The officer didn't buy it and arrested Heather, placing her in lockup at the Marion County Jail. Heather was charged with "simple domestic battery," and the case was later tossed out of court.

CHAPTER 12

THE MSCO TRIED to track down Josh during that late March period of investigating Heather's disappearance, yet, according to Beth Billings's report, she had met with "negative results" whenever and wherever she went looking for Josh during this time. It seemed Josh was keeping a low profile these days and had either left town or was hiding out and did not want to speak with law enforcement.

On March 18, 2009, Billings found Josh's mother, Judy Chandler. Judy had moved to Citra from Mississippi back in 2002. As Judy viewed the relationship, since Josh and Heather had been a couple as teenagers, they would "stay together for a while" and "split up and then [get] back together. They had problems off and on," Judy said. And sometimes those problems escalated into violent, "physical altercations." Throughout it all, however, Judy testified later, "I never seen Joshua hit her. . . . [But] on one occasion, they got into a fight and Heather did bust his head open with a cement block."

Judy talked about how the relationship had progressed over the past year. Josh had come to know Emilia in early 2008 and saw her mainly throughout that summer and into the fall. But on December 26, 2008, a day after Christmas,

Judy said, likely in the spirit of the holidays, Josh and Heather reconciled by getting married! It was a shock to everyone. As Judy saw it, Emilia was like a thorn in the side of Josh and Heather's relationship and marriage by that time—she was always hanging around, getting in the way. The woman would not give up her fight for Josh. She just wouldn't go away. Judy had even told Emilia once to stay the hell away from her son. Emilia didn't seem to get it: Josh had run to her and had a fling, but it was over now and he was back with his family. Emilia needed to go out and find herself a new man, because Josh was finished with her and back with his girlfriend, whom he had now made his wife.

"Haven't heard from Heather since mid-February," Judy related to the MCSO when they tracked her down in March 2009 while searching for Josh. She couldn't recall the "exact date," but had spoken to Heather near that time. Since then, she had not heard a word from the girl.

"What about Josh?" Billings asked.

"Back on February fifteenth, I saw Josh here when I returned home. It was, oh, seven-thirty or so that night. Josh had the kids. We never talked about why he had the kids. I'm not sure how he got possession of them." Judy was just happy to see her grandchildren, better yet with their father. Josh had just gotten out of jail, actually. He had gone in on charges of threatening Heather with a shotgun in January and had spent about forty days behind bars, being released after Heather dropped all of the charges.

To Beth Billings, Judy came across as "defensive," and not at all interested in giving out information about her son.

A mother protecting her child, or something else? Billings wondered.

Changing the subject entirely, Judy told Billings that the MCSO should be looking for a man Josh knew, adding, "He's the one who got my son hooked on drugs!"

"Could you have your son call me as soon as you see him," Billings said, handing Judy her card.

Deputy Billings next made contact with forty-seven-year-old Carolyn Spence, Heather's mother. Carolyn lived in Sturgis, Mississippi, where Heather had grown up. Carolyn was "extremely concerned" for Heather's well-being, she explained to Billings. This sort of behavior was unlike Heather. Not to call or let the family know where she was, no way, not Heather. And the kids! Heather would "never" leave her children for this long a period—especially with Josh—Carolyn explained. The only way she would not contact her children all this time, she added, was if she couldn't.

"I've tried calling and calling her," Carolyn said in a voice that spoke of worry, dread and fear, all at once. Billings could feel it through the phone while speaking with Carolyn. Here was a mother greatly concerned about her daughter. A mother whose gut told her something bad had happened. The deputy could sense it. Carolyn had known Josh since he was sixteen. She'd had a front-row seat to their relationship throughout the years. She knew and completely understood what Josh was capable of.

"Well, we're doing what we can to locate your daughter, ma'am . . . ," Billings said.

"I spoke to Judy," Carolyn then offered.

"What did she say?"

"I asked where Heather might be and she became very defensive and uncooperative—she didn't want to say anything."

Billings asked about Josh. Had she heard from him? Had she seen him?

Carolyn had some rather useful information to share, saying Josh had made "numerous threats" to Heather and the Strong family, as a whole, over the years. He was unstable and explosive. "About three years ago, there was one time when Josh called me to tell me he had tied up Heather, duct-taped her mouth shut and placed her in the trunk of his car. . . ." Carolyn began to cry as she told this story. Concluding,

"Josh then said, 'I'm going to feed her to the alligators! They'll eat her live!' I'm not sure what happened, but the cops were called."

A picture of Josh Fulgham was coming into focus for the MCSO.

"Anything else you can offer?" Billings queried.

"Heather's birthday is coming up on March twenty-third." Carolyn fought back more tears. This was so hard. Carolyn had not been the mother she'd wanted to be. She had her share of problems. "Heather is very family oriented and would never miss this day or not make contact with us or her kids or friends." This meant to Carolyn that Heather did not have the capability to contact anyone. She didn't say it, but she feared that Heather was dead. It was the only answer.

They spoke for a short time more and Billings told Carolyn to call if she thought of anything else. Even little details mattered. Think things through. They were going to find Heather, Billings promised. The MCSO was not approaching this any longer as an adult runaway case: some woman who wanted to disappear with all her problems left behind. The MCSO was beyond that by now. There was something wrong and the MCSO was going to find out what it was.

For Beth Billings, however, as a patrol officer, there was little else she could do at this point. She'd exhausted all of her resources.

"Deputy Billings could only do so much because of her regular patrol work," said a law enforcement source close to the investigation. "She was at a crossroads, essentially."

With that, the MCSO assigned the case to a detective, Donald Buie, a seasoned investigator with over a decade of experience in solving felony crimes and finding people, both those who didn't want to be found and those who did. If Heather was hiding out for some reason, a scenario that many believed could be true in this case, Detective Buie was the investigator to flush her out.

After Buie had a look at the case file on Heather Strong,

he walked over to his supervisor's office and handed Brian Spivey the file.

"Take a look at this and tell me what you think," Buie suggested.

At some point later, they converged again.

"Yeah?" Buie said, walking back into Spivey's office.

"Sit down."

"What do you think?"

Spivey took a moment and sat back in his chair. "Regarding Miss Strong," Spivey said, "she's . . . dead."

CHAPTER 13

SOME CLAIMED EMILIA had a strange and subtle "hotness" about her that men flocked to. She knew how to be sexy and used it to her advantage. She understood how to manage what she had, in other words. And if there was one thing Emilia understood without limitation of any kind, it was how to control men with that sexual allure and confidence. Not necessarily in a bad way, but a way that made Emilia stand out in a crowd of other women. Emilia was living with her mother in McIntosh. She had three children by the year 2007, had been married and divorced once. And yet, since reuniting with Josh after his best friend was killed in July 2007 (they were casual acquaintances then), Emilia and Josh had begun an intimate, intense sexual and romantic relationship.

It was nothing hot and heavy right away, but it progressed through 2007 after twenty-two-year-old Adam Stover was killed in that car accident. Emilia would "occasionally" even stay with Josh at his trailer. It was a strange relationship in many ways, one that had started on a notion of them going to a hotel to make an amateur porn film and then turning into them laughing about it after Adam was killed, becoming closer after that death, leaning on each other for support.

"Like I say, me and Heather's sex life was in the dumps

[when I met Emilia]," Josh told me, adding, perhaps without realizing how insulting and chauvinistic it sounded: "Even though Emilia did not have the prettiest face, she had a nice little set of legs and a nice little fat ass. . . ." It was a few weeks after Josh had left his phone number with Emilia in Tennessee that she called. He picked her up. "We shared a twelve-pack of Bud Light"—ah, those early memories of a budding romance—"and just rode around the back roads for a couple of hours."

Josh pulled over by the edge of Orange Lake. They stared out into the sparkling water, drinking and talking.

"What do you want to do?" Josh asked, looking over at Emilia, smiling, taking a pull from his beer.

Emilia, Josh recalled, straddled him without warning as they were sitting in the car. She sat on his crotch and grinded his penis hard.

Emilia was feeling those beers.

"Well, what do *you* want me to do?" she asked.

"You already know what I want."

Josh drove over to a friend's house. He and Emilia went into an empty bedroom. Of that first sexual experience with Emilia, Josh remembered: "This woman rocked my world like no other woman ever has." He recalled "sleeping with twenty-two women" throughout his life, but none "could hold a candle" to Emilia. She knew her way around a body and how to please a man, Josh insisted.

"Even though she already had three children," Josh explained, once again not realizing how offensive and narrow-minded he sounded, "she was not hurt in that area. I could not believe she'd had her kids naturally, with everything in as good a shape it was in."

Josh had a little taste of Emilia on that night and he was hooked. She had him.

"It got to the point where every day I got home from work, me and Heather was arguing, I showered and ran to Emilia. . . . I was in lust, like a sixteen-year-old schoolboy."

Sex, sex . . . and more sex. Josh could not get enough of Emilia. He had to have her as often as he could. And Emilia was right there, willing and always able to provide him with what he loved.

According to Josh, it wasn't until nearly a year after he hooked up with Emilia that Heather confronted him about his leaving the mobile home all the time. Heather had a feeling, he said, that he had been stepping out, but never really said anything. They had been trying to work things out by giving the relationship a chance.

Still, it wasn't the dope this time around, menacing the relationship; it was this other woman.

"Heather didn't know who it was then, only that I was fucking around on her," Josh recalled.

Fed up with Josh and his running off to another woman anytime they fought, Heather packed up her things and her kids and went back to Mississippi to go live with her mother. It didn't matter who it was that Josh was banging; the fact that he was out and about, sleeping with another woman, was enough.

Heather was done.

"Two weeks after she was gone, I ended up quitting my job and heading back up to Mississippi because I could not live without seeing my kids," Josh told me.

Once again, he chased what he could not have.

Josh's youngest was about to turn one. Josh didn't want to miss his birthday. He needed to be part of the kids' lives, regardless of what Heather thought or wanted. Yet, he also hoped to reconcile with Heather.

It took him a few weeks, but Josh got a job while back in his old stomping grounds. He and Heather hooked up once again and seemed to be getting along. He'd left Emilia kind of high and dry; but according to Josh, he didn't have any sort of deep connection with Emilia besides that unquenchable thirst she put in him for the best sex of his life. There was no agreement between them that they were exclusive,

Josh suggested. The relationship with Emilia was always a rebound, or simply a sexual one.

Problems between Heather and Josh began again because "I was not making any money whatsoever while back home in Mississippi," Josh said.

He had been in Mississippi for about five months and decided it was time to go back to Florida. It was late summer 2008 by then. Josh knew he could make more money in Florida; he had developed contacts and knew where to find steady work. Plus, Emilia was in Florida. All that Josh had thought about since being gone was the sex he had been getting from Emilia before he left. As much as he tried to stay away from her, he later claimed, the sex kept calling him back—especially when he and Heather were not getting along. So Josh drove to Florida and went straight over to Emilia's mother's house, looking for her.

Josh said he knocked and knocked. No one answered the door, even though he could tell people were shuffling around inside.

So he left.

A few days later, Josh ran into someone he and Emilia knew.

"Have you seen her around?" Josh asked.

His friend could tell Josh was looking to hook up. "Um, you don't know?" the friend asked.

"Know what?"

Josh's friend laughed.

"What's so funny?" Josh wondered. He felt like a fool who had not been let in on the joke.

"She went and got married, man. You didn't hear? Emilia and Jamie Carr."

Josh knew Jamie. He couldn't believe this. Never saw it coming.

As he thought about it, Josh began to feel that Emilia getting married might actually be a blessing in disguise—maybe it was that sign he needed, telling him he was crazy for lusting after this woman when he had Heather and their kids. It was a good reason not to get back with Emilia and destroy any chance he had with Heather and their children for a life together. Josh could tell Heather that he was through with his year-plus "fling." But now that Emilia was married, the way Josh saw it, their relationship, whatever it was, definitely had come to an end.

Now Josh was thinking of a way to get back with Heather, who had moved back to Florida that fall of 2008 and had started working at the Petro again. But regardless of what Josh would later say, Heather had no intention of getting back with him. She was done. The history between them was too vast, too violent, too much had happened. It was time both moved on. Sure, they had kids, but Heather didn't care this time around, she was telling friends. She needed to end things with this guy. It would never work. As many times as they had tried, it always turned out the same.

Bad.

As he left that friend after hearing about Emilia's marriage, Josh ran into Emilia's uncle, who was riding down the street on his bicycle.

"Hey, man, can you give me a lift home?" the uncle asked.

Josh put the bike into his car and drove Emilia's uncle over to Emilia's mother's house. As they pulled into the driveway, Josh saw Emilia's truck and realized she was home.

"I'm stopping here," Josh said he told the uncle as he pulled over, parking up the road from the house. "I don't want to see her."

As the uncle got out of the car, Josh claimed, "Emilia came out in some little booty shorts and so I got out and approached her."

"Where's your *husband* at, Emilia?" Josh said in a sarcastic manner. He couldn't believe she went and got married. What the hell!

"How do you know?"

"I found out."

Emilia seemed surprised. She didn't tell Josh then, but the marriage was just about over, anyway. She and Jamie had been kidding themselves. They were planning to divorce.

"Are you happy, Emilia?" Josh asked.

"I was happy," Emilia said, "until right now when I seen you. Now I'm confused."

"Where's your husband?" Josh asked again. Josh knew he was in jail. The uncle had told him.

"At work," Emilia said.

Josh laughed.

"Okay, so he's in jail."

According to Josh's recollection, Emilia's phone rang at that moment. It was Jamie Carr, who explained he had been let out of jail and needed a ride home.

Emilia hung up and told Josh she had to go get Jamie. Turning and leaving, however, Emilia said, "Why don't you drop by here tomorrow—come see me."

Josh knew it was trouble.

"Maybe . . . ," he said. "We'll see."

Who was Josh Fulgham kidding? He drove away counting down the minutes.

CHAPTER 14

THE MCSO FINALLY got a lead on Heather's where-abouts. It was March 18, 2009. Two MCSO detectives took a ride to an Ocala Publix supermarket after receiving information that Heather's debit card had been used there back on March 3, at 9:11 A.M. It was an exciting bit of evidence for the MCSO. The supermarket's ATM machines were equipped with video surveillance, so detectives could sit down and watch the video from that transaction and find out if it was Heather withdrawing the money. Who knew—perhaps Heather *was* hiding out for some strange reason? Ocala didn't seem like a place she would normally go to use an ATM, so it was possible she was trying to stay under the radar.

Forty-two dollars had been withdrawn from the work account where Heather's last paycheck had been deposited automatically. The manager of the supermarket met both detectives and gave them a CD of that entire day. Publix had a camera pointed directly at the ATM machine. When they got back to Major Crimes, the detectives popped in the CD and had a look.

A male, bald, in good shape, wearing what one detective described as a T-shirt depicting a "commercial type leaf blower on his back" had withdrawn the funds.

It surely wasn't Heather. She was nowhere in sight.

After zooming in on the T-shirt the man wore, they learned the shirt advertised a local lawn service company.

"The estranged husband, Joshua Fulgham," said one detective to the other, "he works for that lawn service. . . ."

The MCSO had who it believed to be Josh Fulgham withdrawing money from Heather's account more than two weeks after she went missing.

Huge red flag.

CHAPTER 15

WHEN A CASE opens up, sometimes it moves as fast as detectives can absorb the information and run it down. The MCSO had developed another bit of interesting evidence during that same March 18 day. Once they put their focus on Josh Fulgham as a potential suspect in his wife's disappearance, things started to fall in place. After investigators visited the school where Josh and Heather's oldest child attended classes, they learned from the principal that Josh had actually withdrawn his child from that school and registered her at another school, closer to his home. Apparently, Josh had shown the school a letter signed by Heather giving Josh full custody of the children. The school had a copy of the letter.

While that was happening, Detective Donald Buie had interviewed James Acome, Heather's boyfriend, and a female whom both Josh and Heather knew. During those interviews, Buie heard this from James Acome: "Heather left on a Greyhound bus bound for Mississippi on that last day she was seen around here."

Buie grew up in Gainesville, Florida. Gainesville is south of Jacksonville, in the northern part of the state. There was no family plan of going into law enforcement or some tragic event in Buie's life pushing him toward a career as a cop.

"I just decided one day to go into law enforcement, and there I was," he said.

Buie had been working for Cox Communications when the law enforcement bug bit and he decided to go for it. His first job was at the University of Florida Police Department. From there, Buie found himself working just outside Tallahassee, in a small police department in Perry, where he truly learned the ins and outs of community policing. It was 1998 when Buie took a job at the MCSO and made it into Major Crimes as a detective the old-school way: pounding the pavement, paying his dues. He had eight years in Major Crimes before the Heather Strong case came across his radar and he began to see that it needed further investigation.

Looking at the reports, Buie had a strong suspicion that Heather had not left town. The case just had that feel. But before he had a chance to develop the gut instinct, Buie later pointed out, it was the system the MCSO had in place that actually began to point out that this was more than your run-of-the-mill missing person case.

"To give credit where due," Buie said, "the girls we call 'Star Operators' get the cases . . . and they write them up in the computer." From there, the detectives and other investigators have a look to see where they can help maybe fill in the gaps. Detectives and officers can call into the Star Operator system and dictate a report (instead of sitting down and typing it out), so it gets into the system very quickly. It's an extremely efficient and fast way to get reports into the system so everyone can have access to them. "The Star Operators see hundreds of cases throughout the year they write up in the computers and begin to develop a sense for them," Buie added. "They saw this case of Heather Strong going missing and something just didn't appear to be right. And that's how the case was brought to my attention."

Sometimes it just starts with a cop having a feeling. Buie then had his boss, Brian Spivey, look at it—and that was when he heard Spivey's feeling that Heather was dead.

Buie read through the case one day in mid-March. "And I immediately felt something was wrong. Lot of red flags. There was a lot of history between Josh and Heather. . . . Even if Heather didn't live a grand lifestyle, she still worked as hard as she could to provide for her and her kids. It was unlike her to disappear. This was obvious right away to me."

One thing Buie noticed was that nobody had interviewed Josh and Heather's oldest child. She was eight at the time. He wrote himself a note to get over to Josh's mother's, where the kids were staying, and talk to the child as soon as possible.

Another interesting dynamic Buie found was that Josh and Heather "had a pretty open relationship." Meaning, they often involved others in their sexual fun. Whenever that type of fact emerged, Buie knew, anything was possible.

Love, money, revenge—that's why people kill one another.

Buie needed to run down everything that came in, so he contacted Greyhound in Ocala, the only local bus depot around. Its computers did not have any record of Heather (or Josh) purchasing a ticket to Mississippi or anywhere else.

As investigators were in a meeting that afternoon talking about the case, Sergeant Brian Spivey interrupted.

"We got some information here about Miss Strong's debit card being used right now at the Reddick Supermarket." The MCSO had the equivalent to an all points bulletin (APB) out on the debit card, so any time it was used they'd get a call immediately. "Come on, let's go. . . ."

Spivey and another detective took off for Reddick. As they drove, Spivey said, "We think it's got to be the husband, Josh Fulgham. We're told he's driving a maroon four-door Toyota car."

As they approached a traffic light after getting off the I-75, then headed east on Highway 318, near Highway 441, they spotted a maroon Toyota traveling through a traffic light heading north in the opposite direction.

Spivey called it in.

They followed Josh Fulgham as he drove into the Pine

Grove Mobile Home Park, where he now lived, but they held back and observed Josh walk into his home.

Spivey called for backup. It was time to make a move on Josh and have a more focused chat with him. Put his feet to the flame a little bit and find out what he knew.

They sat surveillance on Josh's mobile home. By early evening, they had a warrant for Josh's arrest on charges of him withdrawing forty-two dollars from Heather's account at the Publix ATM machine. According to the MCSO, Josh had committed credit/debit card fraud.

Sergeant Spivey sat and watched the mobile home as several other detectives arrived to help out. Some were parked near Josh's home; some waited across the way on Highway 441. The MCSO wanted to get Josh into its Ocala Major Crimes headquarters and sit him down, get him on record, maybe get Josh to tie himself to a signed statement. They could question him about Heather under the guise of a potential fraud charge. After all, the MCSO knew that a fraud charge like this would probably never fly in court. Josh was still Heather's husband; maybe his name was even on her account. Still, it was a good ruse to get him downtown.

Detectives Brian Spivey and Donald Buie met down the block from Josh's mobile home and then drove together. They parked in Josh's driveway and walked up to his house. A third detective, stationed across the street, kept a close eye on Josh's maroon Toyota, just in case Josh decided to head out the back door and flee. They kept in contact via radios.

Buie couldn't wash one important factor from his mind: an interview he had done earlier in the day with Josh and Heather's eight-year-old child. Something she had told Buie stuck with the detective. She said that her daddy and mommy were together on that night Heather went missing. Daddy left the house with Mommy and returned many hours later.

Alone.

It was the last time the child had seen her mother.

"During that interview with [Josh's daughter]," Buie

explained, "she puts Josh and her mother together on the night Heather is last seen. This was inconsistent with statements we had that indicated Heather was last seen at the Petro."

This didn't mean Josh killed his wife; but still, the guy had some explaining to do.

Buie knocked on Josh's door at 6:04 P.M. Spivey was standing to his left.

"Come on in," said a man's voice. They couldn't see him.

"Any dogs or anything in here?" Buie asked.

There were no dogs.

Josh stepped out from around a corner inside the house. They exchanged pleasantries. Josh told his kids to go into another section of the house and do their homework.

Buie took in a deep breath through his nose and smelled a strong aroma of weed. Not as though someone in the house had sparked a joint and taken a few puffs. This was much more profound and pronounced, as if someone had been sucking on a bong for hours.

Donald Buie approached Josh and asked him if he had "a wife or anything." Josh said, "I do, but I don't know where the hell she is."

"That's why we're here," Buie finally said.

Buie got Josh to commit to some dates and information about Heather as Spivey, standing by, mentioned that he smelled pot smoke. They discussed where it was coming from as Spivey admitted the weed smell wasn't all that important to them at this point or the reason for their visit.

Josh said he'd fired up a doobie earlier, but that was it. It was just a little toke—nothing more.

Buie asked Josh for a timeline.

Josh said it was February 15 and Heather had called from the Petro. (There was a difference of opinion in who called whom, but phone records would later flesh out that it was Josh who actually called Heather twice at the Petro on that day.) "She told me she was fixin' to get out of here . . . because she was fixin' to get into trouble. . . ."

Buie asked if there was more.

Heather was tossing her boyfriend out of the house and she wanted Josh to come and get the kids, Josh explained. But he didn't want to go over there for fear of being set up and arrested for something he didn't do. So they met, Josh said, "at a little Subway store" near the Petro. As an afterthought, he then said after he got the kids from Heather, he brought them over to his mother's. He was living there at the time.

While he spoke, Josh seemed relaxed and calm.

A little too much, perhaps.

Probably the weed, Buie considered.

"She called me with the keys," Josh continued, referring to something Heather had said to him on that same night. "She wanted me to come and get the keys from Petro. . . . She had two suitcases with her . . . last time I seen her." Josh said he gave her five hundred dollars in cash. It was all the money he had.

They chitchatted a bit more, focusing on when Josh and Heather were married. Then Josh said he had a girlfriend now, "Emilia. But we just came to the conclusion that, you know, we don't need to [argue anymore]. . . . If we can't get along, we're not going to live together."

When they split up—just recently—Emilia went to stay with her mom, he added. She was there now.

Buie found all of this interesting, but not at all revealing in its entirety. He had a sense Josh knew more.

"Any idea where she might have gone off to?" Buie asked.

Josh said he felt he knew where Heather was: Mississippi. He mentioned something about her taking off with some "old guy . . . she used to get money off of. . . . I think she left with him."

Using that point as a launch, Josh did a good job of selling a story that Heather had taken a sum of money from somewhere (he didn't know where) and took off on the run, realizing that cops would soon be after her. He was basically calling his wife a thief, saying she ripped someone off for a large amount of cash and booked town.

Buie said there were no open warrants out for her arrest.

Josh countered by explaining that it hadn't all been figured out just yet. In time, the cops were going to be notified, from what he had heard, and it would all come to light.

Buie asked Josh if he knew Heather's ATM-card pin number.

Josh gave it to them and said he hadn't heard from Heather since she left.

They were sitting in the living room. The kids came in from time to time and asked their father questions about homework and dinner. The situation, despite the foul aroma of stale marijuana permeating the air, soaking into the carpet and furniture, appeared to be a father taking care of his children. Nothing, save for that smell of weed, seemed to be out of place.

Buie said, "Listen, before we leave, can you go and get us any weed you have so we can get rid of it?"

Josh showed them a few roaches in the ashtray and said that was the whole of it.

Spivey asked Buie to hand Josh one of his business cards. "If anything should come up, if somebody sees her . . . we need to know so we can close this case out."

"I mean," Josh said, seemingly confused, "well, what's going on?"

They explained that Heather was considered a missing person. With any missing person case as old as this one, they needed to maybe get a DNA profile of Heather just in case a Jane Doe body showed up somewhere in the future. Would Josh be willing to help with that?

He said he would.

By the time they walked out the door, it was 6:31 P.M.

Spivey and Buie looked at each other as they sat in the car

and prepared to leave. Both had a strong feeling they were going to be seeing a lot of Joshua Fulgham over the next few days.

He's lying, both cops thought. *He knows more.*

Spivey turned the key, fired up the engine and pulled out.

They could have arrested Josh. But for now, as a strategy, both detectives chose to let him be.

CHAPTER 16

SPIVEY AND BUIE waited for a few hours and then returned to Josh's front door. Josh seemed wired and uncertain this second time around, as if something was bothering him. Buie and Spivey were now prepared to tell Josh he needed to go with them down to Major Crimes for a formal interview.

The MCSO knew Josh was the last person to see Heather Strong. Detective Buie had interviewed several of Josh's so-called friends and also one of Heather and Josh's children. Buie had good information that Josh was in one way or another responsible for Heather's disappearance, either aiding her escape from town or facilitating her demise. Buie and Spivey had made contact with Emilia Carr, after finding out that Josh and Emilia had been together as a couple and asked her to come in for an interview. Emilia happily and willingly agreed. They were working on picking her up at the moment.

"We have a warrant on fraud charges," Spivey told Josh. "It stems from the use of Miss Strong's debit card."

Josh said he understood. However, Josh believed that as Heather's husband, he had every right to use the card.

A third detective came in. Josh went with him to Ocala. Spivey and Buie followed.

CHAPTER 17

THE MAJOR CRIMES division of the MCSO investigated homicides and felony assaults, in addition to other serious crimes and deaths considered suspicious or otherwise strange, until proven different: overdoses, suicides, the unexplained and so on. It was Major Crimes that got Heather's case weeks ago when the information the MCSO was receiving told investigating officers that it was highly unlikely Heather had disappeared on her own.

Detective Brian Spivey grew up in Ocala. It was baseball that landed him a scholarship at Santa Fe Community College in New Mexico. Yet, the athlete in him understood that baseball was a springboard for a degree, not a professional contract.

"Every athlete dreams of the pros, but realistically I knew that getting a degree," Spivey said with a laugh, "was the best thing that could come out of my baseball career."

Upon returning to Florida after college and attending a local school to upgrade his education, Spivey went right into the police academy. Not because of a family obligation or some secret desire to chase bad guys, but because being a baseball player all those years and working with a team to accomplish a goal lit a fire within Spivey to carry that spirit into his vocational life.

"Working with a group of individuals to accomplish a goal," Spivey told me, "law enforcement just seemed to be the next step."

His first job happened to be with the Marion County Sheriff's Office. He started like everyone else, in patrol. From there, he worked his way up into Major Crimes as a detective. That was 2002. Spivey's initiation into Major Crimes was a homicide involving a guy who had been stabbed seventy-eight times.

"Two guys put him in the trunk of a car and took him out into the woods after killing him and were in the process of burying him when a patrol car just happened to drive by and see the car. . . ." There was blood all over the vehicle, some even dripping down into the wheel wells and from the trunk. The officer called it in and they found the body soon after, along with the two guys hiding in the woods. It became Spivey's first case.

Now he was supervising Major Crimes.

When Spivey and Buie arrived back at Major Crimes that night, Emilia was already sitting, waiting to be questioned. She had come in voluntarily and said she wanted to help any way she could. Spivey and Buie knew that Emilia possibly held the potential to open up this case. She knew Josh's secrets. She had spent time with both Josh and Heather. Someone had even told the MCSO that Emilia had been Heather's babysitter at various times.

They asked Emilia how long she had known Josh.

"Two years . . . we dated for four months last year when Josh and Heather split up," Emilia said. "When they reunited in December, though, Josh and I parted ways."

Emilia came across as articulate and intelligent. Her voice was tethered to a Southern twang prone to those native Floridians more to the north of the state. Later it would be determined that she had an IQ of about 125. Emilia was no dumb street chick; she was a bright girl who knew exactly what she was doing.

This relationship—Josh, Heather and Emilia—had a sordid, rather confusing history over just the past seven months. When Emilia was with Josh, she, of course, had words with Heather and they didn't get along. On occasion, both women had even tossed vulgarities at each other, shouted insults and argued. Your typical back-and-forth scorned-lover bickering.

"So you dated Josh?" Buie asked Emilia.

Emilia looked off to the side. She was a bit impervious in regard to sharing something—that much was obvious by the look on her face. Emilia had a secret. This much they knew to be true.

"What is it?"

Emilia looked down. She put her hand on her tummy.

"We parted ways, Josh and I, but I was already pregnant with his child."

Buie had noticed a bump. One doesn't ask a woman if she's packing, however—just in case, she's not!

"How long are you now?"

"Eight months," Emilia said. This posed a problem, Emilia explained.

For Buie and Spivey, this was now a major development. The stakes had suddenly changed.

"So you've seen what's been going on with Josh and Heather?" Buie wanted to know, asking for a bit of insight into the relationship from a third party.

"Yeah," Emilia said. "Back in January, Heather claimed Josh pulled a shotgun on her—the gun belonged to my father. He went to jail."

Buie and Spivey were well aware of Josh's time in jail on that charge. They had gone back and listened to several recordings of Josh making phone calls from jail during that same time in January until he got out, just before Heather went missing. Those tapes, and whom Josh was speaking to, told an interesting tale all on their own.

"When he got out of jail, did you two get back together?"

"We tried to work things out," Emilia said. "It was very rocky, though."

"How'd you and Heather get along?"

"We weren't necessarily friendly, so we pretty much maintained our distance. We never fought or anything like that, though."

This was untrue, both detectives knew.

The impression Emilia gave was that she and Heather stayed away from each other. When they followed that rule, things were okay between them. When they didn't, well, they argued like junior high school girls in the hallway between classes, fighting over a boy.

"When was the last time you saw Heather?"

"Oh, geez, probably like January tenth, a few days after Josh got hit with that gun charge. I babysat their kids while Heather worked."

"You *watched* their kids?"

"Yeah . . . when she got home that night, we argued because of her calling the cops on Josh and him going to jail."

Emilia went on to say that Josh never threatened Heather with a gun. He took the weapon so he could clean it. That charge was bogus. It was Heather and her new boyfriend making it up to get Josh out of the picture for a while.

"Did you put your hands on Heather?" Buie asked.

"No way—she would have had me in jail!"

"Did you fight with her, like grab her hair or anything?"

"No! When we got into it, I chose to leave. I didn't have a problem with Heather. I didn't," Emilia claimed. It sounded sincere.

They took a break. Emilia was tired. She was feeling the day, the week, the month. She was going to be giving birth to Josh's child in a matter of weeks. His wife was missing. Josh was sitting in jail on a fraud charge. Emilia felt helpless and unable to do anything. Her life seemed to be once again spiraling downward, and there was no way she could find to stop it.

Near 10:00 P.M. on March 18, after a break, Emilia sat down with Spivey and Buie for a second time. She said she wanted to clear something up and then be taken back home so she could rest.

"Sure," Spivey said.

"I did grab Heather once. It was two or three nights before Josh went to jail. But I made sure not to have any contact with her *after* that. I stayed away from her."

They talked about a few inconsequential pieces of information and then Buie got a patrol car to bring Emilia back to her mother's house in Boardman.

As she left, Spivey and Buie stood, watching Emilia Carr walk out of the building. They looked at each other. Both investigators knew that they'd be speaking to Emilia again. She definitely knew more. That much was clear in the way she answered questions and her body language.

CHAPTER 18

JOSH FULGHAM SPENT the evening of March 18, 2009, in the local Ocala jail. Detective Donald Buie, not much convinced by the answers Emilia had given them, called Emilia just after midnight, indicating that the MCSO wanted her to come back in and chat some more. Would she mind?

"Yeah, okay," Emilia begrudgingly said.

Buie sent a patrol car to pick her up. What he didn't tell Emilia was that between the time she had gone back home and then, he had developed new information about the case.

And it involved her.

It was 12:39 A.M. when Emilia sat back down in the interview suite at Major Crimes to give her third interview within the span of about ten hours. She didn't know it, but Josh was getting rustled awake from his cell to be interviewed, so they could record it and then play back sections for her if Josh said anything that could help—a standard police tactic when two people are thought to be involved and know more than they are sharing. Buie and Spivey were certain that between the two of them—Josh and Emilia—they would figure out where Heather was and what had happened to her. The hope at this point was that she had been kidnapped and was being held somewhere. Or perhaps Josh had threatened Heather and had scared her into leaving town.

Thus far, there was no indication that anything deadly had happened to Heather.

"How are you?" Buie asked Emilia as she settled in.

"Exhausted," Emilia said.

"You and me both." Buie took a pause. "Listen, I had you brought back here because we developed some new information, okay? However, you are not under arrest."

Emilia, who seemed calm, but very tired, nodded, indicating that she understood. Still, that last comment from Buie seemed to be serious. This was not a conversation anymore, Emilia knew. She was being interrogated.

Buie got serious. He said, "Because I had a patrol car bring you back here, okay, I need to question you—okay?" He explained that before he asked his first question, the MCSO needed to advise Emilia of her rights. "These rights are just so you and I can talk."

Emilia said she understood.

After Buie read Emilia her Miranda rights, as a professional formality, he asked if she was ready and willing to talk to him. At this point, Emilia could have said no, that she wanted a lawyer. But it sounded as though she had nothing to hide.

"I mean, I don't see why not," Emilia said.

Buie stood. He approached Emilia and explained: "Before we start, I want to go get something—I want you to listen to something, okay? Then I want you to tell me your thoughts after that. Okay?"

Emilia again nodded yes. She was curious as to what was going on.

Buie had interviewed Josh during the intervening time Emilia had left the MCSO, returned and sat down again with them. Josh was actually just in the adjacent room from where Emilia was now sitting. Buie had recorded that interview with Josh. When he returned to Emilia after a brief break, Buie had a tape recorder with him. He had obviously gotten something he could use from Josh. He placed it on the table in front of Emilia, who looked up, as if to say, *"What the hell are you doing?"*

Buie didn't say much. He hit the PLAY button and pointed to the tape recorder. "Listen."

The interview ran several hours. In it, Josh had admitted to knowing where Heather was, without giving away the location, what happened to her, why she was gone, or if she was alive or dead.

While the tape played, changing his tone from friendly to very serious, Buie said, "You can stop me at any time, okay, but Josh has got *you* driving the bus! He's saying that you told him. . . ." Buie was obviously no longer the good cop, who was just having a friendly conversation with Emilia. The MCSO had information that Emilia was involved in some way. She needed to explain her role.

Emilia was confused. *Told him what? What is going on here?* she wondered.

She felt blindsided. What had Josh gone and done now? Had he turned on her? Was he lying to them about her? This worried Emilia greatly.

"You told him . . . ," Buie began before stopping himself again. Then: "I'm telling you, he told me that *you* told him that! We know that he brought her (Heather) back to the house that night." Buie was referring to February 15, though he never mentioned the date. By "house," he meant Emilia's mother's house in Boardman, where Emilia lived.

"What house?" Emilia pleaded. She sounded entirely confused by what Buie was saying. "I was home that night."

"Listen! Listen!" Buie said sharply. "See there," he added, playing the tape and stopping it after Josh mentioned Emilia by name.

Emilia looked at him quizzically. She was puzzled by the detective's sudden change of demeanor.

What in the world?

"I was at home at my momma's," Emilia explained.

"Your heart is about to jump out of your chest," Buie said, trying to perhaps put a jolt into Emilia to scare her.

"That pisses me off," Emilia said.

"Don't do this to yourself."

"What?" Emilia asked, confused. *What is this detective talking about?*

"Don't *do* this to yourself," Buie said again.

"Ask my momma," Emilia insisted. "I was *home* that night."

"Don't. Do. This. To. Yourself." Buie said it slowly. It was clear, in the cryptic way the detective was explaining things, beating around some bush Emilia had no idea existed, that maybe Buie was hoping to get Emilia to say something to bury Josh. Was Buie playing Emilia? Trying to make her think that the MCSO had more on her and Josh than it did?

"What is he saying I did?" Emilia wanted to know. She couldn't explain herself if she didn't know what the hell this detective was referencing.

"That you set it up!" Buie finally said.

"Set *what* up, though?"

According to what Buie now told Emilia, Josh had told them that "you told him you guys took care of Heather, and for him not to worry about her anymore."

"You guys"? Who else is he referring to?

Emilia was no dense, stupid woman, unaware of what cops were legally entitled to do within the scope of an interview. Cops could completely lie to a suspect or a witness. Cops used this tactic all the time. They said things with the hope of getting a suspect or a witness to admit to something he or she did or didn't do. As far as Emilia could tell, Josh never said any such thing on the tape she was listening to. Where was this coming from?

Thinking more about it, Emilia indicated that she had no idea what Buie was talking about. She encouraged the detective to clarify exactly what Josh was saying if the cop wanted to have a conversation with her she could follow.

"Who's 'you guys'?" Emilia asked. If Emilia had helped Josh, as Buie seemed to be suggesting, where did the "you guys" portion of this come into play? The way Buie worded things, it didn't make sense.

"You," Buie said, further confusing the situation.

"But how, if I was at home?" Emilia asked.

"He told me about the incident of you grabbing Heather at the house when you were supposed to be babysitting . . . ," Buie said, explaining in a bit more detail what Josh had allegedly said happened on a night back in January when Emilia and Heather had supposedly gotten into an altercation. There was much more to it than a simple argument between two women, Buie suggested, as Emilia had told them recently.

Emilia looked down and started shaking her head side to side.

"He was in jail [then]," Emilia finally said, responding to that argument incident between her and Heather.

They went back and forth a bit more and Buie said, "Listen, listen . . ." He held up his hands for Emilia to stop talking. She was becoming somewhat impatient. They were dancing around the issue. Then Buie got a little aggravated. He said, "Listen . . . I'm telling you *right* now, he's admitted to his stuff. He lawyered up, but he chose . . ."

Buie stopped, then thought for a moment.

Then he continued, "You know what? I think I need to tell you *all* the truth. That's why you are back in here."

This got Emilia's full attention. What was Josh doing? What had he said? Emilia and Josh had been fighting lately. Ever since Josh had married Heather back in December 2008, this after making a promise to Emilia (not to mention getting her pregnant), she'd had reservations about the two of them and a future together, child or no child. Emilia knew Josh was pissed off at her lately—but what had he gone and done now? Had he made up stories about her, implicating her in Heather's disappearance? Had he told the MCSO things that were untrue in order to get back at her? She wouldn't put it past him to set her up.

I need to find out what they know, Emilia thought.

Emilia explained to Buie that the MCSO could ask her mother about her whereabouts on "that night" and her mother would confirm that Emilia was at home. Even her sister would vouch for Emilia being there. There was a family friend over at the house who would also verify Emilia's presence.

"Emilia, *what* night?" Buie said. He had never mentioned a date.

"February fifteenth, the day after Valentine's Day that she supposedly left . . ."

Detective Buie now took on a sarcastic tone. He said, "Let me explain something to you, sweetheart . . . okay!"

"Uh-huh," Emilia said.

"You had been soliciting people to do something to [Heather]."

Emilia wanted to laugh. "That's hearsay," she said.

Who is the MCSO's source for this nonsense? Emilia wondered. *Josh? Huh! He's a violent person with a criminal record and a penchant for telling lies. Why believe him?*

"You call it what you want," Buie responded.

Emilia laughed again.

Buie got a little perturbed. "We ain't down here," he said sternly, "to have a picnic."

"I know that," Emilia responded. ". . . but this is why I'm upset—"

The detective interrupted her. "You can be upset all you want to. I'm telling you *right* now that your boyfriend has thrown you under a bus. He's admitted to lying. He's admitted that he is involved in this and knows about it, okay?" Buie got himself going. He continued, telling Emilia that she "could sit there and play this game" all she wanted, but it wasn't going to do anybody any good—to which Emilia laughed again as Buie continued: "I told you the first time when I held your hand and I looked you square in the eye and I told you this is your opportunity to come clean and be straight . . . but I'm going to walk right out of this room if you lie to me."

Emilia kept saying she was home on that night. She didn't say it, but she thought, *Go ahead, Detective, walk out of the room. I could not care less.* From Emilia's viewpoint, she hadn't done anything wrong. She couldn't understand how they could take the word of a guy like Josh Fulgham against hers.

Bottom line here was that if they had anything solid, Emilia would be wearing metal bracelets and sitting in a holding tank, facing charges, same as Josh.

But she wasn't.

Buie hinted at what they had, adding, "You can listen to every jail phone call."

What did *that* mean? Emilia knew she had spoken to Josh when he was in jail—but did those conversations amount to anything?

They went back and forth, and Buie was then called out of the room.

Inside that interview suite just next door, Josh Fulgham was talking. Buie later explained how they had Josh situated in what Major Crimes called a "hard room," a square box with a few chairs, devoid of anything interactive, like photos or pictures or even color. It was just a room—small and serious.

Next door, however, where they had Emilia, was considered the "soft room." Part of her being interviewed there was because Emilia was eight months pregnant. Inside the soft room was a leather couch and carpeting. It had a much homier, comforting feel. The only thing that separated Josh from Emilia was a wall.

Buie was trying his best to turn one against the other—and he was getting somewhere.

It wasn't a "good cop/bad cop" plan, Buie clarified.

"We just wanted Emilia to feel comfortable so she could open up."

Major Crimes understood that the key to getting Josh to admit his role in whatever had happened to Heather was making Emilia feel as though she held the cards. Josh was clearly giving them an indication that he'd had something more to do with Heather's disappearance, but at the same time minimizing his role in any of it.

"Where is Heather Strong, Mr. Fulgham?" Buie asked Josh after walking into the hard room, pacing a bit and approaching his suspect.

Josh was sweating. He was tired. It was late, somewhere near four in the morning now, and everyone had been up all night. Josh was also hungry. He said he wanted this over with so he could get out of there, get into a cell, eat, and get some sleep.

"She is probably with this guy Wayne . . . ," Josh said again.

"Wayne?"

Buie and Josh talked some more. Buie said he would be right back.

The detective opened the door, turned, and walked into the soft room.

"Emilia, listen, who is Wayne? Can you tell me about Wayne?"

"Heather could be with Wayne, sure," Emilia said, and even gave Wayne's cell phone number to Buie.

Buie explained later that Wayne was a guy Josh knew Heather would get with at times and have some fun. Wayne was a Santa Claus–looking truck-driver type that came around once in a while. He was old and fat and smelly. He liked Heather. He spent money on her.

Buie left the room. He called Wayne.

Wayne actually answered and gave his full name after having no trouble admitting he knew Heather. "I have no idea where Heather is," Wayne said. "She's not with me."

"When was the last time you saw her?" Buie asked.

"Probably like the middle of January. She was working at Petro. I stopped in."

"Do you know the whereabouts of Heather Strong?" Buie asked again, more professionally.

"No, man. I have no idea."

It seemed to Buie that the MCSO was getting the runaround from Josh Fulgham, the husband of a missing wife. He was tossing information out and hoping something stuck. Was Josh's story about Emilia part of his plan to drag her into whatever game he was playing with cops?

Buie didn't care at this point. He was tired of the nonsense. He wanted answers.

CHAPTER 19

DETECTIVE DONALD BUIE went back to the soft room, where Emilia was waiting, after going over several pieces of evidence he had developed overnight in the case. It was 5:31 A.M., on March 19, when Buie entered the soft interview suite for what was, officially speaking, his fourth interview with Emilia.

The first thing out of Emilia's mouth gave the increasingly impatient detective an indication that maybe Emilia was ready to share some of her secrets.

"Where is he?" Emilia asked. She was referring to Josh.

"He's . . . out there," Buie said.

"Out *there*?" Emilia was taken aback by how close Josh was to where she sat with Buie. "Can you make sure nothing happens to me?" Emilia said next. She was obviously scared of Josh, shaken by the idea of him being just outside the door.

"Okay." Buie wanted her to get on with what she had to say. There wasn't a chance Josh could get to her. Enough with the drama!

"I'm serious," Emilia said. She looked toward the door. She gave the impression that she was terrified of this man. There was no telling what he could do to her. If Josh had taken it upon himself to implicate Emilia, she believed he was prepared to do anything at this point.

Buie told Emilia that he was under the impression after speaking to Detective Spivey, who had spoken to Emilia between her previous interviews, that she had "new" information she was now willing to share. Buie didn't want her to worry about Josh. He was in no position to get to her. She needn't be concerned for her safety. She should feel free to talk as openly as possible. Buie was a little upset at Emilia because she had told Spivey she had something to say, and yet it felt to Buie as if she was wasting their time.

What Emilia wasn't telling Buie, just yet, was that she didn't trust him. She felt more comfortable talking to Spivey. Emilia knew Spivey outside of the police department. They had a history of sorts. Spivey's former wife was an instructor at the technical college where Emilia had gotten her massage certificate. His ex-wife had taught Emilia, and Spivey had met Emilia at the graduation ceremony. Within that relationship, Emilia felt that Spivey, unlike Buie, was not one to go about making accusations against her, or using an accusatory tone, which Emilia clearly did not like. Spivey was more of a listener. He sat and took in whatever Emilia wanted to say without coming back at her, wagging a finger. Spivey took in the information—and Emilia appreciated that.

"You understand your rights still apply," Buie explained as they again acclimated themselves to the soft room. "Okay. You've got to tell me the truth from point A to Z. Okay? Tell me."

Emilia said she had been thinking about everything they had discussed and something "hit" her as she thought about her mother's trailer the last time she and Buie had talked.

Trailer?

That much was new.

Buie encouraged Emilia to tell him the story. Get on with it. Let's hear what you have to say.

Emilia took a deep breath. She got comfortable in her chair. This was tougher than she thought. It was as though figuring this revelation out herself for the first time scared the hell out of her.

Nevertheless, deciding to come clean with what she knew, Emilia Carr cleared her throat and told her story to Detective Donald Buie.

CHAPTER 20

IT WAS FIVE-THIRTY, the morning of February 16, 2009—the night of February 15 was the last time anyone had seen Heather Strong. Josh generally called Emilia when he wanted to come over. But on this morning, as the sun was just edging its way up over the Atlantic horizon, Emilia was asleep, in bed, when she was startled by a knock on her bedroom window.

Who's that? Emilia thought as she woke up, still partially asleep, and looked toward her window.

"Josh?"

According to Emilia, Josh was standing outside her window.

"What are you doing here?" Emilia asked. Josh looked disheveled, out of breath, spooked and wired, as though someone had been chasing him. "It's cold out there. . . . Come around to the door so I can let you in."

"I just came by to tell you that I love you and I am on my way to work," Josh said.

This was a bit strange, even for Josh. He had suddenly turned into Romeo, showing up at Emilia's bedroom window just to say, "I love you"? Emilia was used to Josh calling her every morning to share this intimacy, but he had never come to her window before this day.

Emilia wondered, *Why is he here? It's so early.*

"Okay . . . Josh," Emilia said.

"I thought he was kind of weird," Emilia told Detective Buie as she told this story on the morning of March 19. Things had been "really, really tense" between them, Emilia later said. She had told Josh on more than one occasion that they needed to stop arguing so much. If all they did was fight, the relationship needed to end.

The gulf growing between them, Emilia recalled for Buie, was centered on Heather and the kids. According to what she explained during her March 19 interview, Josh kept telling Emilia, "I will not let Heather take the kids." Heather had taken them back to Mississippi once and Josh had followed. He wasn't about to allow that to happen again. He was constantly in fear of Heather moving the kids away and him never seeing them again. "What are you talking about?" Emilia said she asked Josh whenever he mentioned not allowing Heather to take the kids. Was Josh planning on taking her to court?

While at Emilia's bedroom window, Josh said, "I cannot come in. You *don't* want to help me."

Emilia wanted to know what was going on. What did he mean by that? Why was Josh at her window? Why was he saying he didn't want her help? Emilia couldn't understand what was happening—it all seemed so foreign to her. Josh wasn't himself.

"Where's Heather, Josh?" Emilia asked after Josh again referred to the fact that Heather was gone. "She back in Mississippi?"

Josh looked down. Then he whispered: "She's closer than you think."

They argued about this comment later. Emilia saw Josh that evening and she asked him again, "Where is Heather?"

She wondered, why was he being so mysterious? All this business about "she's closer than you think." What was he talking about?

"That's when he told me," Emilia explained to Detective Buie. "I don't know if he said he strangled her or he choked her or whatever, but he said he did that."

The reason Josh was at her window on that morning soon became obvious to Emilia, she said. Josh carried on in the days following that visit, telling her one night, "She's in the back trailer."

There was an old trailer home in the back of the main house in Boardman. It was abandoned and nobody generally went near it. Weeds and brush had grown up around it. They sometimes used it for storage; but for the most part, the trailer was full of junk nobody used.

"Now, see, what I don't understand," Emilia continued telling Buie, "is when he told me that he killed her, I don't know where at. But I know he had her in my momma's back trailer is what he told me." Emilia stopped. She thought about it. "Look, she wouldn't come there willingly. There's no way that girl would come there willingly."

Emilia said the trailer didn't lock. The door had no latch. Josh knew all of this. He even offered to clear all the brush and clean up the area surrounding the trailer. Emilia's mother told him not to worry about it, but Josh had made a pile of odd junk in back of the trailer one day. No one wondered why. They just assumed Josh wanted to help clean up the yard.

Buie wanted to know exactly what Josh had said. It was important to get the language correct. Buie wondered: Why was Emilia just coming out with this now? Why had she waited so long? Why hold back a potential admission of murder spoken by the father of her child? Was it to protect Josh?

"He told me that he choked her, strangled her, whatever. He told me, 'I choked the bitch out. . . .'"

Emilia explained that when Buie had mentioned the trailer earlier, it all began to click for her. This was not something she had come to easily. She couldn't believe what she was hearing from Buie as he explained some of what Josh had said. She told herself, *Oh, my God, he wasn't playing. 'Cause he says things to try to scare [me] a little bit sometimes.* Emilia claimed she didn't tell Buie this from the start because she "didn't put two and two together. I thought he was full of crap. Then when you said something about my mom's back trailer is when it clicked in my head and that's when I asked to talk to Detective Spivey."

Though he didn't express it just then, Buie had a tough time with the fact that her boyfriend told her he had killed Heather, and Heather had been missing for weeks, and Emilia didn't want to believe it.

There was a sense here that Emilia might have been protecting Josh. Yet, Emilia came across sincere in her explanations regarding what she knew and when. She appeared to be the eight months pregnant girlfriend of a guy who was explosive and had exhibited on many occasions an unstable, unpredictable, even violent temper. There was also a bona fide threat on the table from Josh, Emilia explained further—and that had played in the back of her mind, keeping her from revealing all she knew right away.

"He said if I was ever to pull anything with our baby"—meaning taking off so he couldn't see the child—"that he was going to do to me what he did to her."

When Josh told Emilia that he had killed Heather, she asked him, "Where is she?"

"Well, you know the gators in Orange Lake and you know they digest bones," Emilia recalled Josh telling her. This now gave Emilia the impression that Josh was telling stories to frighten her—because he had said already that Heather was "closer than you think," meaning inside the trailer. Not in Orange Lake.

"Where is she, Josh?" Emilia asked, not sure what to believe. The guy was acting insane, as if something had come over him.

Josh looked her in the eyes, becoming very serious. He

said for the third time since Heather went missing: "Closer than you think."

It was then that Emilia thought how she "hoped [Heather] wasn't in my mom's backyard—because that is sick. . . ."

As she told Detective Buie this part of her story, Emilia added, "I'm scared. His mother is crazy. She will hurt me if I testify."

There had been several run-ins that she'd had with Josh's mother, Emilia explained. She was clearly afraid of the woman.

It was later during that night of February 16, Emilia said, that Josh called her.

"Heather left," Josh explained. "I have the kids."

Josh showed up at Emilia's at eleven that night. He was wasted, Emilia recalled, drunk and talking out of his mind. Stumbling around, mumbling things like, "I'm gonna burn [his] house down. . . . Get all those motherfuckers back for making me look like a fool." Emilia didn't know what people he was referring to.

Because they had split up—by February 16—Emilia said Josh would stop by her mother's house, where she was living after leaving Josh, to drop off some of her belongings. It was during those times, Emilia explained to Buie, when Josh would disappear into the backyard of the house for ten or fifteen minutes and then return. She had no idea what he was doing. She had no reason, she claimed, to question what he was doing. At the time, Heather had not been reported missing.

But as time went on, Emilia told Buie, it was beginning to sound as though Josh took Heather back into that trailer and did bad things to her. What, exactly, she did not have a clue, and she never asked.

Anytime they fought after that day Heather disappeared, Emilia continued, even up until March 12, threats would easily roll off Josh's tongue, as if he could keep Emilia in check by mentioning Heather's disappearance. The guy was paranoid that Emilia was going to leave, she claimed. And when he got really angry, he'd say something like, "Well, you know Heather *ain't* coming home, Emilia."

"What are you talking about, Josh? I thought she was in Mississippi," Emilia would answer. Up until that week of March 12, she was still under the impression that Josh was making it all up, acting like a big shot, tough guy, as he sometimes did. Emilia claimed she had no notion that maybe Josh had done something to Heather, other than what he had said.

Josh would repeat himself: "She's closer than you think."

Buie and Emilia had a heated exchange over when Emilia knew what she knew and why she didn't divulge any of it to the MCSO when she first sat down with Buie. Detective Buie was definitely annoyed that she had kept these things from him. And because of that, Buie believed Emilia was hiding even more.

Emilia said she was "intimidated" by Buie (Josh aside), a cop who had put some pressure on her, maybe a little too much. And according to Emilia, it wasn't until she sat down with the MCSO that she began to believe that Josh might have really done something to Heather. Emilia was always under the impression that Heather, scared of Josh, had run off to Mississippi or somewhere else. And Josh had used her not being around as a means to intimidate and threaten Emilia. Josh had even shown Emilia a letter allegedly signed by Heather in which Heather, Emilia said, had supposedly given him complete custody of the kids. Josh had brought the letter to the kids' school. So as far as Emilia saw things up until this day she had sat down with Buie, Heather had abandoned her children and had taken off.

Buie wanted to know one thing from Emilia: "If you *saw* her in that trailer?" Had Emilia ever ventured out into the trailer herself to check things out?

"I haven't seen her," Emilia said, a touch of *how-dare-you* in her voice. Emilia was getting tired of being bullied by this cop. All she did, she told Buie, was lie by omission. Big deal. She didn't tell the MCSO everything she knew. Was it any reason to be badgered like this?

"I'm terrified," Emilia told Buie.

"*You're* scared?" Buie asked.

"I'm scared of that man. I thought he was full of crap."

Buie took a breath. "He said *you* gave him the cards!" Buie shared with Emilia.

She was struck by this. Heather's debit cards? That's what Josh was now claiming?

It felt like Buie was fishing. He wanted Emilia to know that he was not going to let up. The suggestion to Emilia, again, was that she was trying to hide things to protect the father of the child in her belly. But by now, it seemed Emilia was done with Josh. He'd shown her who he was and what he was capable of; she wanted no part of it.

"He said *you* gave him the cards . . . ," Buie repeated.

"Why would she (Heather) come to my mom's house?" Emilia asked, posing a hypothetical question. "Let me ask you that—these are the things that don't add up. Why would she come there?"

"I didn't say she came there alive," Buie countered.

CHAPTER 21

AS EMILIA WAITED for Buie to return to the interrogation room, the busy detective sat down with Josh Fulgham in the hard room next door. It was 6:20 A.M.

"Josh, you hungry?" Buie asked.

The investigator had a different tone and approach with Josh. Not quite a buddy-buddy vibe, but there was a mildly friendly touch of *"come clean and everything is going to be okay"* in Buie's voice. He wanted Josh to realize that he could trust the MCSO. They were there to help him as much as they could, regardless of his level of involvement. As Buie saw Josh, "He was a big talker—all over the page. He liked to hear himself talk. As much as he liked to talk, at that time he was trying to convince us that he had nothing to do with any of this, that he is totally innocent."

As Buie listened, he studied Josh's body language closely—which, to Buie, told a story in and of itself. The way Josh moved, the facial expressions he used, Buie felt Josh knew what had happened to Heather. Josh couldn't hide it in the way he shifted in his chair, dropped his shoulders at times, the way he'd flare his nostrils while trying to stay calm. They were subtle movements telling Buie that Josh was hiding something.

The detective asked Josh to pick up where he had left off

during an earlier interview. Buie asked Josh to finish what they had been talking about then. And it was clear here with Josh's response to this question that Buie was definitely playing both sides against each other. A tactic any good cop would use in this same situation. Regarding this common method of law enforcement interviewing, Mike Mongeluzzo, another detective involved in the investigation, would later say, "That's not an attempt to play one against the other—it's an attempt to get the truth out of two people that are lying. . . ."

"Something about . . . ," Josh said to Buie, "she (Emilia) told you I took [Heather] in the trailer and I knocked on her door at four in the morning?"

"Five in the morning," Buie corrected.

"But it never happened," Josh said.

"That's not true?" Buie asked, somewhat surprised.

"I never . . . no. I'm going to tell you something. . . . There's *no* way I could kill that girl. I love her too damn much."

Buie dropped his head. They were going backward.

After a few additional questions, Buie got back into what he claimed Emilia had told him concerning Josh being responsible for Heather's disappearance and ultimate demise. They talked about the trailer and Emilia's mother's yard—those piles of brush, newly excavated earth, junk lying around the property, debris, wood, tree limbs, sticks and dead trees. The way Buie played it with Josh was that Emilia had sold him out: Emilia had told the MCSO that Josh had killed Heather and her body was buried somewhere on Emilia's mother's property. Why was Josh denying this?

Josh said no way. It didn't happen like that. He couldn't have done it.

"So everything she's telling me is a lie?" Buie asked, clearly becoming impatient. He was frustrated that either Josh or Emilia—or both—had been giving him the old-fashioned jerk-off.

"If she's telling you that I took that girl in that trailer, that's a lie."

"What about putting her in the hole?" Buie suggested.

"No!" Josh snapped back.

"What about killing her?"

"No!"

Buie backed up. He started from the top. "What about knocking on [Emilia's] window that morning?"

"No. Listen. I know that family well enough. I can go to the door and knock. . . ."

"So everything she is telling me is a lie?" Buie asked again.

"Yes, sir. I didn't take that girl to that trailer and put her in a hole."

"The only person that has any means to do that is who?" Buie asked.

"Heather is my wife," Josh said. "I would *not* kill her." Josh sold it well. He made it sound as though he cared about Heather.

Buie talked about how he was just "relaying stuff back and forth." He explained that Emilia and other witnesses were giving him information he was trying to verify through Josh. A lot of that information, Buie seemed to say without coming out with it entirely, pointed directly back to Josh. The trail led to the husband. The MCSO was following that trail. How was Josh going to respond to all of these fingers pointed at him?

"Where is [Emilia] now?" Josh asked.

"She's still here."

"You going to let her go home?"

"She *ain't* going home," Buie said. That was not necessarily true. Buie implied that Emilia wasn't going to be allowed to leave any time soon. The truth of the matter was that Emilia had not been placed under arrest. She could get up and leave whenever she wanted.

Buie then enlightened Josh by stating how the MCSO had caught him in "numerous, numerous lies," and there was some explaining that had to be done in order for Josh—who had been complaining about being tired and wanted to be put in a jail cell so he could sleep—to get his way.

Josh continued to say he hadn't done anything to Heather; he had no idea what the MCSO was talking about or where Heather was. He believed she took off. Josh was no rookie offender, some green street kid in the hard room for the first time. He understood the games cops played with suspects and witnesses. He knew how cops juggled information and played the "good cop/bad cop" scenario with multiple suspects at the same time. The fact that Emilia was in the next room and being questioned as though she'd had something to do with Heather's disappearance told Josh he was dealing with a cop who had embarked on a fishing trip. So Josh decided he was going to play his cards close to the vest here. He would be careful with what he divulged, and would try to figure out what the MCSO knew.

"You taking us to the spot?" Buie asked. The question seemed random—out of nowhere. Implying that the MCSO had information leading them to a particular place where Heather might be. There was a certain feeling in how Buie spoke letting Josh know the MCSO might have found out that Heather was either buried on Emilia's mother's property or left dead inside that trailer. The MCSO was working on obtaining a search warrant as Buie and Josh spoke. However, Buie wanted Josh to commit to at least this one request before they could go any further.

Josh was rattled by the suggestion. "I don't even know if that's where she's at, man. I don't know that's where she's at. I *hope* she's not in the ground."

"All I got to say, Josh, if somebody did this with you, you need to expose that person also. Don't take this power rap by yourself."

Josh sighed. Then he rubbed his face, as if doing this would refresh him, maybe wake him up. Using his hands to articulate, he said, "I didn't do it. I'm telling you, I *didn't* do it. I mean, I know I lied to you, and you cannot trust me—"

Buie interrupted: "I'm not saying I can't trust you. I just don't *totally* trust you."

"I ain't got it in me, man. I really don't. I know I've got a violent background, but I ain't got it in me to kill my wife, man."

Buie wasn't getting anywhere. That much was clear. When he realized Josh wasn't yet ready to be honest and talk about whatever he was hiding (if anything), Buie asked Josh if he was willing to give up a DNA sample. Let's start there. Extract some DNA in good faith and see where the investigation went. Buie didn't explain why. He left it hanging again, suggesting that the MCSO had forensic evidence.

"Okay," Josh said.

Buie got up and walked out of the room, letting Josh know he was going to get a DNA kit and the paperwork. He'd be right back.

When he returned about twenty minutes later, Josh asked about Emilia and how she was doing. He came across as though he was generally concerned. Then: "How long before I get moved over to the jail?"

"It's going to be a little bit. So if you need to relax, go ahead," Buie encouraged.

Josh said he was freezing "his ass" off inside the room. "Is [Emilia] okay over there?"

Buie stuck his head inside the room where Emilia sat patiently.

She was fine.

Back with Josh, Buie said, "Uh-huh. Just went and checked on her. . . ."

Josh wanted to know if Emilia was giving a DNA sample, too.

Buie told him yes, she was—though they had yet to ask her.

After Buie got his DNA sample, he left, telling Josh to hang tight, and he'd be back in a few.

CHAPTER 22

DETECTIVE BUIE PUT on his Emilia Carr cap and walked back into the soft room, where Emilia was waiting. Emilia had been firm in her position, but also a bit standoffish and not so cooperative as far as everything she knew. The MCSO was well aware of this.

In Emilia's defense, her lack of cooperation didn't mean she was covering up for her old flame; it only meant, Emilia said later, that she was not in the business of giving cops everything they asked for, just because they asked for it. Emilia knew the rub: Buie was playing her as much as she was playing him. Far as Emilia considered, Josh could be anywhere. Josh could even be out, walking the streets. Emilia didn't trust cops to tell the truth all the time. Bottom line for her was: Could Josh get to her? This was a genuine concern for her. Emilia understood Josh's internal rage; she had seen it firsthand. Emilia recognized what Josh was capable of. And now, after talking with Buie and Spivey, Emilia claimed to have figured out that Josh actually had killed Heather, when for the entire time Heather had been missing Emilia claimed to believe Heather had taken off.

Last time they chatted, Buie and Emilia were trading

barbs over a particular point of contention: Did Emilia know Josh had taken Heather into the trailer? Buie was firm in his position that he believed Emilia might have even been at her mother's when Josh brought Heather over there. One of the last things Buie had shared with Emilia before he stepped in to speak with Josh was: "He could have brought her to your house. I don't know if she was dead or alive when she came."

"Oh, dear God," Emilia responded to that comment.

When Buie returned, Emilia spoke up immediately: "I remember something."

Of course you do.

"What's that?" Buie asked.

"I don't know how relevant it is, but you said you asked his daughter some questions."

"Uh-huh," Buie agreed. He was interested in this.

Emilia explained that she didn't want Buie to run out and sit down with Josh's daughter, because the girl was only eight years old, but if they did speak with her again at some point, Emilia wanted them to ask the child if "she remembers the day we were all out at [my] mom's house and Josh told me that there was a stray dog in the back he was scaring away." Emilia went on to explain how Josh demanded on that day that she keep the kids "up front" and away from that backyard area. "Just ask her if she remembers that. That was one of the days he was out in the backyard. . . ." As Emilia now saw that moment, she was thinking Josh was doing something that involved the child's mother out back and didn't want anyone to sneak up on him—especially the kids.

Buie didn't seem too excited by this revelation. He moved on.

After some conversation about getting her something to eat, Emilia said, "I'm hurting."

"Where are you hurting at?"

Emilia Carr, eight months pregnant, said, "My belly."

Buie explained that he was going to be keeping her another several hours and was sorry it was uncomfortable, adding, "We got to find out what's there at the house."

The strategy the MCSO was working under (without sharing it with Emilia or Josh) was to get Josh out to the trailer to point some things out for them. If they could get him into the situation—and what they now believed was a crime scene of some sort—they could begin tossing hardball questions at Josh and maybe crack him. This was the virtual-reality version of taking a crime scene photograph as a suspect talked and sliding it across the table, placing the end result of a serious crime in front of a perp's face, hopefully, to unsettle him. It often worked when you had a suspect on the verge of a major break.

The detective asked Emilia if she would be "okay" with them questioning her some more.

"Yeah," she answered. "I hope to gosh she ain't there."

"You want a candy bar?" Buie asked.

"I just want to go home to my babies."

Buie said something about how an investigation was ongoing; and because of that, and because of Emilia "misleading [them] a lot in this investigation, covering up and lying in this investigation," she was a "potential suspect in this investigation," too. Emilia had done this to herself, in other words. It was a warning to come clean and stop lying by omission if she wanted them to work together toward her needs.

Emilia said she understood.

Buie explained how she was now being "detained." Her presence there at the MCSO was no longer voluntary. Emilia was being held by the MCSO.

She could no longer leave on her own.

The DNA question came next.

Emilia said the MCSO already had her DNA. "I was

arrested a few years back on a felony charge and they did my prints and took a swab."

Buie said he wanted a fresh swab.

Emilia said she was okay with that, adding, "I'm not going to let some sick man cost me my children."

After Buie took the swab, he ended the interview.

CHAPTER 23

JOSH FULGHAM WAS drained and couldn't really think straight. Yet, he was not tired enough to be interested in what Emilia had been saying. Detective Buie later noted, "The guy would not stop talking. All he wanted to do, once he got going, was talk and talk and talk."

Buie told Josh he couldn't share any of the information Emilia had given them just yet. Then he read Josh his Miranda rights again, surely trying to send a message that Emilia had divulged information causing the MCSO to believe Josh knew where Heather was and had been involved in her disappearance.

Josh then decided he wanted to go back to his jail cell and get some sleep before they continued. He was too tired. He wanted to be fresh.

"You wasting my time?" Buie asked. "Do you *not* want to do this?"

"Start over in the morning," Josh suggested casually.

"Do you *not* want to do this?" Buie asked again. He was under the impression Josh had something important to share. That's what Josh had told one of Buie's colleagues while Buie was out of the room.

"I guess not," Josh said. "'Cause I want to sleep and we'll start over in the morning!" He sounded a bit more firm.

Buie decided to play a card: "I'm *not* coming back in this room."

"Tomorrow can we?" Josh said.

"No," Buie snapped back. He then stood and walked out of the room without saying anything more.

"Wait . . . ," Josh said, pleading.

Buie had made it as far as the hallway outside the room, when he turned and walked back in.

"What?" Buie asked as he faced Josh.

"We're done?" Josh asked. He sounded shocked—surprised that Buie had given up on him so quickly.

"Listen . . . Josh. I have no—I *don't* want to play games."

"I'm not trying to."

Buie said he was finished with the dance they had been doing all night long. It was close to sunup on March 19. Buie was tired, too. He said he'd rather not talk at all if Josh was going to play him for a fool, adding once again how, if he left the room for a second time, Josh would be entirely on his own.

A look of worry came over Josh.

Buie sat down. "You want to talk to me or not?" the detective asked quietly.

"Yes, yes," Josh said. Then he said if he was "going down for something, I don't want to take somebody that might have did something down [too]. . . . You see what I'm talking about?"

However confusing it had come out, Buie said he understood.

Josh admitted that what he had shared earlier during a conversation with Buie out in back of the building, while he was allowed to smoke a cigarette, wasn't exactly the entire truth. In fact, Heather had never called Josh's mother's house on the day she went missing. Josh said he wanted to clarify this, because he had reported that to Buie previously. Apparently, Heather had never asked him to meet her at the

Petro because she was taking off and wanted to leave the children with him.

"That was not the truth," Josh admitted.

Detective Buie now knew they were getting somewhere and encouraged Josh to continue.

While at Heather's house that night, Josh explained, he had sex with her (probably another lie). Afterward, he didn't hang around. He left almost immediately. Things were okay between them. They were acting civilly toward each other. They were even talking about getting back together (also a lie). But now Josh had this other woman in his life, Emilia (who was pregnant), which posed a major problem for Heather. Josh never said whether Heather knew if Emilia was pregnant with Josh's child, or if Emilia knew that Josh was thinking of getting back with his wife. These were two very important facts Josh did not share at this time.

Josh arrived home to Emilia that night, after supposedly having had sex with Heather, and Josh said his girlfriend never suspected anything. But two weeks later, long after Heather went missing, Emilia approached Josh and said something about Heather being gone. The way Josh told it was, although Emilia might have never come across as knowing Josh had slept with Heather, she certainly knew he was seeing her again.

Josh explained to Buie that he asked Emilia on that night if she knew anything about Heather's disappearance. She had made remarks that led him to believe she might.

According to what Josh told Detective Buie, Emilia had responded to Josh as follows: "She's 'gone and not to worry about her.'"

Was this a tit-for-tat situation? After he realized Emilia had obviously told the MCSO something and had used his name, was Josh now putting the onus back on her?

Buie, who didn't care one way or another how Josh felt

about their conversations with Emilia, asked Josh if he had questioned Emilia further about that particular comment.

Josh said he didn't, adding, "I don't know. . . . I didn't believe her. I figured Heather would be back by [then] and take the kids. To be honest with you, I really did. . . ."

So Heather had never left the kids with Josh?

That much, it appeared to Buie, Josh had just admitted.

"Do you think Emilia had something to do with it?" Buie asked.

"I don't know."

According to what Josh said next, Emilia told him Heather's boyfriend, James Acome, along with a friend of James's, were both involved in Heather's disappearance.

"And Heather told me something, too," Josh said.

"What's that?"

"That them two boys were offering money to get rid of her."

None of this made sense to Buie. He questioned Josh further about it. Josh said he never took any of it seriously because Heather was known to take off and leave "for a long period of time." So Josh never really worried too much that something awful had happened with her being gone all that time. But now that he'd had a period to think it through, considering that James and his friend were involved (as Emilia had implied and Heather herself had seemed to back up with that comment), Josh said he believed they might have tossed Heather into Orange Lake to be eaten up by the gators. He concluded that thought by saying, "I don't want to believe something bad happened to her."

Buie broke into a long rant about Emilia and how pissed off he was at her for running him around in circles, clearly using Josh's feelings for Emilia—and these new admissions—against him. Buie could tell Josh was on the fence with Emilia: Josh was ready to give her up totally, and, at the same time, he was trying to keep her close by, as an ally.

Near the end of a long back-and-forth between the two men, as Josh noticeably felt completely comfortable with Buie and surely understood Buie was on his side, the detective said, "Listen to me . . . hold my hand. Let's get through this. It's late. You owe it to your kids."

Josh nodded yes.

"It got out of hand. . . . Be a man."

Josh nodded yes again. He was slipping, falling into Buie's arms.

"Let's go get this girl . . . ," Buie suggested. "Let's do the right thing. You got me to fucking tear up here . . . 'cause I know how you feel." Buie talked about how Emilia didn't "give a fuck" about Josh or the fact that Heather was "the mother of your child. . . . She gave *birth* to your children."

"Can I get a phone call—and I will find out right where [Heather's] at?"

What?

Buie thought he had Josh on the ropes. What did he mean by "phone call"?

"Who are you going to call?" Buie wondered.

By then, Josh was under the impression that Emilia had been driven back home and was no longer across the hall.

"Emilia," Josh said. That's who he needed to call in order to find out where Heather was. According to Josh, she would know.

Buie said he was going to get Emilia picked back up and Josh could speak to her once Emilia returned to Major Crimes.

Josh wanted to know if Buie was going to be speaking with Emilia as soon as she arrived.

"I'm not talking to Emilia," Buie said. "Because . . . you know what? She's a coldhearted bitch, and you don't *owe* Emilia shit. She done set sail on you already. . . . Think about your daughter. Think about your son. Let's do the proper thing for their mother. You ain't gotta tell me nothing in between. Nothing. Just take me to where she is. I just want to see her. I just want to get her from where she is."

Josh paused. He was thinking about what Buie had said. Then: "Well, say I did something to her—I didn't have *nothing* to do with it."

Detective Buie breathed a sigh. His suspect appeared ready to give it up.

CHAPTER 24

EMILIA WAS WITH Detective Sergeant Brian Spivey at her mother's house in Boardman, Florida, an Orange Lakeside small town just north of McIntosh, Reddick and Ocala. But they were not at Emilia's for a social visit or a break from Emilia being questioned. Spivey and Emilia were conducting a "walk-through" of that property, specifically the abandoned trailer in the backyard. A lot had gone on behind the scenes with several detectives working the case as Buie and Spivey kept their focus on questioning Josh and Emilia. The MCSO had learned many new bits of information about the case overnight, all of which pointed to one conclusion.

The house was a lime green clapboard, small, box-style ranch, with obvious roof decay (a blue tarp covered a portion of it). The house required some much-needed renovating or, rather, a large bulldozer to push it down so they could start over. Paint crumbled off the clapboards, the doors, the windowpanes. It seemed that invasive vines had overtaken the back of the home and sections of the carport. To the right of the front door were two signs: PRIVATE—KEEP OUT and BEWARE OF DOG. There were several ficus trees loaded with hanging Spanish moss, giving the yard your typical Deep South feel, as if Spivey and Emilia were wading through the swamps of Louisiana.

Spivey and Emilia were outside now, in the back, standing near the trailer they had talked about at Major Crimes. That trailer, located not far from the house (maybe a two-minute walk), had also seen better days. It had a film of mildew and organic growth all over the outside. It was white at one time, but now had taken on a greenish, black, moldy color. Much of it had been overcome by brush and weeds. There were beautiful palm trees all around, but it was hard to see them because the forest had grown in so thickly.

Revealing a fact she had held back until now, Emilia explained how she had walked out there just after Heather went missing and noticed that the door was closed. It seemed to Major Crimes that every time they spoke to Emilia, they learned more about this case—a fact that told Spivey and Buie that Emilia was holding out and possibly knew what had happened.

"I opened the door and came in," Emilia clarified.

"Was there anything outside?" Spivey wanted to know. (Though he didn't let on to her, during this interaction, Spivey believed Emilia was playing the role of *"Oh, my gosh . . . I cannot believe this is happening. I had no idea. I didn't know what Josh is capable of. . . . I'm afraid of him."*)

"Her stories began to sound self-serving," Spivey said later, "which made me think that she was involved in some way. She played the role of the poor, little, innocent girl."

It was all bullshit.

"Glass," Emilia answered Spivey's question, ". . . and I looked down and I saw glass, and I came in and that's when I looked up and I saw the broken window."

It was that broken window initially sparking Emilia's interest, she explained to Spivey as they stepped into the trailer. She had walked by and noticed the broken glass and eventually looked inside the trailer to see if there was anything out of place. That is, the broken window was the impetus for her to go inside the trailer—it led her to believe something was wrong. Or something had happened inside.

Spivey expressed some concern after Emilia revealed how she and her mother had gone out into the trailer the previous week (the week before her interviews with the MCSO) to move a desk.

What were they doing? he thought.

The timing seemed odd.

Or maybe convenient.

With a quick cursory look inside the trailer, however, once Spivey walked in, he could tell that the family definitely used it as a storage facility. There were bags of clothes, bikes, toys, garbage, old bed frames, furniture, boxes of diapers, old electrical appliances, shoes, coolers, art supplies and crafts items, box springs, a refrigerator, empty food boxes, cleaning products, suitcases, and other household furnishings strewn all over the place, even stacked in the corners, on top of tables and chairs, some turned over as if someone had ransacked the place. Emilia told Spivey she had moved the desk and some other items "to get to the kids' clothes," which were in boxes. It was the main reason why she and her mom had gone out to the trailer to begin with.

Now it made sense.

But there was something inside the trailer she saw on that day, Emilia explained as they walked around, that was shocking.

Something terrible.

Something horrific.

Spivey asked Emilia to elaborate.

"I just kept walking and that's when I came in here"—another room inside the trailer—"and I saw her in the chair. . . . She was taped to it. I just kind of stopped for a minute. I didn't know what to think or what to do. And then I just went up to her and I was checking for a pulse."

Saw *her*? Heather? Was Emilia now saying she had seen Heather strapped to a chair and checked her body for a pulse?

Quite the revelation Emilia had been holding on to.

Spivey turned a corner, walking down a short hallway, and there in front of him was a black desk chair, some used gray duct tape on the floor nearby, and a large, black, leaf-type plastic bag next to the tape. They were not simply tossed into this section of the trailer like all of the other junk; these items stood out. Something had happened here. A space had been cleared: the chair in the middle, a blanket or sheet of some sort on the floor, next to the bag, and the tape. It had a Mafia feel to it, as though a hit man had put a snitch in a chair and had tortured him before killing the son of a bitch.

Spivey looked at Emilia. *What the hell happened in here?*

CHAPTER 25

IF THAT HAD been some sort of admission from Josh Fulgham, it was poorly worded and vague, to say the least. Detective Buie needed more than "Well, say I did something to her—I didn't have *nothing* to do with it."

In the scope of the night and the interviews he'd conducted with Josh, Buie wondered, just what in the hell did this mean? Was Josh trying to say he knew where Heather was, what happened, but he had no hand in getting her there? How could he expect the MCSO to buy both: Josh had done something to Heather, but he didn't have anything to do with it at the same time?

"That's fine . . . ," the detective said at one point, clearly frustrated yet again at Josh's unwillingness to be straight with him.

"What would happen to me, though?" Josh wanted to know.

Buie explained that he didn't want to make any promises. All he needed from Josh was for him to show Major Crimes where Heather's body was located. That was the most important action Josh could take for himself at this point. Stop all the nonsense of Heather being kept captive somewhere. Buie indicated that they all knew Heather was never coming home. She was dead. So there was no need to talk as if she had been kidnapped by James Acome and his buddy and was being held in a warehouse somewhere, like some rich man's daughter would be. That was all nonsense.

Get to the damn truth.

"I'm worried about losing my babies for life," Josh said. Then he changed his story once again, adding, "I don't know what they did with her, but I can find out. I give you my word. I can find out."

It took Buie some time to explain to Josh that nothing else mattered except locating Heather. He ignored Josh's previous statement and instead asked: "Is she in the water? Is she in the dirt? Is she in a building? Is she in a car?"

Where the hell *is* she?

Josh went back to insisting that all he needed was some time alone with Emilia and he could get out of her what James Acome and his buddy had done to Heather. He was certain of it. Emilia knew something, Josh kept saying.

Buie asked Josh if he actually believed and thought James Acome and the other guy were holding Heather. It sounded ridiculous the way Buie put it. It was so asinine that Buie didn't even want to talk about it anymore. You could almost hear Buie thinking: *Come on, Josh . . . you're a seasoned criminal—you have been fingered, friend.*

Let go. Give it up.

"You think they got her somewhere for thirty days and they're feeding her?" Buie speculated with a touch of sarcastic impatience in his tone. There was nothing worse for a man in Josh's position than to patronize an irritated, fatigued detective on the cusp of getting his man.

"I cannot see nobody killing [her]," Josh said.

"But you *know* she's dead—you *know* she's dead, Josh."

"Man, I *don't* know. . . ."

Buie found it hard to believe that James Acome, a man he had interviewed earlier that day himself, had a motive to kill Heather. He wanted Josh to humor him with his idea of a motive.

Josh said, "If they did, it would be for getting laid."

Rape?

No way.

"James was *with* her!" Buie pointed out. "He was *living* with her."

"They split up that day, man," Josh said. "She put his ass out."

Now Josh was trying to say it was revenge?

Buie wasn't buying it.

Josh said, "Listen . . . listen . . . they split up that day. She was getting rid of him because he was trying to take over everything, and I told her, 'Heather . . . there's something else. He was fucking a fourteen-year-old little girl.' . . . I told her that. . . ."

Buie recalled an interview with James Acome, which the MCSO had done, wherein James had admitted that Josh would say something like this, but James had said it was a sixteen-year-old girl. Perfectly legal. (Acome had never been charged with a crime even remotely connected to young girls.)

Buie made a good point when he next said: "He ain't been convicted of it." The detective was somewhat disappointed in Josh's feeble attempt to claim James Acome and his friend had kidnapped Heather. He kept telling Josh the MCSO wasn't buying his pack of lies anymore and Buie, personally, was sick of it. They had caught Josh, time and again, in lies. Time was running out for Joshua Fulgham, Buie made perfectly clear. Josh needed to come clean with what he knew or there wasn't much left that Buie could do for him.

Then Buie made the suggestion that Josh knew where Heather was because he'd had something to do with murdering her.

Suddenly things had just gotten very serious for Josh Fulgham.

"I didn't do that . . . ," Josh balked.

Buie said he was done. He was going out to find where Emilia was.

CHAPTER 26

JOSHUA FULGHAM HAD talked himself into a corner of problems that the MCSO was not willing to hear. Josh insisted that all he needed to do was speak with Emilia and he could tell them where Heather was and would clear everything up.

The MCSO wasn't biting, though.

"You need to take us to that body," a detective who had stepped in after Buie walked out told Josh. "You need to take us to where she's at."

"I can't do that . . . until I talk to [Emilia]."

"Josh, you can't."

That ship had sailed, the detective made clear, telling Josh, "She's denying the whole thing."

Josh continued to say he didn't know what had happened.

Buie came back into the room.

"Josh, she's telling me that you're full of crap," the other detective reiterated, referring to Emilia, as Buie got settled.

"Full of it," Buie added.

Josh slipped down into his chair. They clearly had him on the ropes. The lies Josh had told all night were catching up with him. It's one reason why cops allow a suspect to lie their way through an interview without being challenged (at first)—because sooner or later, the suspect cannot keep track of the lies. And that was the spot Buie and his team believed Josh Fulgham was now in.

"Sit up, sit up," Buie told Josh.

Josh insisted he did not know where Heather's body was located.

Buie told him repeatedly that they were not accepting that statement any longer.

Both detectives started to badger Josh, coming at him from both sides. "You know where's she at. . . . Just tell us . . . just tell us. . . ."

Josh complained of being sleepy. He said he wanted to go back to his cell. Josh said: "I don't know where the body is. . . . I haven't done anything. I did nothing to her."

"You are the *last* person that was with her," Buie said.

Josh snapped: "Damn, I should not have . . . fuck!"

"You shouldn't have been *what*?"

"With the bitch, man . . . *damn*."

"Tell me about it."

"Fuck her!"

"Tell me . . ."

"It's time to sleep."

"Tell me about her, Josh." As any expert interrogator in the same position would do, Buie appealed to Josh's anger, and what was potentially churning in his mind. It was time for Buie to take a real crack at him. This was the opening Buie had been waiting on. Clearly, Josh was becoming angry with Heather as he sat there. Rage was building. Buie fed off it and used it against Josh, banking on what the MCSO believed to be a motive.

"She was taking your kids away!" Buie shouted.

"She couldn't take them from *me*. . . ."

Josh then ranted about Heather and how he had always gone back to her—no matter what. He'd demand she toss out whichever man was living with her at the time after they split up and he would move back in. This seesaw love affair went on for eleven years. Josh loved the woman. He said this, over and over. There was no way he could ever do anything to hurt her. It was Emilia. They needed to speak with Emilia. She knew. Josh said he needed to get some sleep before he passed out on the table right there.

"Let me go talk to [him] for a minute," Buie said, indicating that he needed to step outside the room and speak with a colleague.

Did Buie have an idea?

CHAPTER 27

AT SOME POINT on March 19, Josh Fulgham gave it up. Sort of.

"He was getting, so to speak, worn down," Buie said later. "He had let a few things slip out, which he then pointed to Emilia and blamed her."

Either way, Buie knew they had him. Josh, too, realized he was going to be better off in the end if he told them what they wanted to hear.

Buie explained to Josh that the MCSO was going to go ahead and charge Josh with the flagrant use of Heather's credit card. It wasn't much, but it was enough to hold him.

"Wait," Josh said.

Buie asked what he wanted.

"Look, if you allow me to take my wallet to my mom and kiss my kids, I'll . . . I'll . . . take you to where Heather is."

Detective Buie . . . advised that Josh had disclosed to him about an area in the back of the [Maria Zayas, Emilia's mother's] residence that possibly could contain the body of Heather Strong, said a report filed by the MCSO.

"He told me he was ready to go out there and find her," Buie explained later.

There was a team of detectives and crime scene investigators (CSIs) assembling to head out to the Boardman property and have a look around. Josh had claimed there was possibly a "freshly" dug grave and some "disturbed" dirt in an area near that abandoned trailer in the back of Maria Zayas's property. And that was where they would "possibly" find Heather's body buried in a shallow grave.

Buie went to Maria and found her underneath the carport on the left side of her home. Maria said she had some information regarding Josh and a shovel.

This, of course, was of great interest to Buie. "Can we go inside that car over there and speak?" Buie asked her. He wanted to get the conversation on tape.

She said sure.

"It was the fifteenth or the sixteenth," Maria said, referring to February, "around three or four in the afternoon. Josh came by here and asked to borrow a shovel."

Maria was curious why Josh needed a shovel, so she asked him.

"Oh, damn, wouldn't you know, I just hit a dog on the highway and need to bury it," Josh had reportedly told her.

Maria gave him a spade shovel and then walked back into her home to finish cooking dinner.

"I didn't see where he went with the shovel," Maria told Buie.

"I see."

It was forty minutes later when Josh returned with the shovel. He said thanks and left.

"The next morning," Maria explained to Buie, "Emilia woke me up and said Josh was banging on her window. I went outside and saw him there. He said he wanted to come by and see Emilia. . . ."

Josh came back later that same day after he got out of work. There was an argument between Emilia and Josh, Maria said, so Josh left and went back to his mother's house.

And that was all Maria Zayas could offer.

CHAPTER 28

WHILE EMILIA AND Detective Brian Spivey were inside that trailer talking later on during the day, on March 19, Spivey asked Emilia to point out for him exactly which chair she was referring to. Where was it Emilia had seen Heather strapped to a chair? Spivey was beginning to have a problem with Emilia and her sudden revelation of seeing Heather's body inside the trailer.

It all seems like a show she's putting on, Spivey thought.

Emilia pointed to the black chair closest to them: "Right there."

"Okay, then tell me what you mean, 'She was *taped* to it'?"

Emilia said Heather's hands were bound and her body was fastened to the chair with "silver, gray tape. . . . She was kind of slouched in the chair and her head was leaning back."

Spivey asked for specifics: Where, exactly, was she taped? On which parts of her body? These facts would become important later. The detective wanted them coming out of Emilia's mouth, into his ears, traveling then onto the pages of a report.

Documented.

That way Emilia would own them.

"The tape was around her neck, where the bag was, and

there was tape around her wrists, and there was some tape around her ankles."

Bag? *Now* there was a bag involved?

This was astonishing information. It seemed to suggest that Heather had been kidnapped, held, and either tortured and murdered, or left to die.

Emilia said she panicked when she saw this. It was startling. She had a tough time registering what she was looking at. It didn't seem real. She then told herself she had to check to see if Heather was still alive. Staring at Heather, Emilia had no idea. So she put her fingers on Heather's wrists to check for a pulse and then tried to find out if she was breathing.

To Emilia's dismay, Heather was dead.

Spivey asked Emilia what she did next. The detective had a few issues with this story. Here it was a month later, for one, and Emilia was just now relating it to the police. Why would she hold on to such a sordid, horrific tale for such a long period of time? To protect Josh? Or had Heather's killer (or killers) threatened Emilia, keeping her quiet?

"I just kind of looked at her and started to cry," Emilia claimed. "I didn't know what to do, what to think. I turned and started walking out. Then I sat on the back step and I cried and then went inside."

Emilia needed a breath. She was back there, reliving that moment when she found Heather. It was exhausting and emotionally taxing, she said. She put both her hands on her belly and rubbed softly. The stress was not good for the child.

Spivey needed to know what other information Emilia had been holding on to. He asked if she recognized the tape as coming from somewhere inside the main house or somewhere else. Had she ever seen that tape before?

Emilia said, "Everywhere you can find rolls [of tape like that]. . . ."

"That's all you remember seeing that day?"

Emilia looked down. She knew something. "That he . . . had told her there was money stashed somewhere."

He?

"And who's 'he'?" Spivey wondered.

"Josh."

If Emilia had thrown Josh under a bus earlier, as Detective Buie had suggested, well, now she had invited an eighteen-wheeler to come by and run over him. Because, according to what Emilia Carr was now saying, Joshua Fulgham had strapped his wife to a chair inside this trailer and murdered her.

Yet as Spivey would soon learn as Emilia continued talking, there was more.

Much more.

CHAPTER 29

IT WAS DARK outside, heading toward the morning sunrise of March 19. Detectives Mike Mongeluzzo, Brian Spivey, Donald Buie, along with Josh Fulgham, traveled down Highway 441 in an unmarked black Crown Vic.

Josh had given it up—mostly. He now said he was willing to take them to Heather's body. He wanted to go see his mother and his kids after escorting the team to where they wanted to go.

Buie said sure.

"Why do you shave your head?" Mongeluzzo asked Josh. This was something investigators did. They were Josh's friends now. They would do what he asked—within reason—and cater to what he wanted while he was providing detailed, truthful information—all of which could help close this case and get Heather's family some answers. Making small talk like this, building on a rapport, was part of being a good cop. It made Josh feel like he was a human being, not just some lunatic killer taking them to see his work.

"It's cooler," Josh said. He rubbed his bald head.

Spivey and Mongeluzzo talked together about the case as Josh sat, listened and then piped in, apparently wanting to make something clear.

"Man, I'm going to tell you how it is right now. . . . I

didn't do this shit. I didn't have it done. But I *know* it was done."

Mongeluzzo said, "Okay. And you're taking us to her. It's the right thing to do."

"Where I'm *told* she was," Josh clarified. "I didn't see her, but from what they tell me, she's dead, man."

Josh kept saying he didn't have anything to do with Heather's death. He only knew about it from what others had told him. He said this, over and over, without offering any insight or new facts to back it up. Here was a guy taking cops to a dead body—a woman who just happened to be the wife he had been battling with and separated from—and he was saying he had nothing to do with killing her or dumping her body. With that, these cops had to wonder if Josh was blowing smoke up their asses, or was he beginning to come clean?

As they got closer to Maria Zayas's house, Josh said, "A pile of shit in front of the trailer, behind her mother's house." He was explaining—to the best of his knowledge, he claimed—where he thought Heather was buried, based on what he had been told. As Josh explained it, Heather was underneath a pile of brush and trash, buried in a shallow grave. He started to freak out a bit inside the car as they got closer to where her body was supposedly buried.

Buie asked if Heather had been moved since she had been put out there.

"I don't know, man. I'll tell you what I was told. . . . Please don't make me see that shit again."

What did Josh mean by "again"? Had he seen it once already?

The way he explained it, Josh didn't want to view the body. He was getting nervous that they were going to make him stand by as CSIs dug Heather up from out of the ground.

"You just point it out to me and I'll go see it," Buie said.

They arrived at the trailer and Josh insisted he stay inside the car. In the back of the main house, where Emilia and her mother lived with Emilia's sister, was the trailer. In back of the trailer, heading northeast about ten to twenty paces, was a pile of debris.

After some prodding, Josh got out of the car.

"He walked around the yard," Buie explained later, "pointing to various places. . . . 'Maybe there, or there. . . . No, it's over here . . . ,' acting like he wasn't sure."

Buie didn't believe him. He felt Josh was jerking them around, but he kept it to himself for the time being.

Then Josh said it was there (pointing), underneath that pile of garbage, based on what he had been told, that they'd possibly find Heather.

Buie walked out into the yard. He looked around. He saw the pile of debris. Someone had done a poor job of raking leaves over a cleared area to make it look natural. Buie found the spot in the ground where, he believed, the earth had been recently dug. He grabbed a stick and stuck it into the ground—and the stick went down into the earth like a toothpick through a perfectly cooked cake.

"And I knew that's where she was," Buie said.

Before he walked away, something else struck Buie. There was a chair there, turned over. But it didn't look weathered, like all of the other debris. It appeared to be much newer, as though it had been placed outside only recently.

Buie called in the CSIs to navigate the search. It had to be done delicately. You find a body and that's a win, but there is also evidence that needs to be collected at the same time.

After the team assembled and Spivey went off to speak with other colleagues at the crime scene (he would ultimately stay at the scene), Mongeluzzo and Buie took Josh to his mother's house, as promised, so he could see his "babies" one more time before he and the officers went back to Major Crimes and allowed Josh some sleep before interviewing him again.

Josh was shackled and chained; Mongeluzzo carried a shotgun. There were not going to be any surprises for Buie and Mongeluzzo inside the house. They felt Josh's mother had been hostile when they interviewed her earlier that month and here they were waking her up, her son chained, two detectives escorting him as he told them where to find his wife's body. The situation lent itself to volatility and uncertainty. Buie and Mongeluzzo were not taking any chances.

"Are they saying you killed her?" Josh's mother, Judy Chandler, asked him as they walked in. She then said something about seeing on television that Josh could get life if he'd had something to do with Heather's death. "Well, how you going to get life in prison if *they* killed her?" she asked him. Then she turned her attention toward Buie and Mongeluzzo: "I don't know how you are going to prove it."

"Where the babies at?" Buie wanted to know.

"In bed," Judy said. Judy might have come across as crass and a little bit perturbed; but from her point of view, Judy was a mother whose son was being accused of killing her daughter-in-law. Judy had temporary custody of their children. Two detectives had shown up at her door without warning, her son arrested and shackled. There was a detective standing in her living room, holding a shotgun. Her life had been turned upside down overnight.

Buie and Mongeluzzo told Josh not to wake the kids. They'd allow him to give them a kiss on the cheek, but they gave him strict instructions not to disturb them.

"Why you carrying that shotgun?" Judy asked Mongeluzzo. At first sight, it seemed a bit over the top. But Mongeluzzo was a seasoned investigator—he knew the difference between things getting out of hand or things staying calm was sometimes the presence of power.

"Because my partner's in here with somebody . . . for his own protection," Mongeluzzo said.

"You got his ankles chained," Judy responded, clearly alarmed.

"I don't know who's here."

"I beg your pardon?"

"I don't know who's here—who could jump out of a closet."

Josh's mother was frightened and taken aback by the weapon. She felt they were taking things too far.

When Josh came out of the kids' bedroom, he stared at his mother with a look of utter defeat. It was as if he knew she was never going to see him again inside this house.

"You are not going to prison for something I know [James] and them [did]!" Judy said.

"I love you" was all Josh could muster.

After a short exchange between Josh and Judy, Mongeluzzo called on Josh's mother to listen to him while Buie escorted Josh outside to the vehicle.

Judy paid attention.

"To let you understand why we're here in this area, okay," Mongeluzzo said as Judy watched Josh leave the house with Buie. "He just showed us where she was buried at." Mongeluzzo allowed the information to settle with Judy.

Judy put her hands over her mouth. Then, surprised, she asked: "Where she's buried at?"

They talked some more, and Josh's mother said: "If Emilia told everybody that her and [James] . . . did it—"

Mongeluzzo interrupted: "Emilia didn't say that. . . . Emilia put it all on him."

"We'll see. That's what I figure."

"It's a 'he say/she say.'"

Mongeluzzo clarified best he could all of the evidence they had against Josh—as much as they were willing to release (publicly)—and told Judy that her son had done nothing but lie to them. If Josh was telling the truth now, that he had nothing to do with it, those facts would eventually emerge and he had less to be concerned about.

Josh's mother talked about that February night in question. She said he wasn't gone that long. How could he possibly have killed Heather?

Mongeluzzo said it didn't take long to murder someone.

As he began to walk out the door, Mongeluzzo apologized to Judy for the show of force and the intrusion.

Outside, Josh said to Buie and Mongeluzzo, "Sorry my mom got mad."

They drove away.

A window was down in the car and a nice breeze blew in. Josh could smell the heat of the day just beginning to rise. It had been a long night, he said to the guys as they made their way back to Major Crimes.

Buie told him, yeah, long night, but they still had more questions they needed answers to; the situation was far from over.

The noise of traffic going by was loud.

Josh leaned his head against the door, now thinking about putting the entire murder—the idea, the plan, the crime—on Emilia. If he was going to get out of this, he needed to take drastic measures.

CHAPTER 30

EMILIA COULD BE persuasive, Josh explained to me in a letter. He was referring to that period of their relationship when he returned from Mississippi to find that Emilia had gotten married. Josh said he found out, after speaking with a friend, that her husband was in jail at the time. Emilia came out in those skimpy "booty shorts" that day (because she knew how to tempt Josh) and told him not to worry about her husband. She wanted Josh to stop by the next morning and pay her a visit.

"And I did and we had sex in her mom's backyard," Josh explained.

From that day on, Josh insisted, he would tell Heather he was going out to "apply for jobs," but he was actually stopping by Emilia's house to "have sex with her in her and her husband's bed."

This went on for about "three or four months," Josh claimed. After that, Emilia would send her husband to his father's house to stay so Josh could spend the night. As for Emilia, Josh suggested, when she decided to be with him, "she had to have all of me." As time went on, Emilia would "make comments" about Heather, knowing that Josh was still in love with her, indicating that Heather was consistently and routinely going to come between them. Josh and Heather had kids. The way Emilia saw it, Josh later explained, she and Josh could never have a complete life together unless Heather was totally out of the picture.

By "comments," Josh implied that Emilia began talking to him about getting rid of Heather at this time.

"I laughed it off," Josh told me.

He believed she was joking around. He never took her seriously, he said.

Nonetheless, when Heather finally found out what was going on, the relationship—involving the three of them— became unpredictable and insalubrious, if not downright sleazy and salacious. There was one afternoon in late summer 2008 when Josh was on his way home from Emilia's. At this time, according to Josh, Heather had no idea he was seeing Emilia. (However, I have an issue with that: Heather was smart. She knew damn well what woman Josh was sleeping with.) Nevertheless, as Josh drove home that day after having a sexual escapade with Emilia, his cell phone rang.

"Yeah? What do you want, Emilia?"

"Heather called here," Emilia said.

"What did she say?" Josh asked quickly. He felt an adrenaline rush. This statement got his attention mighty quick.

"She was pissed."

"What did *you* say to her, Emilia?"

Heather was fishing, Emilia explained. She had found her phone number in Josh's things, but she had no idea who it was. So Heather called and began asking questions.

"I told her we spoke on the phone once before . . . but she asked me, 'Are you fucking Josh?' I told her she needed to ask *you* that question."

Josh became enraged. "What the hell, Emilia!"

Emilia explained further that Heather hung up on her after she said that.

"I'll talk to you later," Josh said.

Josh pulled into his driveway. There was Heather, waiting for him. She had her arms on her hips, shaking her head.

"Look, look . . . I don't know who that was," Josh pleaded with Heather after he got out of the car and Heather flung the accusation. "It's just someone trying to stir up some shit with us."

Heather bought it, Josh claimed.

After he did some additional explaining, calming her down, Josh went to bed that night, thinking the situation was behind them.

Heather got up as Josh slept and went through his phone. Emilia, by then, had left Josh six "crazy-ass text messages," Josh recalled. Among them, these two:

Did little boy blue get into trouble?

Are you going to be able to come out and play anymore?

After the sarcasm, Emilia asked Josh where he wanted to meet up for sex the following day. Emilia knew what she was doing, throwing it into Heather's face.

Reading this, Josh said, Heather now knew for sure they were getting together.

Josh woke up the following morning and looked at his phone. He scrolled through the text messages, both outgoing and incoming, and saw fifty texts between Emilia and Heather from the previous night. They had spoken throughout that entire night. As he scrolled through them, Heather got up and stood behind him.

Several of those texts, Josh later alleged, referred to perhaps the three of them getting together for a "threesome" sometime soon. Heather had told Emilia it "would make

Josh happy to do this because he always talks about being with another woman."

"I knew I had been caught, so there was no way out of it but being honest," Josh explained.

The three of them got together later on that day—but it certainly wasn't for a ménage à trois.

CHAPTER 31

SPEAKING WITH EMILIA inside that abandoned trailer, Detective Brian Spivey felt he was finally getting to the truth of what had happened. They'd discussed the duct tape and agreed it was that common silver/gray tape most households had on hand, but Emilia had no idea where it might have come from (Josh had probably brought it with him was Emilia's feeling).

Emilia said Josh brought Heather into the trailer under the guise of giving Heather some money he owed her; that was how Josh had convinced Heather to meet him at Emilia's house and walk into the backyard.

Spivey planted his focus on the bag Emilia said she had seen placed over Heather's head. He wanted specifics.

"I know there was dried blood on her forehead," Emilia said as they stood, staring at the chair, that black plastic bag on the floor, a piece of silver duct tape nearby. The musty smell of old, wet newspapers, dead animals, cobwebs, dirt and mothballs permeated the air.

"There was *blood* on her forehead?" Spivey asked, somewhat startled by this new piece of information.

They talked about the bag being pulled over Heather head, but Emilia believed it was "open."

Spivey wanted to know what kind of bag.

"Garbage bag . . . like a black garbage bag."

Just like the one on the ground by their feet.

Spivey thought: *We're standing in a crime scene.*

They agreed that the bag must have been torn open, or Emilia wouldn't have been able, as she put it, to "see her face."

If there was any reservation on the MCSO's part about whether Emilia was giving Josh up, the pregnant mother of three put it to rest when she next said: "[Josh] told me he hit her over the head with something to kind of shut her up. And that she tried to run for the door, and that's when she hit the window—she broke the glass out of the window and he dragged her back. . . ."

Spivey asked a few more precise questions regarding this new disclosure and then wanted to know if Emilia had any idea what happened next.

"While he was tying her up, she urinated on herself," Emilia revealed. "And I was told that he tied her up, put a bag over her head"—Emilia took a deep breath and sighed as she explained this—"and suffocated her, and he just . . . he just held it there till she stopped moving."

The way Emilia described Josh killing Heather Strong, his wife of not even eight weeks, he came across as a cold-hearted, cold-blooded sociopath, killing the mother of his children without a shred of guilt or mercy, the same woman he had been involved with for eleven years. From what Emilia claimed, Josh murdered Heather, without a second thought, luring her to this trailer under a ruse, indicating premeditation, and sparing Heather no respite from a painful death she knew was coming.

Spivey asked Emilia where she had heard all of this. He wanted Emilia to be clear here in what she was saying.

Emilia said, "Josh."

The reason why the bag was open, Emilia explained

further, was because Josh had torn it open to check if Heather was still alive after he finished suffocating her.

The way Emilia described this scene, with the detail she had added, it seemed as if she had been there and witnessed it all herself.

Heather was fully clothed when Josh killed her, Emilia said. There was no tape over her mouth, but he did use tape to hold the bag in place around her neck. Emilia knew this because she said she had to tuck her fingers in between the tape and Heather's carotid artery to see if she had a pulse.

A motive came into play when Spivey asked Emilia if she recalled anything else Josh had told her in relation to this terrifying tale of murder. Spivey had reservations about Emilia's story, but he was keeping them to himself at this point.

"Just that he was going to make sure that she wasn't going to take her kids from him again. . . ."

There was still an odor in the trailer, Emilia said, for some time after she saw Heather in that chair. She wondered what it was, and she drew the conclusion it must have been Heather's body. She'd assumed then that Josh had stuffed it somewhere inside the trailer and left it there.

They discussed whether Josh had taken anything from Heather: jewelry, her wallet, any money. Evidence he was maybe hiding, which the MCSO could find and further tie him to the crime.

Emilia said she hadn't heard anything from him about that.

Then Spivey hit Emilia with the obvious question: "I mean . . . everybody else who asked, or everybody else who inquired, I mean, you . . . you *knew* what happened. But you just went along with—"

Emilia didn't allow him to finish. She said, "Well, nobody ever asked. Everyone always asked Josh."

They were outside the trailer now, standing near the door. A slight breeze blew the palms and tall grass easterly, making a calming, oceanic, *swoosh* sound. Spivey looked around. There was brush and overgrowth everywhere. He was searching for disturbed earth, maybe an area of over-turned ground indicating someone had maybe dug a fresh hole recently.

"[James Acome] never talked to you about her?" Spivey asked.

"No," Emilia said. She hadn't had any contact with James for quite some time.

Spivey was a bit confused, or, rather, he came across this way. He wanted to know if Emilia was now saying that James and his buddy were *not* involved. And if so, why were they at the house that night? Spivey had an issue with them being at the home on the same night "that she's dead, and, all of a sudden, they never come back."

"Because that night when he came here," Emilia said, "he (James) had left Sparr (a town's name) at nine-thirty, and that's when he had come here drunk to tell me she had stolen his phone. She (Heather) had stolen his necklace, and that he was looking for Josh because he was going to have Josh arrested for stealing property." She maintained that James's entire motivation for stopping over that night was to con-vince Emilia that Josh and Heather were "back together" and also working together to rip him off.

"And then he never came back?" Spivey asked.

"I haven't had contact with him."

"You have not talked to him since then?"

"No."

Spivey paused as they walked back to the front yard.

"Is there anything else?"

Emilia looked at him. She had more.

CHAPTER 32

JOSH WAS STILL tired. As they left his mother's house on March 19, Josh, Mike Mongeluzzo and Donald Buie continued talking. Josh might have pointed out where he thought Heather's body was buried, but he had never implicated himself more than having knowledge of the murder. That alone was a serious charge—but not as severe as having actually killed the woman he had been telling cops was "the love of [his] life."

Josh explained that it was Emilia who had given him Heather's ATM card, his kids' Social Security cards and birth certificates on the night Emilia moved in with him. That was right around March 1, just over three weeks prior to Josh's arrest. Telling that story, Josh said Emilia came home one night and told him: "'You never have to worry about Heather taking the kids again.'" She was acting cocky, all high and mighty. There had always been a spiteful rivalry between Heather and Emilia, who could be extremely territorial when it pertained to her men. Heather, too, had not held back her feelings toward Emilia.

One neighbor reported that on the date Heather went missing, somewhere around 10:30 P.M., she heard a vehicle pull up to Emilia's mother's house and a "female" voice shout, "Joshua? . . . Joshua!" The house door opened. Josh stepped outside. That same female voice then shouted, "Fuck you, Joshua! Look what you traded me in for!" Then the vehicle took off speedily. It was then that Lily, as the neighbor described Emilia by her common nickname, came outside to find Josh fuming, ranting and raving. Lily yelled: "It's not worth it. She is *not* worth it. Why are you even wasting your time?"

"What?" Josh told Buie he asked Emilia that night after she told him he did not have to worry about Heather any longer.

"You don't have to worry about her ever interfering with our lives again," Emilia supposedly added.

"Where is she at, Emilia?" Josh asked.

As Josh recalled this tale while they drove back to Major Crimes, Buie piped in: "Josh, let me bring something up. . . . You used that card. You used that card *two* days after." The point Buie made was that Josh couldn't have gotten hold of the card on or near March 1, as he had just claimed, because he had used it to withdraw money before that date.

Josh wrote this off as him being confused about the dates, asking Buie, "When did we move into that trailer over there in Pine Grove, man?"

Buie said they'd check into the date and let him know. But Josh had some explaining to do, Buie made clear. Here he was now trying to push the blame on Emilia when the MCSO had backed him up against a wall with dates.

What had happened?

It's the smallest details—always—that catch liars.

"Josh, we need to know the truth, bro?" Buie said. His voice was calm. He was pleading more with Josh than trying to bully him. It was clear that Buie was saying there wasn't much time left for them to discuss particulars of the case— and once the lawyers got involved, it was over. Josh was going to be on his own for good.

Josh took this in and stared out the window.

CHAPTER 33

BACK AT EMILIA'S house in Boardman, the investigation was dramatically picking up pace. Yellow SHERIFF'S LINE—DO NOT CROSS tape went up around the entire property, and law enforcement troops of all kinds arrived as daylight began and streaks of sun jetted through the palms like rays from God. Law enforcement vehicles lined the dirt driveway alongside the house. Save for the purpose of the MCSO's presence, it was a nice morning. Not too hot, not chilly at all. For March, it was ideal weather. Some of Florida's best (and worst) days of the year were upon the Sunshine State. Early spring in Florida was when all the idiots from colleges across the nation came down and displayed their vilest, drunken, most sexist behavior. Locals hated this tradition. Most of the scandalous, insane, alcohol-induced conduct was centered south of the Orange Lake in Fort Lauderdale, Miami and Tampa. But all of Florida was touched by the attendance of Neanderthal college kids getting wasted and acting like knuckleheads.

On the side of the trailer facing the back of Maria Zayas's house, there was a window completely busted out. To the left of a door going into the trailer's left side was that window Emilia had told Spivey about—the one Heather had smashed while trying to get away from Josh, its glass on the ground leading Emilia into thinking something had gone on inside the trailer. Oddly enough, there was an old recliner in front of the door; there was a busted-up case of unused baby formula strewn about. Beyond that were food wrappers all over the ground; empty soda and beer and booze bottles rolled about. Car and bike tires, hubcaps and dirty plastic toys lay around. And leaves—lots and lots of dead, dried leaves—making a confetti-like layer of organic matter on the yard floor. Next to the trailer on the right side was what appeared to be the bed of an old box truck, much like an ice-cream company would use to haul its frozen products from store to store. The cab and the remainder of the truck were gone, but the rusted tail section and box, with doors, was intact and resting on blocks and old tires.

Standing there, as several investigators from the MCSO surely had throughout that night and early morning, one had to think there were better places—even surrounding this home—to bury a body. Hell, the lake was just a chip shot away. This area they were focused on seemed so close to the road and main house, which told cops that not a lot of thought had gone into the aftermath of the crime and the burying of Heather's body—that is, if her final resting place had truly been here, as Josh Fulgham seemed so certain.

Not far from that beaten-down storage trailer, where Emilia claimed Josh held Heather and strapped her to that black desk chair—about twenty paces northeast—was that pile of debris, including an old box spring mattress, a red office chair (turned upside down), some building wood, large logs and other garbage, atop another area of thick leaves and dense, weathered brush. In several places around the yard were piles of junk. But this pile, unlike the others, had a "staged" feel to it, as though someone had placed these items carefully, one on top of the other. The investigator behind the camera taking video of the entire scene soon turned the focus of the lens to this pile and moved the camera into it and toward the ground. He might have been

thinking, *Right there—that's where she's buried. . . . You can
see the cleared dirt and overturned earth.*

Just underneath the red chair, placed just to the left of
the junk pile, was a spot of open ground that looked to be
recently tended to, as in moved around and disturbed. Most
of it was sand, much like all of Florida. But if one looked
closer, there was a clear indication that someone had been
active in that area and perhaps maybe even digging. At no
other location within the entire yard was there a cleared
space of earth where dirt and sand were as visible as they
were in this particular area. For that reason, it stood out,
mainly because the yard and the home had been so neglected
and unattended.

One of the CSIs got a blue metal rake and began to scrape
the surface of the sand, pushing back any leaves and small
sticks that had since covered the area where they believed
Heather was buried. The MCSO needed to wait for the
medical examiner (ME) and additional investigators to
arrive to help in the excavation process. While those experts
made their way there, investigators on the scene moved the
junk away carefully, being certain not to disturb what was
looking more and more like a grave site.

CHAPTER 34

NOTED PHYSICIAN AND surgeon Barbara Wolf had a reputation within the scientific and law enforcement communities as one of those forensic pathologists that any lawyer or cop would want to have on his or her team. Wolf was renowned, sure, but also very respected as someone who didn't muck up the high-profile investigations she became involved in by turning them into sideshows on CNN, Fox, HLN and other cable-news "crime" networks. Admiringly, Wolf did a lot of work on child abuse cases and testified as an expert witness in many of those, helping law enforcement put away what are the scum of the earth: child abusers. She also worked on the O.J. Simpson trial and the Medgar Evers exhumation, and with a team of forensic scientists assisting in the identification of the human remains in mass graves in Croatia and Bosnia, among other cases. All of that said, however, Wolf wanted nothing to do with the true-crime celebrity some of her counterparts had been accused of after routinely appearing on those network shows. To her credit, Dr. Wolf was humble and kept her focus on her work; she had often been called out to actual crime scenes as bodies were recovered. For Wolf, it was never about her; it was about the victim of a crime, or a deceased person's family in need of answers.

With active licenses in Florida, New York, Massachusetts and New Jersey, Wolf traveled a lot. She was in great demand and had been since her initiation into the business some three decades before she took the call to head out to Emilia's.

At the scene, Wolf met with the investigator in charge, Ray Williams, Chief Investigator Lindsey Bayer, several crime scene personnel, investigators from the MCSO and patrol cops there to maintain the integrity of the scene as onlookers and people in general began stopping by to gawk and try and sniff out what was going on.

The MCSO briefed Wolf when she arrived. She then had a quick look at the ground where they believed Heather was buried.

"We partially excavated the site," one CSI told Wolf. They were waiting, he added, for her to show up before going any further.

There was a good indication almost right away that they were onto something. As he dug, a CSI hit a long board buried maybe fifteen inches down into the ground. It was mahogany in color, with a wood grain finish, some fading green and red paint visible. It definitely did not belong underground. It must have been placed there.

Wolf nodded to herself. She had seen hasty burial sites like this plenty enough times to realize that they were perhaps going to find a body.

Digging further around the edges of the board, it appeared to be about the size of an average human being. Pushing it to the side with the shovel, an investigator pointed to what looked like black fabric underneath the board.

They all had a peek.

Certainly, there was no reason for black fabric to be buried this deep into the ground.

"You see that?" someone said.

Everyone nodded.

"The body," Wolf explained later, "was buried . . . [and

placed] partially within a suitcase. . . . The knees were bent and the lower . . . portion of the body was in the suitcase that was partially zipped."

They'd found a body.

The black fabric was a rollaway suitcase with one of those long handles. As they cleared the ground around it, a portrait of a dead body (DB), presumably Heather Strong, came into view. Heather had been stuffed inside this small suitcase as if she were a doll. Her knees had been pushed up in back of her in order to try and force her body into the suitcase, but it was just too small.

She wore a pair of gray/blue Polo Jeans, a Ralph Lauren T-shirt, with a United States flag on the front, *RL* in place of the flag's stars. Heather's shirt was covered in dirt, weathered as though she had been buried for some time. There were indications of dried blood visible all over the bottom corner, armpit and neck regions. Two small pieces of silver duct tape, about the size of a cigarette pack, were also recovered from inside the hole.

Unzipping the bag to have a look at her face and upper torso, investigators saw that Heather's killer had covered her head and face with a blue blanket. Seeing this, any detective on the scene could be certain that Heather's killer knew her. In cases where a blanket or some type of fabric is used to cover the victim's face or head, it's a clear indication that the killer is showing some form of personal connection to the victim simply by not wanting to toss dirt over the face or bury the victim with her head exposed. In many cases, it's a subconscious way, however shallow and fantastic, of the killer saying: *"I care for you."* Cops see this more often when a mother kills her child.

Wolf and two others lifted the suitcase bag with Heather's body inside of it out of the hole after placing a black body bag underneath her, so they could get a good grip on the corners and heave Heather out of this superficial burial site, which her killer had hastily stuffed her in.

Heather had terrible bruises on her arm by her right bicep, where dried blood was present—and also all over her head and face. There was hate written all over this murder, and also the clear mark of rage—inherent, deep-seated anger at this victim for some reason. Heather Strong had been beaten and strangled and/or asphyxiated; the bruises on her neck and upper body told this part of that horrible story. She might have even been tortured.

For the purpose of not wanting to disturb or fail any of the evidence that could be present inside the hole and suitcase, or on Heather's body, Wolf said later, "We lifted the body from the burial site in the suitcase and brought the whole body with the suitcase to the medical examiner's office."

This was where Barbara Wolf could get to work on finding out exactly what had happened to this young, pretty mother whom some monster had murdered and stuffed in a makeshift hole, discarding her as if her life had no meaning.

CHAPTER 35

DONALD BUIE HAD an issue with Josh claiming he did not believe Emilia when she told him he shouldn't worry about Heather anymore. For one, Heather had vanished. That, alone, should have been enough to raise Josh's interest to more than a shrug-off. Secondly, Emilia, according to Josh, gave him Heather's ATM card, among other personal possessions. Where else would she have gotten those personal items but from Heather?

Buie made the point that Josh "had to know something was wrong" after all of that. Also, Buie was curious how Josh knew exactly where in the yard Heather had been buried. By now, Buie had been informed by colleagues that they believed Heather's body had been recovered. Josh's info back at the scene had been spot-on.

"How would you know to go to *that* spot?" Buie asked Josh. They were sitting at a stoplight. Mongeluzzo was driving. The radio went off. Dispatch was looking for someone. The road was loud: cars whizzing by, wind blowing inside the vehicle.

Josh didn't have an answer.

Buie moved on to the letter Heather had supposedly written and signed, giving Josh custody of the children.

Emilia wrote it out on the computer and signed it herself in front of him, Josh now admitted.

Mike Mongeluzzo explained to Josh that they were growing more and more suspicious of him and his stories every moment they spent with him. Buie said the more they chatted, the less they believed what Josh had to say.

The light turned green. Mongeluzzo hit the gas pedal and said, "Josh, we got to keep eking it out of you, man. The number one reason people are most deceptive is self-preservation—you go into survival mode. You know what I mean?"

Josh shook his head yes. He was listening.

Mongeluzzo continued: "And a lot of time, people who do that have nothing to worry about, but they still do it, anyway. . . ."

Buie suggested the best thing for Josh to do at this point was to "clean your slate all at once." Man up and tell them everything. They were going to find out what Josh was hiding or holding back sooner or later, so the best thing for Josh's future was to be straight. Stop waxing poetic nonsense and get to the truth. It was the only way Josh could hope to receive any sort of sympathy from these two cops.

Buie could tell that Josh was thinking. So the investigator then reiterated that he had to put everything they discussed in his report: the good and the bad, the lies and the truth. If Josh helped, that, too, would go into the report and a judge would look at it in Josh's favor.

Josh said again this was his story and he was sticking with it. He repeated himself. Emilia and "them boys," as Josh called James Acome and his buddy, murdered Heather.

Mongeluzzo radioed in: "Mike, six-ninety-one. Ten-ninety-seven back at operations." He was pulling into the parking lot of Major Crimes.

"Did Emilia tell you what they did to her?" Buie asked as

Mongeluzzo turned off the car and they sat for a moment. "What she said?" He looked at Josh. "You're shaking your head . . . yes. . . . So, *what* did she say?"

Josh was crying now. Sniffling and whimpering like a child. Wiping his runny nose on the sleeve of his shirt. "They . . . choked . . . her."

"They did *what*?"

"They choked her out."

"Who did?"

Josh went back to that story. He explained it was James and his friend. He was crying much harder now. Buie asked where it all happened. Josh said, "Honest to God, man, I don't know where it happened, 'cause I didn't want to hear about it. I know how Heather was claustrophobic. . . ." Josh was crying hard; his chest moved speedily in and out as he wiped tears away. "[Emilia] laughed 'cause [Heather] pissed on herself."

"She laughed because of *what*?" Mongeluzzo wanted to know.

"[Emilia] laughed 'cause Heather pissed on herself when they were choking her out."

Buie asked what happened after they allegedly choked Heather "out." Both Buie and Mongeluzzo knew Emilia had said Josh told her Heather had urinated on herself, though they did not share this information with Josh, who was providing a rather detailed account of what supposedly took place.

Josh said, "I guess they put her in that pile, man. They took her from wherever she was, wherever they was. Heather wasn't stupid, man. She didn't *volunteer* to go to that house." Josh took a moment. Then he continued, further explaining how Heather had once told him Emilia "tried to cut Heather's throat," so "Heather wouldn't go around Emilia."

Just as soon as he got himself started, Josh indicated that

was enough for now. He needed to have a cigarette before they filed back into Major Crimes to sit down again in the interrogation box. Josh was wiped out. He was finished talking, he added. All he wanted to do now was lie down and rest his eyes.

CHAPTER 36

ON THAT MORNING after Heather and Emilia allegedly spent the night texting each other, Heather finding out about Josh's affair and supposedly suggesting to him that they enjoy a threesome with Emilia, Josh explained to me that when they got together later on that day, it wasn't for an afternoon of raucous, steamy sex. They sat cordially, according to Josh's recollection years later, and discussed what was going to happen next in the relationship. Josh could not continue handling two women at the same time: living with one, sleeping with the other.

"I had to make a choice right then between the both of them," Josh recalled.

Josh stared at Emilia. He could tell she was livid with both him and Heather. She didn't want to lose him. She'd put up with Josh living (and sleeping) with Heather, but he now needed to drop Heather and move in with her at once. For Emilia, no other choice would suffice. This was something, Josh said, he noticed about Emilia the more he got to know her: Emilia demanded to have her way. If she didn't get it, well, there would be some type of hell to pay for that betrayal.

"Look, Emilia, Heather is the mother of my children," Josh said as Heather looked on and listened. "That is where I am going to be."

Emilia left without saying much more than a few choice curse words for Josh and Heather. What else could she do?

That weekend, Josh and Heather were "playing around," he said (not elaborating on what that actually meant), and he asked Heather about "all that shit you said about you, me and Emilia—that was just talking shit, wasn't it?" Josh was fishing, he admitted; he was testing the waters to see if Heather was serious about arranging a threesome.

"Why, would you like that?" Josh later claimed Heather asked.

"Of course I would."

Josh called Heather's bluff. He took out his cell phone without saying another word and dialed Emilia.

Heather didn't say anything, nor did she try to stop him.

"Emilia, come on over," Josh told his girlfriend, staring at Heather the entire time. Heather didn't flinch; she went along with it. "Let's you, me and Heather get together."

"She came over," Josh explained, "and we had our three-some."

If true, Josh was perhaps living out some men's fantasy: an afternoon of sex and drinking and more sex and more drinking. The three of them were enjoying each other as much as they could, according to Josh. He said Emilia and Heather were both really into it; they liked playing with each other possibly more than with him.

They ended up getting together for sex, Josh claimed, several times after that first afternoon (some reports even have Heather and Emilia getting together on their own, without Josh). But Heather and Emilia grew tired of it and sat Josh down after an encounter one day.

"You've had your fun. Now choose one of us."

The three of them could not go on like this, both women argued. Their lives were not going to be like an episode of *Sister Wives,* designed to give Josh all the pleasure. Josh always seemed to get whatever he wanted, enjoying the best of both worlds. Not anymore. Emilia, especially, made a point to say that she wanted Josh all to herself. Heather seemed a bit tepid and possibly realized she'd had this guy for almost a dozen years by then. Heather could just as easily find someone else to disrespect her and treat her as poorly as Josh had all that time. Josh could sense Heather slipping away from him—maybe this was her tipping point.

Still, Josh chose Heather again.

"I didn't know at the time that Heather was talking to dudes on the computer," Josh recalled. Josh's instincts were off at that time: Heather, apparently, had her own thing going by then.

She had met someone, a slightly older guy named Ben McCollum. Yet, according to Ben, he later recalled meeting Heather for the first time at a bar on Orange Lake while she was drinking with Josh (a second report backing up this claim), not online, as Josh had always suspected.

"She had marks all over her when I met Heather," Ben said. "He was beating the shit out of her."

Ben was a down-home country boy who didn't take too kindly to men abusing their women. He felt sorry for Heather and thought she deserved so much better than "that piece of shit," Josh Fulgham. Ben also said his relationship with Heather started out entirely professional. Ben had two kids of his own from a broken marriage. He inquired about Heather babysitting for him. "Josh didn't want her to," Ben remembered.

It was June 2008. Ben had gotten to know Heather and spoke to her one day when Josh wasn't around. Heather was, of course, looking for any reason to step out of what was a bumpy, unhealthy and dangerous relationship with Josh. That pull of codependency, though, was powerful for her. Heather thrived on the chaos in her life, without even realizing it. She was locked in a cycle with Josh, not knowing how to break free. But when Ben came along, Heather saw a light. She realized there was more for her out there—a better man, number one, and also a more calming, normal life, which she had always dreamed of, but had no idea how to live.

Ben asked, "Come and watch my children for me? I'll provide you with a vehicle to drive, money and a place to live." Ben said later he viewed the relationship as a "live-in nanny" situation because it had been made clear to him that Heather wanted to move out of the home she shared with Josh, but not in order to begin another relationship. By then, Heather wanted to be rid of Josh for good. Her heart wasn't in it anymore. They'd been through too much. Josh had always promised to change, but he would always return to his past behavior. Heather wanted a better life not so much for her, but for the kids.

"Josh was a *bad* guy," Ben said, putting it as plainly as he could. Ben spoke with great respect for Heather. He adored the woman. "Heather wore ragged clothes all the time, and I think Josh liked it that way."

Ben had seen Josh and Heather together around town. He "kind of *knew*" Josh, but he "didn't really *know* him as well as [he] thought [he] did." Ben knew the guy Josh occasionally worked for doing landscaping. Josh would stop by Ben's airboat and vehicle restoration shop in McIntosh and hang around. Because he was so busy with work, taking care of his two girls and running the business, Ben never paid too much attention to Josh. He was just another dude from town scraping and scrapping his way through life—a trouble-maker who didn't get that it was time to grow up.

There was one night after they had met at that bar when Heather called Ben. She asked him to stop by the house. She wanted to talk about that job offer of being his nanny. Although Josh was totally against it, Heather told Ben, she was seriously considering taking it. A few days later, Ben and Heather made plans for her to leave Josh and move in with Ben.

"She was pretty much done with Josh and all of his

bullshit by then," Ben explained. Ben lauded Heather as a "sweet country girl." She had a good heart, wanted decent things and a decent life, but she just couldn't seem to get out of the situation with Josh. Ben considered her wanting to work for him as a nanny to be the first step she was taking toward a new life. Ben was attracted, sure; but he was also a gentleman and would never dream of overstepping the boundaries that Heather had put in place when she said she was moving in as the nanny, nothing more.

Ben borrowed a friend's truck, drove over to Heather's with another friend for support—and maybe backup—and packed all of Heather's belongings ("which wasn't much," Ben said) and moved Heather and her kids into his house.

"Every time I seen her," Ben recalled later, "she was always dressed in these ragged clothes, shorts and stuff—she never really had any nice clothes."

Ben knew Heather didn't want to dress poorly. She wanted nice clothes, like so many other women. But it was Josh who "wouldn't let her." It was another way, Ben supposed, of Josh controlling Heather. He was jealous. When Heather cleaned up and wore the best clothes she had, she would give any top model a run. She was beautiful in every way.

Ben never expected anything from Heather other than for her to work as the nanny.

"That's the way it started out," Ben said. "I gave her like two hundred dollars a week to watch my girls, pick them up from school and take care of things while I worked."

According to what Josh later told me, Heather came to him one night and explained that he'd had his fun, so she wanted to go out by herself and have some fun of her own. Josh made no mention of this business relationship Ben and Heather had entered into.

Josh said he agreed, making his position clear to Heather that although he didn't like it, Heather could go out and sow her oats, so to speak. He'd done it. He was fine with allowing her the space to realize how important her family was.

"I did it, so go ahead," Josh said he told Heather. (Although, this comment seemed to go against all the available evidence, suffice it to say when you take into account Josh's previous behavior and his overall attitude toward Heather in general.)

This sort of dysfunctional relationship went on, Josh insisted, between him and Heather for quite some time. Heather would go out, while he ran back into Emilia's arms. There was one time Emilia told Josh that Heather, who was calling Emilia by then and chatting it up with her as though they were old friends, was speaking to all sorts of guys on the Internet. So Josh said he cut the Internet lines to the house, thus severing her access to the Web.

But he also did something else after realizing that Heather was, indeed, engaging in exactly what he had given his stamp of approval for her to do, he later claimed.

"I roughed Heather up a bit over that," Josh admitted to me. "I am not proud of it, but I just want to be honest with you so you can set shit straight."

"Roughed Heather up a bit" was beyond putting a shine on the truth. Ben saw Heather after this roughing up and said that Josh had beaten the snot out of her.

After Heather moved into Ben's and started working for him, Josh began meddling right away. On the same day Ben moved Heather into his house, Ben and Heather were sitting outside Ben's shop under an orange tree. They were having a nice afternoon together, eating lunch and talking. Normal stuff. Heather felt as though she'd taken a deep breath and had gotten past a part of her life she was ready to leave behind for good. Ben was telling her that everything was going to be okay. She didn't have to worry about Josh, about anything. Ben was going to make sure she was taken care of—and that Josh wouldn't bother her.

As they sat and talked, Ben happened to look down the road and there was Josh heading toward them.

He soon pulled up, rolled the window down and said: "Ben, look, man, you have no idea how far I am willing to take this."

It was a bona fide threat. Josh came across as serious. He was filled with anger. No man was going to swoop in and take his family away from him without paying a price.

Heather started to say something, but Ben stopped her and stood. In the small of his back, Ben had a Glock .45, "a subcompact thirty," he said. Ben was no stooge. He knew Josh wasn't going to walk away from Heather and allow her to move on.

What Josh didn't understand, however, was how far *Ben* was willing to take things.

Ben took the weapon out from the small of his back, pointed it away from Josh, making sure Josh saw it. "Look here, Josh," he said, "I'm willing to take this shit as far as you're willing to take it."

CHAPTER 37

BEN RAN JOSH off his land on that first day Heather moved into his home. Perhaps more than anyone else whom Josh had tried to push around for most of his life, Ben McCollum understood that when you stand up and face a bully, he generally will back down. For now, Josh was out of the picture.

That incident didn't stop Josh from being a pest, however. He even stooped so low as to drive by the shop one day while Ben's mother was working in her garden and harassed the woman. "Hey there, whore!" Josh yelled before taking off.

Real junior high school stuff, Ben said. That was Josh: a name caller. He only beat up women. A man presented himself in front of Josh and he ran away with his tail between his legs, like a bitch dog.

Soon Josh began throwing rocks and other things at Ben's house. A nuisance, sure, but as Ben saw it, "He never would take it as far as I thought he would, and, to be honest, I was absolutely prepared for anything he could bring my way."

For the first few weeks, it was an employee/employer relationship between Ben and Heather. Nothing more.

"But, you know, living together like that," Ben explained, "things grew between us."

Ben bought Heather her own car. They started doing

things together. Normal stuff. That sparkle hit their eyes whenever they passed each other in the house. Heather was so happy. Her life did not revolve around enduring turmoil or walking on eggshells, controlled by a man who seemed to enjoy the pain he caused her and the power he wielded over her.

"I'd go out froggin' in the middle of the night," Ben explained. "She'd be there when I got back at midnight or later, waiting up for me. I could see that she not only wanted to be there for the kids, but me, too. She was feeling left out."

Josh wasn't going to beat Ben—he knew that the minute Heather moved into Ben's house. So he did what he did best: turned the situation into a trade-off. The night Heather moved out, Josh helped move Emilia in. Emilia had always been Josh's fallback woman. She had never been (and would never be) number one. And Emilia, who understood this, always took Josh whenever he came crawling back. This type of behavior might be a by-product of Emilia's obvious lack of self-esteem, perhaps born from the sexual abuse she claimed she suffered as a child. Subconsciously (unconsciously, for certain), Emilia believed she didn't deserve better than a guy living with the mother of his children or, at the least, sleeping with that same woman and her at the same time.

This went on between June and December 2008, Josh remembered (Ben and Emilia later backing up those dates). If you asked Josh, Heather kept the kids away from him for just about that entire time she lived at Ben's house. He claimed he never saw them, and she refused to allow him to take them for weekends or weeknights.

According to Ben, Heather was terrified, really, to allow him to take the kids. They both knew Josh to be a pill head and into meth. Allowing him access to the kids, they felt, anything could happen. Still, Heather did allow him to see his children, Ben said. She never totally denied him.

"We were both playing games with each other, back and forth with our feelings," Josh said of him and Heather during this period. They even went to court and slapped injunctions on each other to keep the children away from the other. It was a volatile, emotional chess match, pitting the children in the middle. Josh and his abusive, angry rants and threats existed there on the periphery of it all. Heather had gotten tired of the "same old/same old" with Josh. He'd work. He'd quit. He'd do drugs. He'd stop. He'd hit her and say he was sorry. He'd make promises he never kept—and make them again.

Heather was done and Josh knew it. He could not talk his way back into her life again. She had seen through him and realized there was better for her out in the world.

That confrontational nature Josh had set up inside the structure of his relationship with Heather, which carried over into Ben's romance with Heather, occurred during the entire relationship. As much as he tried, Josh couldn't let it go (or let Heather go) and move on with Emilia. Heather was his *possession*—that was clear in the testimonials left behind. What Ben later recalled was a madman who tormented him and Heather any chance he got—even after Ben made it clear that he was willing to take things to a violent level himself and had the firepower to back up his stance.

"[He] couldn't just leave us alone," Ben said disappointedly. It was all Ben wanted. He didn't care about Josh or making sure Josh knew who was tougher. It was never about ego and macho bullshit for Ben. He was in love with a girl. Simple. Pure. Healthy love. And Heather deserved it.

Josh continued tormenting them. He threw "missiles" at Ben's house—projectiles of some sort—one day. He would routinely pull up to Ben's, roll down his window and shout obscenities at Ben and Heather. Josh even came by once with a firearm of his own (probably a shotgun he had taken from Emilia's father after telling him he would clean it for him) and waved it at Ben, threatening him, Ben later recalled.

And yet Josh would never confront Ben face-to-face, no weapons. He didn't have the balls to do that.

The stress of it all was too much on Ben, who was running his business and dealing with a problematic ex-spouse himself. He loved Heather by now, sure. And there's good evidence available proving that Heather loved him and knew how good Ben was for her. But this couldn't go on forever like it was.

Sure enough, it all came to an end one day in December 2008. Heather made quite a strange and baffling decision. She sat Ben down. It was a Saturday, Ben recalled. He couldn't forget because it was one of those days anyone in his position would remember. Ben was fond of Heather and her children, who got along great with his. Ben built airboats. He often took the kids and Heather for rides; they'd meet up with some of Ben's friends, six or seven other airboat owners, and do day trips. Normal things that normal families did. It wasn't constant chaos, as Heather had been used to all her life with Josh. There wasn't that endless tension, always wondering what would happen next, where the day's food would come from, as Heather had been so used to by then. There was calmness. There were family-oriented moments. The pace of Heather's life had slowed considerably while she was with Ben. She was enjoying her life: cooking for him and the kids, cleaning, shopping, acting like a happy home-maker. Yet, ostensibly out of nowhere, Heather went to Ben on that Saturday and made what seemed like an unusual (and very bad) decision.

"I need to go back to my family," Heather told Ben on that Saturday in December. "I need to put my family back together."

Ben thought about it. He was going to play hardball here with Heather for her own good. "Look, Heather, I love you. But if you leave—I have to say, as much as I don't want to— you *cannot* come back."

Through tears, Heather said she understood. It had been a hard decision for her to make. She'd been going over and over it. But in the end, it was for the kids. They were asking about their dad.

Ben took a moment. Then: "Do you understand that if you go back to him, that guy right there, he *will* kill you one day?"

This thought had always been on Ben's mind. He had seen Josh in action, all from a different perspective. Heather's view of Josh was slanted, dulled by years of experiencing him firsthand. She really couldn't tell how dangerous he was anymore because she had lived with that danger for so long. Ben could see it all clearly, though.

"He was just flat-out fucking crazy, that guy," Ben remarked later. Josh even had Heather arrested on a trumped-up domestic violence charge while she was living with Ben. She was taken in, booked and jailed. Ben called his Ocala attorney and put up six thousand dollars of his own money to get her out. "The sheriff came over to my house one day, handcuffed her and took her away—and all she did was go over and drop the kids off at the house so Josh could spend time with them."

Nonetheless, with all they had been through, Heather called Josh on that Saturday. There's a good chance that Heather did this in order to save Ben from all the irritation Josh was going to cause them. It was just easier for Heather, as it always had been, to give in. Heather had sat by and had watched two men wave guns at each other. The last thing she actually wanted was one of them to go through with violence, especially in front of the kids. Although she knew Ben would never do anything to damage the children, Josh didn't care. He'd beaten her before in front of them. The best thing she could do for everyone was to submit.

According to Josh's recollection of that phone call, Heather said, "I'm done [with Ben]. I love you, Josh. I miss you. I am ready to come home and be a family again."

Josh was thrilled, but he had a serious problem. Emilia was now living in the house with him. He wasn't torn, however. Josh was using Emilia—that much was obvious in the casual way he always treated her feelings. Emilia was the go-to girl when Josh had nobody else. Now with Heather beckoning him to rebuild the family, Josh told Emilia, without a second thought or concern that it was going to hurt her feelings, "Get out."

Then Josh made a promise to Heather. He was going to change this time. She'd see. And, to prove it, after all the time they'd been together, after everything they'd been through, he was now ready to marry her.

("I started giving Emilia the cold shoulder after that phone call from Heather and she knew what was about to take place," Josh told me—though he did not tell Emilia then that he was planning on marrying Heather.)

"It's time for you to leave," Josh told Emilia. "Pack your shit and get out."

Emilia was totally blindsided by this.

"What?"

"You have a week to pack your shit and get the hell out!"

Emilia was pregnant by then with Josh's child.

It didn't matter to Josh.

So Josh went and picked Heather and the kids up at Ben's. He took them to a motel close by, where they all stayed the week.

("This way, it gave Emilia time to get her shit out of my house," Josh later told me.)

But as Josh and Heather would soon learn, their new life together was not a road paved with red rose petals and dancing unicorns, as Josh had sold it.

CHAPTER 38

DETECTIVE DONALD BUIE was thinking about Emilia and how she had walked Detective Brian Spivey through her mother's trailer.

Why would she do this? What was her purpose?

"Obviously, Heather's body had been found in her mother's backyard—she *had* to have some type of knowledge of it," Buie said.

What she knew exactly, Major Crimes still wasn't sure. Was Emilia the "terrified" girlfriend, as she had said back in the soft room? Was she actually "afraid for [her] life"?

"She had told us that Josh said he killed Heather, placed her inside the trailer, put some boxes over her and left her there," Buie said.

Josh was supposed to come back that night and bury her, Emilia told Buie and Spivey, but "he worked late." So Josh couldn't do it that day and, thus, Heather had been left inside the trailer for about forty-eight hours before he buried her in that shallow grave behind the trailer—all of which Josh was still blaming on James Acome and his friend.

"It was only out of curiosity, Emilia told us, that she went back into the trailer herself to check things out afterward," Buie added. "To me, obviously, she wants to put herself inside that crime scene if anything is later linked back to her. . . . So if there is *any* evidence found of [her inside the trailer], she's already explained that."

But Buie saw something else when he looked at Emilia and listened to her during those interviews. Evaluating all of her interviews, Buie had developed some ideas.

"She's a smart girl by far," Buie said. "But she is also very conniving and *very* evil."

CHAPTER 39

DR. BARBARA WOLF got to work finding out how Heather Strong died. Inside her autopsy suite, the sobering stench of death and disinfectant permeated the air. The more information the MCSO had about Heather's death, the better they could question Josh and Emilia. Things were coming together on the investigatory side of things with Josh; it was not happening so much with Emilia, who was standoffish and elusive with information. The MCSO knew that, in time, Buie and Spivey could crack Josh and find out what he knew, when, and how deep he was involved. Emilia was another story; she was playing a bigger game here. She knew a lot more. They were going to have to squeeze it out of her, little by little. Most of the investigators involved in the case were now beginning to believe that both Josh and Emilia were telling partial truths and that perhaps the two of them had conspired to kill Heather. Something didn't fit. The way their stories revealed new details each time they talked: Some things juxtaposed, others didn't. The truth, as it is told by someone, should always mesh together seamlessly. There shouldn't be big holes, except for missing periods of time.

This wasn't the case where Emilia and Josh's stories met.

James Acome and his friend, those same investigators felt, didn't have anything to do with Heather's death. There was nothing—not one shred of evidence—pointing in that direction.

The first thing Dr. Wolf did was fingerprint Heather and get those cards into the database to get a positive confirmation on the body. There was no doubt the corpse was Heather Strong, but scientists and cops like to have unequivocal proof, which those fingerprint cards, seeing that Heather had been previously arrested, would demonstrate.

As it turned out, the only finger available to Wolf was Heather's right thumbprint, she said, adding, "Because the body was showing decompositional changes, that was the only fingerprint that was obtainable."

Heather had been buried, by most estimates, for about one month. Even though the body was underground, the Florida weather could change it during that period into an unrecognizable state—they were lucky, as these things go, to have it in the condition it was, which turned out only to be because of the time of year.

Wolf X-rayed Heather's body as it sat partially inside the suitcase on top of her autopsy table. Dirt and debris fell out of the body bag as Heather was hoisted up and onto the slab. Wolf wanted the body X-rayed in the position they had found it in order to best mimic the conditions and placement inside that hole. This would give Wolf an inside look into the contents of the suitcase bag and maybe whatever else had been used during the course of Heather's murder.

Next, Wolf walked over to where the X-rays were processed and placed them on a backlight to have a look. As she studied each picture, it appeared that there were no "projectiles or fractures" present. All Wolf could see from the X-rays turned out to be "the presence of dental restorations [and] fillings. . . ." Heather had not been shot or beaten with a blunt object anywhere that Dr. Wolf could see within the X-rays.

With some help, Wolf removed Heather from the suitcase and spread her out on the autopsy table for a more thorough examination. The doctor then cleaned Heather's body after removing all of the deceased's clothing, as well as any jewelry. It seemed odd, but Heather did not have any shoes on, nor were there any shoes found in the hole or suitcase. Yet, she was wearing socks.

Barbara Wolf carefully studied Heather's body, inch by inch. She noted that Heather was five feet eight inches tall, 108 pounds. However, postmortem measurements can be a bit misleading because Heather's body had been so severely bloated. Thus, "as the body decomposes, it loses weight. . . ."

Still, Heather took care of herself. She was in good shape.

Heather's body was in such a state that her skin had turned mostly green and would "slip" upon touch. Sections of it glided off her body like plastic sheets with the simple touch of a hand. She was in a fragile state. A week more, perhaps, and Wolf would not have been able to conduct the type of autopsy she wanted.

"The hair itself was slipping from the body. Some of the fingernails had become loosened and were actually separate." Those had fallen into the suitcase.

Wolf opened a sexual assault kit and made sure to perform all those tests on Heather to see if she had been raped and/or her killer had left any DNA inside her.

Upon an examination of Heather's shirt, which Wolf had removed, a reddish brown color of the shirt turned out to be body fluids that, because of the advanced state of decomposition, had discolored the shirt from its original gray.

There was a piece of duct tape stuck to the "butt" area of Heather's jeans. Wolf took a pair of tweezers, carefully removed the tape and placed it in an evidence bag. A piece of tape actually had the potential to break a case. You match that piece of tape to a roll of tape in someone's house and you've found your killer.

It took hours, of course, but Wolf finally tore off her surgical mask, unsnapped her latex gloves and sat down to write up a final report of her "findings" so far. These reports can change, actually, as the investigation moves forward. Medical examiners will sometimes amend a report based on what detectives later find. Things that didn't make sense at autopsy begin to become clear, say, if a suspect makes an admission and this explains how a victim was murdered. Medical examiners are always open to learn more about a particular case. The main objective here was to see if anything stood out, or if Heather's killer had left behind any telltale signs or forensic evidence of his crime.

Wolf concluded that Heather's internal organs appeared "perfectly normal." All of her major organs—heart, lungs, the entire contents of Heather's abdomen—exhibited "no evidence or injury" or any "pre-existing natural disease process." Had she not been viciously murdered, Heather had a lot of life ahead of her, it appeared.

Wolf explained how she had made an "incision" in the skull "to examine the brain." And that once she peeled back the scalp in order to saw through Heather's skull, Wolf found "a bruise that was about two inches" located "in the mid-forehead region." Wolf noted how this "wasn't visible from the outside." After peeling back the scalp, the doctor "opened the skull to examine the brain."

The bruise itself was created by "blunt-force trauma," Wolf assessed. She wrote: *Something impacted the body at that point, the head, or the body hit against something with a blunt surface, not a cutting object.*

There was no pattern to the bruise, giving Wolf any indication or clue as to what might have caused it. But, regardless, it was a blow strong enough to cause harm, and yet not a "life-threatening injury."

Although Heather's brain was "very decomposed," Wolf could tell that the blunt trauma she located was not powerful enough to have caused any injury to the brain. Thus, a conclusion could be made that Heather might have been hit in the head while she was alive, or, perhaps, this injury happened when that glass window broke.

So, what had killed Heather Strong? If it wasn't that blow to the head, what happened? In Wolf's professional opinion, Heather died of asphyxia, or lack of oxygen, which essentially, as far as autopsies are concerned, becomes a hidden death. Not to be confused with strangulation, a means of murder that would leave marks and bruises on the neck, asphyxiation leaves nothing behind but a dead body.

Later in court, Wolf hypothetically noted in talking about Heather's murder, "If someone is suffocated and . . . they're not fighting back, they're impaired or in some way incapacitated, the expected finding is actually no finding."

What Wolf made clear here was that Heather's body showed no obvious signs of what killed her. Therefore, the only reasonable, professional explanation, with all of the evidence they had so far, could only be asphyxiation, barring toxicology tests coming back to prove poisoning, which Wolf did not suspect based on her exploration of Heather's internal organs.

"There's no marker in the body for lack of oxygen," Wolf explained later. "There's no way to measure it. In a live person, we can measure blood levels. In a deceased person, we can't."

What Wolf said that made Detectives Buie, Mongeluzzo and Spivey take notice was that Heather's death and the findings of the medical examiner were analogous to what the ME's office had seen "quite frequently." In other words, Wolf wasn't pulling the cause of death out of thin air; there was context and basis for her determination.

Wolf finally said, "Individuals who commit suicide by putting a bag over their head—the suffocation itself leaves no physical findings."

The MCSO had a witness saying she saw a bag over Heather Strong's head. The medical examiner was backing up that claim with her findings.

CHAPTER 40

JOSH FULGHAM WOKE on Friday morning, March 20, 2009, near nine o'clock. A guard stepped near his cell and told him, "Those Marion County detectives are on their way."

"Yeah, thanks," Josh said.

He put his feet to the floor, sitting on the edge of his jail cot. Then he rubbed the sleep from his face and took a deep, long breath. Josh wanted a cigarette. Really bad. The past few days had been both foggy and grueling, not to mention emotional and sobering. Josh had been telling Detective Buie he was tired, but it had actually been a hangover from a substantial bender. Josh had smoked so much weed and taken so many pills the previous day—when Buie showed up at his door and he and Mongeluzzo claimed to have smelled pot smoke inside Josh's house—that it burned him out for the following twenty-four hours. His head was a bit clearer this morning, but he was still feeling the haze of that nasty binge. All of it wasn't necessarily from the drugs, but the fact that Josh realized he had given the MCSO the location of his wife's body. Thinking about this now, Josh gasped when he thought about how much he now had to explain.

Shit, he thought.

Josh found his legs and stood up from his cot. Took a leak. Washed his face.

Buie and the MCSO were not going to let up. Josh knew he needed to come up with something to explain his part in knowing where Heather was buried, beyond shifting the blame to James Acome and his friend. Either that or he was facing potential death penalty charges.

Son of a bitch.

Josh arrived at Major Crimes near 10:00 A.M. "Hey, can we take these off?" Josh asked, referring to the handcuffs, as they entered that familiar interrogation room.

Buie nodded yes.

Rubbing the pain from his wrists after the cuffs were removed, Josh said he didn't want anything to eat or drink after Buie asked him.

Buie then left the room and brought Detective Brian Spivey back with him.

Josh said he was "at least clearheaded today." He was looking forward to talking, setting some things straight.

Before they could talk, however, Buie said he needed to read Josh his rights again.

"Inconsistencies," Buie brought up right away after he finished Mirandizing his suspect. This, Buie added, was where they were at, effectively. Josh had told too many stories, kept so many things to himself, Buie felt. He wondered if Josh could be trusted anymore to tell the truth, now that the MCSO had a body?

Josh took a deep breath in and let it out slowly. He said he understood their frustration with regard to all the lies he had told.

Buie put it simply: "We [now] know someone's been killed. We got our own idea what happened. Just be *honest* with us."

Spivey piped in, "That's all we're looking for."

Josh stared at the both of them. He wiped his mouth. He scratched the back of his head. "Well, I'm going to tell you all, man. I mean, I know I've lied to you. I know that I have lied to you. But I did not kill her. I did not. That's my wife. I did not kill her."

Buie looked at Spivey. Then at Josh: "What happened?"

"Well, like I told you . . . Heather did come in that day. I wasn't home. . . ."

And from there, Joshua Fulgham gave Buie and Spivey his version of the events that led to the murder of his wife, Heather Strong.

CHAPTER 41

SO WHAT HAPPENED to Heather Strong, the twenty-six-year-old mother of two? The MCSO had so many versions of what they now believed to be one truth: Heather Strong was lured to Emilia's house under a ruse of some sort and brought back into that abandoned trailer. (Probably, it happened forcibly, not under a guise of being paid money she was owed.) From there, she was bound to a chair, likely asphyxiated, and dumped in a hole about ten paces in back of the trailer. They had Josh and Emilia both pointing fingers at each other, a "he said/she said" farce. At one time, both of them had also made it sound as though James Acome and his friend had killed Heather.

But as the evening sun of Friday, March 20, 2009, set on Ocala, Florida, the MCSO investigation into this murder took a turn. That space in between—from the time Heather left work and met up with Josh—was now the MCSO's central focus.

It had taken a night in solitary confinement for Josh to think about what had happened to his wife and to come clean.

"We put him in there (solitary) to limit his use of the telephone," Buie explained. "We didn't want him having contact with anyone else or him causing harm to himself. It also gives him a lot of time to think about what he has done."

It was a Saturday, the following morning, when Josh called for Buie.

When Buie walked into the room, Josh looked up at him—and Buie knew.

"He wanted to wipe his slate clean," the detective later said. "He was ready to tell us everything that had happened."

What happened to Heather did not actually begin when Heather left work on that day, Buie and Spivey learned—it actually had started back in 2008, as the love triangle of Heather, Josh and Emilia turned into something Heather never really saw coming. And in a not-so-surprising twist to these cops, they now had a new suspect on the radar: the orchestrator and mastermind behind what they believed to be a terribly violent murder.

CHAPTER 42

AFTER SPENDING THAT week in a motel, Josh, Heather and the kids returned to their trailer in Citra. Josh had made it clear to Emilia that she needed to pack her belongings and be out of the house by the time he showed up a week later with Heather and the kids. They were a family once again. He'd tried calling Emilia to see if she was gone, but she wouldn't answer her phone.

"Josh always went back to Heather," said a source close to this case. "Emilia would always play second fiddle. She knew that."

But this time Emilia was taking charge.

Josh talked about how he was splitting his time, at least for a while, between the two women. Buie asked him: "You always went back to Heather?"

Josh responded, "Look at Emilia and look at Heather."

The implication from Josh was that Emilia could not hold a candle to Heather as far as beauty.

Hearing this, Buie shook his head. How superficial. How shallow. And yet, that was how Josh thought.

Emilia simply wasn't about to allow Josh and Heather to ride off into the Florida sunset together on their high horse, leaving her in the dust once again. After all, Emilia was carrying Josh's baby (or so she claimed).

When Josh and Heather pulled into the driveway after that week at the motel, the first thing Josh looked for was Emilia's truck. She hadn't responded to his calls, maybe she was still there.

He didn't see it.

She's gone . . . , Josh told himself. *Good!*

Josh got out of his car and told Heather and the kids to wait. He tried the front door.

It was locked. He didn't have his keys on him.

He had always left a window in the back unlocked for this reason. He told Heather he was going around to the back in order to crawl in through the window.

Josh fell onto the kitchen floor after going through the window. He got up and brushed himself off. He walked into the living room to go open the door for Heather and there was Emilia. She was sitting on his recliner, a blanket over her legs, smiling. "Like everything was fine," Josh recalled.

Josh walked over. "What the hell are you doing here?"

Emilia started laughing.

"You need to pack your shit and get the hell out, Emilia. I told you that a week ago."

Apparently, the situation was funny to Emilia. According to Josh's recollection, she sat there, not moving, not saying much of anything immediately, and laughing this strange sort of giggle underneath her breath.

Then, after some time, Emilia said, "I'm not leaving."

Josh put two fingers on his temples and thought for a moment. His carotid artery was throbbing, adrenaline pumping. Anger rose in his body. In the past, Josh would react to these situations by blowing his top, screaming at Emilia (or Heather) and threatening violence. Instead, he later recalled, he looked at Emilia and said, "I'm going back to the motel for a night. You had better be gone by the time I get back tomorrow."

As he was leaving, Emilia said, "Josh, you don't want her! You just want your kids. So, why don't you just bring her back over here tonight and we can get rid of her? Then we can be a big family and have all of our kids here." (This chilling statement actually occurred, according to a letter Josh sent me. Emilia, of course, denies that she ever said this—and there is reason to believe her. The only source beyond Emilia is Josh.)

"Me and Heather are going to work on our relationship," Josh said. "We *want* to be together again, Emilia."

Josh said he left. And throughout that day, after "raising hell" with Emilia on the phone, badgering her to get the heck out of his house, she finally left. The last thing she said to him on that day: "It does not have to be this way, Josh."

Josh said he "stayed away from Emilia after that day" and he did not have contact with her until the day he and Heather were married, December 26, 2008. He couldn't help himself, he claimed. Emilia had been calling Judy Chandler, Josh's mother, the entire time and telling her that she needed to be with her son. She also said she'd found out the sex of their child and wanted to share it with Josh.

So, not exactly saying why he chose of all the days to call Emilia back, just moments before he married Heather, Josh humored the woman and dialed her up.

"What do you want?" Josh asked.

"It doesn't have to be this way," Emilia said again (according to Josh).

"I have to try this," Josh responded. "I need to see if the marriage will work out."

Emilia knew Josh would come back. He always did.

CHAPTER 43

IT WAS TEN days later, Josh explained, when Heather's true intentions came to light. This marriage, claimed Josh, the so-called reconciliation Heather wanted, the idea of being a family once again with her and the kids, was nothing but a ploy by Heather, with the help of Ben McCollum, who was still together with her at this time, according to Josh. In fact, Josh explained, Heather and Ben had devised some sort of diabolical plot to get rid of him for good.

"Ten days after we were married," Josh told me, "Ben and Heather concocted this plan to . . . put me in jail."

"That's not true," Ben explained to me. "But let me tell you, Heather pawned that ring Josh gave her when they married."

She did it, Ben added, because she had nothing. Josh gave her nothing, and Heather needed to take care of her children.

Josh had Emilia's father's shotgun in the house because he had told the old man long ago he would clean it for him. It was the same gun Josh waved at Ben once before. The way Josh told it, Heather called the cops on him one day in early January, saying he was threatening her with that shotgun.

Josh was arrested immediately and held in jail without bond.

"I did tell her to go down and press charges against him,"

Ben said. "Because, hell, he pointed that same shotgun at me one day while we were riding down the road. I reported it a day after it happened, because I told the cops that, basically, I wasn't worried about him. I could take care of him on my own."

"Three days after I was put in jail," Josh said, "Ben told her . . . that it wasn't going to work out." Ben bailed on Heather, according to Josh. Yet, while Josh was in jail, he said, James Acome stopped by the house and "had sex with Heather . . . while the kids were [there]. . . ." And James and Heather became a couple then.

As soon as Josh was locked up, he began leaning on Emilia, calling her from the jail, asking her to keep an eye on things at his house. During these recorded phone calls, Emilia sounded—as she always did—as though she and Josh had always been together and never separated. Emilia came across as though she and Josh would continue their relationship when he got out of jail.

"Do you want me to find out if [Heather] is going to leave [the house]?" Emilia asked Josh during one phone call.

Josh wasn't sure. He was curious what Heather was now saying (since she'd gone and had him arrested and tossed in jail). It was clear Josh was pissed, even enraged by this. He felt a tremendous betrayal on Heather's part. Just the idea—which wasn't true—that Heather had married him as part of a plan with Ben to set him up made Josh fuming mad to the point of fury. He felt demeaned and scorned and played. He could not (nor was he psychologically equipped to) deal with the emotions that followed.

Emilia explained how she'd spoken to Heather: "She said she was now scared that you'd kill her, that she'd gone and had you arrested."

"She's so crazy . . . ," Josh said in his noticeable Southern accent. He came across as relaxed and calm.

"You want me to see what she's gonna do—if she's gonna stay or she's gonna go?"

"She can stay there," Josh said. But now there was a touch of possible retribution—a hint that Heather would get hers, later on—in his voice. "She can have that house. Ain't no problem." Then, with sarcasm, as if he had ulterior motives: "Ain't no problem at all."

Emilia sounded desperate. Josh cared only what Heather was thinking and saying. The call was all about Heather. It was obvious he was using Emilia. Playing her. Laying on that old-school charm, telling Emilia what she wanted to hear.

"Will you come and sign a bond [for] me?" Josh asked.

Emilia sighed. "Yeah," she said, but there was an uncertain tone to her voice, a subtle reluctance indicating she was perhaps going against her better judgment.

Josh knew how to reel her in, though. He laughed coyly, then: "I love you."

"I love *you*," Emilia responded.

They were officially back on.

Next they talked some more about what they should have done so Josh could have avoided jail altogether. What became obvious from this first conversation while Josh was locked up was that they had been talking and seeing each other for quite some time. Josh might have married Heather in December, but he was still keeping Emilia on the side. He'd never really let her go.

Emilia said she had approached Heather and asked her what she was going to do: Was she going to press charges, drop the charges? What was her plan?

"Heather told me, 'I don't know. . . . If he gets out, he's gonna kill me.' And I told her, no, he's not. 'Heather, I mean, he wouldn't hurt you because of them kids, and if you don't know that by now, well, then, you are really fucking stupid.'"

Again playing "Mr. Smooth," Josh said, "Anyway, I don't even care about her. . . . I want to talk to *you*. What have *you* been doing, baby? What things been going on?"

On January 6, 2009, Josh and Emilia spoke several times

throughout the day. Josh kept calling her back when the line went dead or their time limit had expired.

"Baby, what's going on?" he asked once. Remember, Josh had married "the love of his life" eleven days prior to this.

"Okay," Emilia explained, "now she's saying to *me*—this is fucking retarded—if I want to hang out with her!" Emilia further explained that she had spoken to Heather before talking with Josh, and Heather supposedly had told her that she could get a babysitter that coming weekend if Emilia wanted to come over and hang out.

"We did hear from sources that there might have been a relationship between Heather and Emilia," one law enforcement official told me. The information was that Heather and Emilia, after getting involved in that threesome with Josh, continued fooling around on the side without Josh knowing. The extent of this supposed lesbian relationship was never known, but several sources close to the case agreed it was something that went on from time to time between the women.

On that day Emilia spoke to her, Heather said she "needed someone to talk to." According to Ben, he later recalled Heather being frightened of Emilia. "She told me once she went over to Emilia's mother's house to see Emilia," Ben remembered. "And Emilia held her down, put a knife to her throat and threatened her. I told her to call the cops."

Emilia told Josh she would pick Heather up and take her out.

There was a pause. Josh was listening.

"Is that okay with you?" Emilia finally asked when Josh didn't respond immediately.

"For what!" he snapped. "Look where she's done put me. You wanna go hang out with someone who put me in here . . . and I might be here for seven days?"

"Listen, you know why I would hang out with her," Emilia said. "Right?"

"No," Josh responded, laughing nervously, as though something was being kept from him. "I don't know."

Emilia talked about her "cousin" being around town, a fictional person she had made up to try and disguise herself. There was an unspoken agreement between them that they were trying to hide from whoever might be listening to the call.

"Unless you don't want me to," Emilia said.

The idea seemed to make sense to Josh now—it clicked. He said, "I don't care." Then he talked about being locked up for the next week. Seven long days behind bars. Plus, when he got out, he was going to have to go stay with his mother. On top of that, Heather had his car, which he didn't think she'd give back.

Emilia reminded him that she had a set of keys to the car. "Like I'm saying, if I get invited to hang out, I might just go. Baby, you know I'm not stupid."

"Oh, I know."

Emilia could get dropped off, in other words, and, with her set of keys, drive away with Josh's car at the end of the night.

When Josh called again later on, he sounded depressed and alone. "Baby, I'm gonna tell you, go ahead now and move on." He wanted Emilia to let go and find someone else. He was finished.

"You are so damn dumb."

"No, I'm not. I'm not gonna keep dragging you the fuck around. I already have for a month now. I want you to do that, okay?"

"Why do you keep telling me that?" Emilia asked. Her voice spoke of a woman who knew now she had the upper hand in this relationship. She had Josh where she needed him: crawling on his hands and knees, desperate, behind bars, needing her. Emilia embraced the sense of power she manipulated through her relationships. She embodied the idea of controlling the relationship anyway she could. Here she was now driving the bus.

"This is the first time I have ever told you to move on," Josh said.

"Nope. You told me that when you went to Mississippi last year. . . ."

"And you did."

"No. I did what I had to do to get the fuck out of my momma's house," Emilia said. She was fired up, defending herself.

"Well, you may have to do that now."

When they connected again, Josh was crying. "All I ever wanted was my babies and you," he said, sounding more distressed than ever—though Emilia did not pick up on it.

"What?" she asked.

He said it again.

"You know we could have had that," she said. "But you had to do shit *your* way. Right?"

"I tried to keep from ending up here and look what's happened?" Josh said, again complaining about being locked up. He was still crying.

"I know," Emilia said. "But like I told you, no matter what, I got everything under control. You *know* that."

They talked about how Heather was responsible for him being locked up because she wanted to be with Ben, but Ben had since run from the situation and wanted nothing to do with Heather any longer. Josh was too terrifying, too volatile and too damn fly-off-the-handle; Heather was too unpredictable for a more stable guy like Ben.

Emilia explained further how she'd just had a conversation with Heather. Heather was going around to mutual friends, acting big and bad, bragging about being the person who had put Josh in jail. She was telling people how she could get Josh's "ass locked up in prison" if she really wanted to. Not just the town pokey, where he was, but serious prison time. Emilia said she had suggested to Heather that she go back to Mississippi if she had felt so scared and threatened by Josh. Then Emilia implored Josh to "do some serious thinking about a lot of things" while he was locked up. They'd have to make a few decisions when he got out. She never alluded to what, exactly, but there was an unspoken implication in Emilia's voice that drastic measures were going to be called for.

Josh interrupted Emilia's little rant. He sounded confused: "*What* do I need to think about?"

"You better kiss a lot of ass when you get out, buddy," Emilia said, making her point heard.

"To who?" he asked, surprised by this.

"To *me*. You put me through some shit this last year and a half."

Josh grew defensive. "You've done the same to me."

Emilia laughed. "How? What did I do to you except be there *every* time you wanted me?"

"I know . . . I know," Josh said. A sense of defeat came over him. White flag. There was nothing he could say to counter or argue that statement . . . and he knew it.

"*Every* time," Emilia slowly repeated.

Josh realized he needed to conduct a bit of damage control. "I ain't never had nobody done love me like you," he said in his best homage to Billy Dee Williams. "Never. I really don't know how to deal with it."

"I know—you just keep running from it."

Emilia wanted Josh to understand that she was going to "handle things" out in the world while he sat in jail. There was no need to worry about Heather. Emilia encouraged Josh to trust her. She had everything under control. She said "right now," Heather was "kissing [her] ass," and she had no idea why, but she was going to use it to their advantage.

"I'm gonna milk it," Emilia said, meaning Heather's ass kissing. "You know I'm not stupid. I know how to play games, Josh."

Josh was quiet. He was thinking, listening.

Emilia came up with a plan. She suggested that if the judge asked Josh about the gun and why he hadn't registered it, "Why don't you just tell him you bought it off of a friend—and if that judge asks for a name, you just tell him [James's buddy]. And you're just using it for skeet shooting."

"Okay," Josh said as Emilia laughed at her suggestion.

The conversation then shifted to Josh wondering what Heather "really, really planned on doing." Josh said he desperately needed her to drop the charges so he could walk out of the jail. Josh was also concerned about Heather packing up her things and taking off with the kids somewhere. He feared this. The time to do it would be while he was in jail. He couldn't imagine her leaving without saying a word, getting a few weeks' head start, leaving him to do the time before he could even try and track her down.

Emilia said she didn't really know what Heather was planning, but she did mention to Heather that she loved Josh's kids. And Emilia had also recently told Heather, "'Look, whether you believe it, [Josh's kids] have a sister on the way. . . . I'm tired of all the bullshit. But I want to know where you stand.' And she's just like, 'I don't want to leave.'" Heather said something about getting another job in order to pay her bills. Emilia then offered to drive her around so she could fill out job applications; and if Heather needed, Emilia would even watch the kids while Heather went out and looked for work.

Josh liked what he was hearing. He thanked Emilia.

"I'm not dumb, I know what I'm doing," Emilia said. "Keep your friends close—but keep your *enemies* closer."

CHAPTER 44

AS JOSH AND Emilia continued to talk while Josh was behind bars, they came to the conclusion that Heather was—and always would be—a nuisance in their lives. She would never go away on her own. There was no getting around this problem. If Josh was ever going to be able to see his kids regularly and move on with his life without interruption from Heather, something was going to have to be done. The first step, though, was getting Josh out of jail so he and Emilia could work together on this task—most important, perhaps, without anyone else listening to them on the other end of the line.

During one phone call, Josh explained to Emilia how he had just spoken to Heather. She sounded upset, he said. He mimicked her crying to him over the phone, and he and Emilia shared a good laugh at Heather's expense.

"Listen, I want you to just go along with whatever she says," Josh explained to Emilia. He had a scheming, devious sound to his voice, as though he had some sort of plot developing to fix everything.

Josh talked about getting out of jail the following day, January 7, and taking the day after that off from work and going "straight to the state attorney's office" with Heather. "She's gonna tell them that she lied about me." Based on the last phone call he had with Heather, Josh was under the impression Heather was prepared to drop any charges.

"You know what," Emilia said, "they ain't gonna drop the case. 'Cause the state done picked it up, no matter what." There was a sense here that Emilia liked the idea of Josh being behind bars right now. At least there, she knew where he was at all times and he wasn't sharing his bed with anyone else.

They spoke about the prosecutor still pushing forward with a case against Josh, even though Heather might drop the charges.

Emilia told him not to worry. She was seeing Heather the following day and would find out exactly what was going on.

"I got this," Emilia said. "You leave it to me from here on out, do you *hear* me?" Emilia sounded pissed. She had taken control and wanted Josh to trust that she could handle Heather. And she also wanted Josh to keep his damn nose out of it. The more he meddled and tried to control Heather, the more he mucked things up and made Heather suspicious that something else was happening.

"All right," Josh said.

"I'm serious!" Emilia yelled.

"Okay. Don't get all [crazy]."

"I'm not. I am just *tired* of you telling me how this is gonna happen. I'll play along like I've *been* playing along. . . . I'm gonna have to, because you seem like too much of a *pussy* to do shit."

Their time was up. The call was over.

CHAPTER 45

THE NEXT MORNING, Josh called his mother, Judy Chandler.

"Momma?"

"Yeah, baby . . . it's me."

Something was up. Josh was crying. He didn't say anything.

"What's wrong?" Judy pressed.

Josh still wouldn't speak.

"You okay, baby? What's wrong?" Judy could hear her son whimpering. "You there?"

"Yup, Momma, I'm here." Josh sounded like a little boy, as if Judy had scolded him and he was coming back to apologize.

"Oh, God, you got some bad news, don't you?" Judy asked.

"Yeah . . . ," Josh said through tears.

"Oh, God . . . here's Lily." Judy handed the phone to Emilia, whom she called by her nickname.

"What's wrong?" Emilia asked.

Josh was breathing heavily, crying and sniffling. He could barely speak. In a whisper, he said, "I gotta stay here. . . ."

"What? No bond?"

"No."

Josh had gone to court and faced the judge, who indicated Josh wouldn't be getting out that day or the next, or even the following week. He was going to be spending forty-five days in the can and might end up with even more time. Walking into court, Josh assumed he was going home that morning. The news was devastating.

"They said I'll go back to court February ninth." That was one month and a day away. He had no idea what would happen on that date, but he would face the judge again. For all Josh knew, he explained to Emilia, he could get some serious time in the state pen.

"Are you serious?" Emilia asked. She sounded both livid and confused.

"Yup," Josh answered, crying even harder.

The line went quiet for a time. Then Josh said, "Oh, my God, I should have killed that bitch."

CHAPTER 46

A FEW DAYS later, after some time reflecting on things, Josh was back to his normal self, the blow of being locked up for a month (at the least) finally not throbbing any longer. He had accepted his sentence. He had that warrior tone to his voice again. Revenge was on Josh's mind now. He had been betrayed. He was ready and willing to accept punishment, but there would be a price.

He encouraged Emilia to stay close to Heather.

"I got this," she said. "You don't worry."

"I'm gonna leave it in your hands."

Heather and Emilia were communicating just about every day by now. Emilia was helping with the kids and playing it cool with Heather, being her friend.

Josh told Emilia how he was "fixing" to "do ten years" for the gun charge—years stripped from his life that he, of course, blamed Heather for. He had just spoken to Heather himself, Josh said, and she now promised him that she was definitely going to drop the charges, but she had done nothing to support that claim just yet.

"No, you're not," Emilia said about the ten years. She sounded certain.

Their time was up. Josh said he'd call again soon.

CHAPTER 47

EMILIA AND HEATHER were driving back from Ocala. Emilia had taken Heather food shopping and was planning on watching Heather's kids that night when Heather went off to work. Heather drove. When they got to Emilia's house, Heather started crying.

Emilia asked what was wrong.

It was Ben McCollum, Heather explained. She was sad that it hadn't worked out. Heather liked Ben a lot and realized that she loved him and it was real. She knew he was good for her. But she'd gone and screwed it all up, and now Ben wanted nothing to do with her, even with Josh out of the picture.

Emilia asked why they broke up. For Emilia's benefit, Heather and Ben together would be the ideal scenario; it would take Heather out of the picture—sort of—and allow Emilia to have Josh to herself without having to worry about Josh and Heather getting back together.

"'Cause he said if I dropped those charges against Josh, he didn't want to have nothing to do with me. He didn't want to be looking over his shoulder no more and it wasn't fair to him."

Heather explained that although they had broken up back in December before she and Josh married, there was still a chance for Ben and her to be together. She was planning on pleading with Ben to reconcile.

They sat in the driveway. Emilia didn't know what to say. She needed Heather to drop the charges, but she also wanted Heather and Ben together. Emilia had gotten hold of a police report from the incident. She knew by reading the report that the prosecutor had no case without Heather—despite what she had been telling Josh. Ben had said in the report he wasn't sure if Josh had a gun, so the case relied solely on Heather's testimony. Without her, the prosecutor would have to drop the charges and release Josh.

"He's done so much to me over eleven years," Heather told Emilia. She was still crying. "He shouldn't be pissed off if he sits in there a little while, because I deserve to have a life, too."

Not taking sides, Emilia consoled Heather, telling her it was all going to work out. Not to worry. They'd think of something.

Together.

"Can you come and babysit tonight?" Heather asked Emilia.

"Of course . . . I miss those babies."

"Yeah, I need some time to talk to Ben." Heather was hoping to convince Ben that the relationship was worth reinvesting in, that Ben shouldn't be frightened away by Josh.

"I am so glad I got you, Lily," Heather said.

Before taking off, Heather mentioned that perhaps Josh should stop calling her, because there was a restraining order in place.

CHAPTER 48

THEY WERE ON the way to the store: Emilia, James Acome and his buddy. Josh had no idea Emilia was hanging out with these guys, but Emilia had a plan. As they drove, she started blathering on and on about Heather and Josh and how much of a nuisance Heather had become for the two of them. Emilia was reeling.

"I'm getting some money back for taxes," Emilia said. She was speaking to both men, but addressing James's friend, a guy who knew Heather and James well, and also hung out with them at times and partied. "I'll give you five hundred dollars. You get Heather drunk, lure her to [a place where I am] so I can snap her neck."[2]

James's friend felt that Emilia "was serious," he later said.

While Josh was in jail, James Acome had moved in with Heather and the kids. Heather had realized Ben was totally not into her anymore. She needed to be with someone. But whether it was Ben or James, this pissed Josh off royally. James wasn't only sleeping with Heather, he was now living with her, spending copious amounts of time around the kids, which infuriated Josh even more.

[2] In a deposition, James Acome's friend claimed it was "seven hundred dollars," not five hundred, and that was the only discrepancy in his interviews and testimony.

But after James heard Emilia's offer, he hightailed it over to the house and, according to his friend, moved out of the house and told Heather he wanted nothing to do with either Emilia or Heather. The idea that Emilia wanted them—whether she was joking didn't matter—to get involved in a conspiracy to hurt Heather was something James and his friend wanted nothing to do with.

Emilia started to call everyone that she, Josh and Heather knew. One friend took a call from Emilia soon after she had approached James and his friend. Emilia didn't hold much back.

"I'll pay you five hundred dollars to kill Heather," Emilia said, according to several sources, including law enforcement. "I would do it myself, you know, but I cannot move the body."

She had that baby bump, after all. She didn't want to strain herself and hurt the child.

The friend laughed it off and thought Emilia was kidding.

CHAPTER 49

MUCH OF THE focus surrounding the conversations Emilia and Josh had from January 10 through January 28 centered on Heather continuing to press charges, despite her telling Josh otherwise. If she dropped the case, Josh kept repeating, the state could not hold him longer than ninety days. If that scenario played out, he'd be out in March, just in time for the arrival of his baby.

But Emilia kept telling Josh she was certain that the same woman who had let Josh down, time and time again, was going to push forward with the case. Heather was lying, Emilia explained. She had no intention of ever dropping those charges.

"Yeah . . . she's *going* to," Josh said.

Emilia became angry.

The next idea Josh had was for Emilia to call the Department of Child Services to report abuse going on inside the house so Heather would have to face a bit of trouble herself. It would all help Josh's cause. If James was still living there (even though they had heard he moved out), then he and Heather would be caught up in a state child abuse investigation.

Emilia went quiet. She was beginning to feel used. She was a bit uneasy about doing everything in her power to get Josh out because she feared Josh would, as he had so many times before, run right back to Heather and the kids. She didn't say it to Josh, but Emilia wondered if she was just the "other woman" for the time being once again, like all those other times Josh needed a woman in his life.

"Listen, Emilia . . . you never have to *ever* worry about me and Heather again . . . ," Josh said, picking up on Emilia's trepidation. He sounded sincere, selling this very well.

With an obvious unease in her voice, in a nearly inaudible whisper, Emilia said, "I know. . . . I'm not worried about that."

They got into a discussion about James Acome's friend and "that thing," as Emilia put it, she had asked him to do. Emilia told Josh she needed to spend more time with James's friend so she could try and convince him, obviously. But she didn't want to go into too much detail about it over the jail phones.

"Why do you got to spend time with [him]?" Josh wanted to know. He genuinely seemed to be in the dark here about what Emilia was referring to when she said "that thing." Josh even had a dash of jealousy in his tone.

All she could answer, "I hope you know what I mean when I say 'spend time.'"

"No, I don't," Josh responded. He sounded confused.

"It's not in a sexual way. I hope you don't think that. Please don't *ever* think that," Emilia said with a nervous laugh.

"I don't know. What's going on?"

"Baby, I cannot talk to you over these phones. You know that."

Josh got loud: "You need to send me some . . . damn kind of indication."

"Well, it's not nothing *dirty.* Geez."

"Okay," he said, calming down.

"What you and me had talked about," Emilia said, pressing on. The sense was that they had broached this topic in the past and Emilia was simply revisiting a prior plan.

"What you and me had talked about . . ."

"Okay, okay, okay . . . ," Josh said, as though he had an epiphany—*Oh yeah,* that *thing*—and it had hit him and he suddenly understood what she had been referring to all along.

"What you and me had talked about . . ."

The ambiguous nature of this conversation went back and forth for a few days as they hashed out plans for something Josh claimed not to be entirely clear on. Emilia kept saying she had his back, and she would take care of everything. All Josh needed to do was the time he had in front of him. Josh indicated on several occasions that he was upset for being kept out of things on the outside, but Emilia stressed the importance of being quiet about her plan because their conversations "could be"—and actually were—"recorded."

CHAPTER 50

BY JANUARY 15, 2009, Josh and Emilia were at odds. Josh had said some things to Emilia a few days before and she was still upset with him. He had called her, but she didn't want to talk. He kept telling her how sorry he was and how much stress he had been under in jail. He kept up the "baby this" and "baby that" pillow talk to try and win her back.

But Emilia was clearly feeling like the other woman. It seemed all they ever talked about was Heather. It was never about Emilia or their future together. How was Emilia feeling? What was their plan to be together when Josh got out? Hell, in all of the recorded phone calls, Josh never once asked Emilia how her health was or how the pregnancy was going.

"What's wrong, baby, why aren't you talking?" Josh said at one point.

"Been doing a lot of thinking," Emilia stoically whispered. "I really get pissed off when you start telling me [what I got to do]. I'm gonna tell you now, Josh. . . . For some fucking reason, me and you cannot just see each other and be okay. . . . It's either you are there or you are not." Emilia used the child she was expecting in order to explain that Josh needed to step up, be a man, and either choose her and the child, or just go away forever. She promised she would never keep the child away from him if he chose to leave her, but

"I don't know if I can handle it if you were just coming around to see the baby." Emilia either loved this guy sincerely, or had become obsessed with him. It was never clearer than during this one conversation that Emilia needed to have all of Josh or none of Josh. There was no way she could share him again. It was no longer an option for her.

"Could you?" she asked Josh, wondering if he would be able to come around on the weekends and spend time with their baby and not be in a relationship with her.

"I could," Josh said without hesitation.

"Huh?" Emilia responded. She was both shocked and hurt by the answer.

He said it again.

The line went totally silent. Emilia did not respond.

Josh finally broke the silence. "It's not what I *want* to do, but I could. I would not want to leave her without no daddy. You know I'd support her and take care of her. . . ." Then he went on to bad-mouth the two fathers of Emilia's other children. He called these men lazy, deadbeat "m-f'ers," who had left her high and dry, with kids to fend for by herself.

There was a weird cadence and tone to Emilia's voice during this part of the call. She sounded very different. Quite subdued. Even a little bit crazy. She spoke softly and methodically—though not much. She had become someone else.

"With me and you, it's just . . . well, hanging out in limbo, just ain't fun," Emilia concluded. The impression she left with Josh was that she was finished. It was over. *Don't call again.*

But Josh called back later that day. Emilia was in a better mood. Josh had something on his mind, though. He'd heard a rumor in the jail. He wanted to know if it was true and if Emilia was serious about it.

"How you gonna help me out of jail by giving James and [his friend] money?"

There was "that thing" again.

"What are you talking about?" Emilia asked.

"Are you gonna help me out or not? Straight out, baby."

"Yes," Emilia said, unable to respond fast enough. "Yes . . . ," she said again.

"Don't do it like that. I'm not doubting you, and I'm not, *not* believing you. But, baby, I'm . . . I'm scared right now. I really am. I am fucking scared. Just to be stuck here."

"Look, I gave James ten bucks just to run me to the store, just so I could buy diapers."

"I don't know. I don't know. All I been told is that James done and gone taken money from [you]. . . ."

Josh then talked about how, if only Emilia could get him out of jail, they would get "it" right, meaning the relationship. There was no doubt in Josh's mind, he claimed. All of that history with Heather, it was enough to send him packing. He was done with her for good. The time in jail had made Josh realize that Heather was poison.

"Baby, I know everything's gonna work out—I don't worry about that," Emilia said.

Josh put on a domineering tone and said sternly, "You don't do *nothing* as far as *that* goes. You just get me out of here. . . . That's your main focus right now. And that's kissing ass right there. We got this. We gonna be the motherfucking team we supposed to be. You *got* that?"

"I know."

CHAPTER 51

ON JANUARY 20, Josh called Emilia with something very specific on his mind. He wanted to know how close the next-door neighbor to her mother's house was and if the wooded area between the two houses was thickly settled. He came across like a man on a mission, trying to figure out part of a plan.

"Is there people living in the house back there?" Josh asked. He had obviously been thinking about something in particular.

"Uh-huh," Emilia said, agreeing. "Why? What . . . next door?" Emilia was genuinely confused as to why Josh would care about this.

"But listen, it's pretty woody in between by where your momma's is and they's house and where that old trailer is?"

"Yeah . . ."

". . . And they can't see out through there?"

He meant the neighbors: Could they look from their house windows—any of them—and see through the woods to that trailer?

"No," Emilia said.

"Okay, okay . . . ," Josh answered. He had been full of adrenaline, but now realizing no one could see out into the backyard of Emilia's mother's and that trailer, he was suddenly calmer. It was as if the plan he had mapped out in his head had come to fruition right then and there.

"Why?" Emilia wanted to know.

"I was just wondering, baby," Josh said. He had an unabashed and obvious patronizing tone to his voice, as if he knew something no one else did. "I was just wondering."

"O . . . kayyyyy," Emilia said, stretching out the word. Then she laughed.

"I was just wondering . . . but anyway . . . I been in jail. I been thinking a lot."

Emilia started cracking up, as though she had just gotten the punch line to a joke.

There was another word for what Josh was suggesting here: "premeditation."

Without Emilia knowing about it at first, Josh Fulgham was planning the murder of his wife, Heather Strong. At least that much was obvious in this one phone call.

Over the next several days, after they understood perfectly what they were discussing, now both on exactly the same page, Josh began asking questions designed around a definite plan he was concocting. He wanted to know what "the neighbor" was going to do eventually with all that land around Emilia's momma's house, especially the old trailers. Did the owner of the land have any plans that Emilia knew about? Was he going to be excavating or building or selling at any time in the near future?

Emilia explained that she heard the guy was going to be clearing the lot, getting rid of the trailers and turning the land into pasture for some horses.

"All right, all right . . . I was just wondering," Josh said, again with a diabolical, smug, self-assured tone. Her answer seemed to give him great comfort that the land—along with the trailer—would be cleared and taken away. "Because this motherfucker," he said, referring to himself, "has been doing some *thinking.*"

"About?" Emilia said, laughing.

"This shit."

She laughed harder. She and Josh were a team now. Working together. Understanding each other. On the same page entirely.

They were coming together.

"We'll talk when I get home."

"Okay."

During another call, Emilia asked about Heather and if things didn't work out for Heather and whichever guy she was seeing when Josh got out. What was going to happen then? Was Josh going to drop Emilia again and go running after the sweetheart from his teenage years?

Josh became livid. There was something different in his voice. He had written Heather off—completely. He had wiped her from his mind and his heart. He was finished with her, but there was more to it. He had erased Heather. And one of the only ways he could be certain of never going back was to make sure she wasn't around.

"You don't *ever* worry about that," Josh scolded Emilia, referring to him getting back with Heather. "Listen to what I am saying—Don't worry about that."

"Okay, I believe you."

"You don't be worrying about me and Heather *no* more. I promise you. You'll see when I get out."

Emilia hung up and stared at the phone. For the first time, she felt Josh was being straight with her.

CHAPTER 52

JOHNNY STRONG GREW up in Lebanon, Indiana, where his father was a hardworking construction foreman subjected to long, grueling hours out on job sites. As a young boy, Johnny and his family packed it up from Indiana and moved south to Tennessee because his father got a better job offer. The Strong family finally ended up in Mississippi, where life took a turn for the worse. Johnny's dad developed cancer at a young age, so Johnny, his brother and his sisters wound up in foster care after their momma couldn't take care of them.

By the time he was fourteen or fifteen, Johnny said, not quite able, these days, to recall exactly when, he was already working a steady job roofing houses. School wasn't something Johnny thought about much ever since he could swing a hammer and pound nails. Johnny needed to take care of his siblings and get back with Ma. And by the time he was nineteen, Johnny reunited once again with his sisters and aunt and mother. Johnny's brother was in Nashville, staying with family there. It wasn't the ideal situation and some time had passed, but the family was back together again.

During the late 1970s, when Johnny was cutting his teeth as a teenager, he was hanging out at a local bar one night, shooting pool, when a young gal who tickled his fancy walked in.

"We was dranking, you know, and partying like young people do," Johnny explained later.

"Carolyn," the young girl said her name was.

Johnny liked what he saw. He had seen Carolyn around town. But here she was right in front of him.

"Johnny, pleasure to meet y'all."

Johnny said he and Carolyn "wound up getting together that night" and shacked up "together for about six months" before Carolyn demanded that they "go ahead and get married."

So he proposed.

It was 1980 when Carolyn and Johnny wed and moved to Texas to begin raising a family. For construction workers, like Johnny and his father before him, they followed the work. Johnny had become an all-around laborer, like his old man: roofer, framer, concrete, whatever he could do to earn enough to drink and take care of the family. At the turn of the new decade, the fabulous 1980s, Texas was a booming mecca of construction with all of that oil money floating around and being pumped back into infrastructure and new housing. Johnny wanted his piece of it.

After a year in Houston, however, Johnny saw his work decline sharply and he was getting laid off a lot, so he decided to follow the trail once again. But this time, work was drying up everywhere in Johnny's chosen field. He couldn't find much, so they moved to Mississippi, where Johnny's mother had a house and she could take him and Carolyn in.

Then, on March 23, 1982, Carolyn gave birth to Heather. Now Johnny needed steady work. He had a daughter. He started asking around.

"Dallas," someone told him. "They're hiring down there."

Johnny, Carolyn and Heather left for Dallas shortly after Heather was born.

In Dallas, Johnny and Carolyn both found work: security

guards for Gateway Bank One. With some cash in their pockets, though, an itch started. They were looking for something to do, something exciting, something fun for once. It seemed to be nothing but a struggle since they married, and now that they were working different shifts, Carolyn and Johnny rarely saw each other. Johnny worked a twelve-hour shift—half a day—and Carolyn the other. It got to the point where they decided they wanted to move back home to Mississippi.

"Big mistake," Johnny said later.

That excitement and fun they were searching for in Dallas came when they got back home—in the form of partying to excess, at least for him, Johnny explained.

Carolyn and Johnny were equally responsible for drifting apart and leaning on other things to get them through tough times. And Johnny admitted that he was not nearly close to being the father that Heather deserved.

As a young girl, Heather believed life was what you made of it. For some strange reason, later on, she felt connected to Josh Fulgham forever simply because they had kids, even though she knew he was never going to give her what she wanted and, in turn, would likely cause her grief. Maybe it *was* the kids? Perhaps she didn't know any better? Some claimed Heather was raped repeatedly when she was young by someone she knew. If that was the case, well, what chance did she have without any psychological help to cope? Her codependency was placed inside the wiring of her brain long ago as she witnessed her parents slowly begin a struggle with not only each other but with life in general. Heather turned ten, and Johnny and Carolyn were constantly at odds.

"She was a wonderful child," Johnny said of his daughter. "She was always trying to help around the house. Washing clothes, washing dishes, cleaning. Heather was always there for her mother."

Heather was your typical teen. She liked having friends over. She liked watching television, playing outside, heading off to the local teen hot spots, laughing under her breath about the neighborhood boys she had a crush on.

"In fact, every birthday she had," Johnny explained, "Heather didn't like cake. So she had to have her pizza. That was her main food love."

Heather did well in school, Johnny said. All was fine and her life was going on as any typical teen until Heather, as a fourteen-year-old, put her focus on boys. That was when her studies started to slip.

"Them boys began to come up to the house," Johnny said. "She had a few boyfriends. I guess my discipline wasn't what it should have been, maybe not enough." Johnny went on to say he and Carolyn were seriously involved with their own difficulties then, especially Johnny's heavy drinking.

"I was a pretty bad alcoholic myself," Johnny said. "I drunk a lot."

As a teen, Heather became pregnant with Josh's baby. Johnny didn't have any problem with Josh before the young man got his daughter pregnant. Josh was a "yes, sir/no, sir" kind of kid, Johnny recalled.

In the beginning.

"He had a steady job, nice pickup, kept his hair nice and clean, dressed nicely, and I thought, 'Well, he seems to be a pretty nice fella and all. Looks like he's trying.' All the other guys she was going out with or dating didn't have nothing. They didn't even work."

But maybe, Johnny said, the Josh he knew then was just for show. Johnny understood that maybe Josh wasn't who he appeared to be. Years later, Johnny saw this firsthand as one of the last to find out that Josh and Heather had even gotten married. It wasn't until after Heather was dead and missing that Johnny was told she and Josh had married that previous December.

Heather and her dad lost touch during those years Heather had taken off to Florida with Josh and had more kids of her own. It was just one of those things that happened, Johnny said, clearly disappointed in himself for not pursuing a more intimate father-daughter relationship.

"Heather acted like she was twentysomething from the time she was maybe fifteen or sixteen," Johnny recalled.

It's always the case: Someone dies unexpectedly and we go back and think what we could have done differently. Johnny recalled a daughter he wished he'd had another chance to raise; a second go of being the dad Heather deserved. There was once, he explained, when he took Heather fishing. She loved to fish. Mississippi had some monster catfish. Well, she and her dad were sitting in the boat talking when Heather hooked herself a whopper.

"And the thing dragged us in the boat around for a time until it broke the line," Johnny said. "We laughed and laughed. . . . Heather even done liked to hunt," Johnny remembered.

The "close time" they shared, Johnny pointed out, was always minimal because of his work and then later he was unavailable because of his own demons. Johnny was quick to point a finger at others, but he realized that when he did that, there were three fingers pointed back at him. He wished like hell that he'd done things very differently, but life was the way it ended up. You can't rewrite it. You have to live with it and accept your mistakes, and he has.

"I just remember my kid as loving and caring and always willing to share with people, and would help you out any time in any way. She always had a smile on her face. I never done seen her upset or angry. It took a lot to get Heather mad."

All of this made Heather's life in Florida, and what happened, that much harder to take for Johnny. He was at home, much older, much weaker, fighting several health ailments, including the removal of a kidney and two bouts of cancer, when the sad news came. His health had deteriorated after years of excess partying. Johnny lived in Mississippi and saw Heather and his grandchildren whenever Heather came up from Florida and stopped by. But there was one day when Johnny heard that his daughter had turned up missing. He didn't want to believe it, of course. But Heather's brother had called Johnny to tell him how cousin Misty had spoken to the Florida police to report that Heather had not been seen or heard from in a fortnight.

"Missing?" Johnny asked. "Heather?"

Johnny knew Heather's children were her life and she would not leave without them. "She would have given up her own life for her children." He considered Heather to be streetwise and street-smart. "Missing" and "Heather" did not sound right to Johnny.

Lord, there's got *to be something going on,* Johnny thought when he heard Heather had vanished. His next thought was *Foul play . . .* Johnny found out that the kids were with Judy and, to him, that could mean only one thing: "I knew [Josh] had to do something with her, either have her put away, or . . . Well, look, I knew she wouldn't leave her kids."

In the days that followed, Johnny said, "I felt like killing myself. I realized I was not a good daddy. I was not there."

Those memories (good, but mostly bad) flooded back and made the impact of Heather's disappearance all that more penetrating and powerful. Johnny was helpless.

And then, as Johnny sat one day on his porch enjoying a rather mild Mississippi early spring day, he looked on as two cops pulled into the driveway and got out of the car and walked up to him.

"Florida authorities found your daughter's body," Johnny recalled the local cops telling him that day. "They have her husband . . ."

Johnny wanted to vomit. He wanted to end his own life right there, he said. But not before, "going down to Florida, and if I could get my hands on Josh, choking him to death!"

Heather's murder was a devastating blow to a guy who

didn't see himself as someone who showed her the love he truly felt in his heart.

"Josh took her air," Johnny said. "He is still down there eating, living and breathing, and my daughter is not. I'm still not over it." Johnny paused. Then: "I guess it is something you never get over."

CHAPTER 53

JOSH GOT OUT of the local jail on February 6, 2009. By then, he had heard, James Acome was back living with Heather. From all he had been told, Josh was livid at the idea that James and Heather were not watching the kids the way Josh thought they should. Imagine: Josh was stepping out of jail after forty-plus days of not seeing his kids and the first thing he did was judge the adults taking care of them. It seemed absurd when placed into that context, but that was Josh Fulgham. Josh never looked at himself. He was always concerned with what others were doing to him.

According to Josh, he had heard stories about the kids being neglected. This was never proven, mind you, but Josh didn't need proof to be enraged about anything—he needed only to get it into his head that it was going on and there it could fester like a tumor, growing each day, becoming more of an annoyance to his thought process.

Josh thought about it, though; after consulting with Emilia, he decided that he had better watch himself messing too much with Heather and maybe ease his way back into the kids' lives. His great concern was that Heather would make something up about him and he'd be right back in jail. Nevertheless, he needed to abide by all of Heather's rules whenever he had the children. Or else . . .

"She did set him up for that gun charge," a source later said. "She made it all up."

One night shortly after Josh was out, he took his mother's car (Heather still had his car; Emilia had never gotten it back, as she had promised) and drove over to see Emilia. After picking up Emilia, they were at a stoplight in town when Josh spotted his car coming through the intersection, going in the opposite direction.

"Look at that, Emilia!" Josh yelled.

"Oh, my."

Josh could not believe his eyes. James Acome was driving *his* car. Not only driving, but "spinning the tires out," Josh recalled. "[He was] cutting in and out of car lanes like he was in a race. . . ."

Josh followed him. James ran out of the car after stopping at his parents' house.

Josh decided to call the cops, instead of chasing James inside and putting a hurt on.

The police came and Josh proved it was his car and James did not have permission to be driving it. The cops got the car back.

"But this pissed Heather off," Josh recalled.

A day later, Heather called him: "If you don't give me that car back, you will *never* see your children again," Josh said Heather threatened.

"You will not get the car and I am taking your ass to court to get my kids back!" Josh screamed.

The War of the Roses was back on, in full force.

As he thought about it in the days ahead, however, Josh thought he'd had enough this time around.

By the following weekend, February 14 and 15, when Heather disappeared, she kept to her word and told Josh he wasn't going to be seeing the kids.

Not then. Not ever again.

So Josh decided to put into action that plan he'd come up with while in jail.

CHAPTER 54

ON FEBRUARY 14, 2009, Ben McCollum stopped by the Petro with his kids for something to eat. He hadn't even re- alized Heather was working there. By then, Ben had severed all contact with Heather. As much as he loved her, he had moved on with his life.

Heather walked over to the table.

The kids went wild; they loved her. For a fleeting moment, there it was, like old times at Ben's house when they were all a family.

Ben and Heather didn't say much of anything to each other right away. Both just stared. Here it was Valentine's Day and Ben was out with his kids. He hadn't moved on, as far as finding someone else yet. Ben could tell Heather was still thinking about him. She had that look Ben knew all too well.

However, she also seemed nervous, Ben thought. Not in an anxious-to-see-him way, but unlike anything he had seen while he was with her. It wasn't because Ben was there. He felt that. Heather's anxiety stemmed from something else. Something was going on. Something major was bothering Heather, Ben considered.

"How are you?" Heather asked.

"Good, Heather. I'm okay."

They had been through so much it seemed that Ben and Heather were destined to meet on this day (which, Ben did not know then, would be the last time he ever saw her).

Heather sat down. "I have something for you."

"What?" Ben asked. He was curious.

Heather reached into her pocket. She'd happened to have a letter she was about to mail to Ben. With tears in her eyes, she handed it across the table. Ben was feeling the moment himself.

"What's this?"

"Read it," she said. Then Heather got up and walked away.

After eating, Ben took the kids and went out to his vehicle without seeing Heather again. He sat for a moment before starting his truck. Then he opened the letter and read.

Heather wanted him to know that she was sorry for everything. She wished she could come back and live with him. Her life with Josh was a joke. The guy was an animal. That chapter of her life, Heather explained, was over for good. There would never be Josh and Heather again. Regardless of her reconciling with Ben, Heather wrote, she and Josh were finished for good. The guy was toxic; she needed to be rid of him.

Ben believed her and was taken by the letter. He thought maybe he should reconsider his strict stance on not taking her back once she had left and dropped those charges against Josh. Maybe he was being pigheaded and inconsiderate of Heather's situation. Giving her another chance might be just what Heather needed.

So Ben took a ride over to his father's house. He wanted the old man's advice on his dilemma.

"Should I take her back?" Ben asked his father. "What do you think?"

"Nope, nope . . . stick to what you decided and said, you know."

Looking back on his relationship with Heather, Ben

thought that maybe she couldn't handle being truly loved. He'd treated her with respect and kindness, like any lady deserved to be treated. He bought her classy clothes and nice things, and she felt like a real woman, an appreciated mother, as though they had a natural relationship devoid of the dysfunction she had lived with her entire life. Heather felt good about herself when she was with Ben. He was good *for* her. But when Josh watched all of this taking place, it messed with his head, Ben believed. Josh couldn't fathom that she could move on without him and lead a "normal" life—or Josh didn't want to let her.

Not taking her back when his heart told him to, Ben said later, was a decision that both him and his dad later greatly regretted. Also, not doing something about Josh when they had the opportunity was a consequence of that same regret.

"I should have killed that motherfucker long ago myself," Ben said as he concluded his thoughts about his life with Heather Strong.

CHAPTER 55

ACCORDING TO JOSH'S version (the one he shared with me) of what happened that weekend of February 14 and 15, it all started with a drug and alcohol binge Josh had begun on Saturday morning.

"I went and bought me a bunch of pills and a bottle of liquor and decided to stay the weekend at Emilia's house."

He rented a "bunch of DVDs . . . watched movies and got fucked up."

On Saturday night, Emilia and Josh hit the bedroom and "had hot, wild sex for four hours," Josh explained. It was so intense, he added, that he woke up the following morning with a severe back issue. Emilia, however, wasn't hearing any of it.

"That morning, the little nympho had to have more," Josh said. This just screwed up his back even more, so he popped whatever pills he had left from the night before. Josh fell asleep, then woke up to his sister calling him.

"What? What?" Josh said. He was still in a fog.

"Heather has been calling and calling. You need to come home and talk to her."

Josh got dressed and drove to his mother's house. Michelle Gustafson, Josh's sister, was there. She talked about how Heather had been at work and calling, looking for him. It sounded urgent. He needed to straighten his ass out and call her back.

"Okay," Josh said. His head was pounding. His back was sore. His mind was scattered.

Josh told me *he* called Heather at work, but he later told police that Michelle called Heather for him.

Either way, "Where are the kids?" was the first thing out of Josh's mouth.

"Listen to me . . . ," Heather said.

"No, *you* listen to me . . . where are my babies?" Josh had little patience at this point. He knew that Heather was now finished, as was he, with the relationship. And a battle had ensued between them. Both were jockeying for position in what was presumed to be a fight for the kids—one that Josh had to know he would never win.

The next thing Heather said, however, enraged him. Maybe it was the hangover? Or everything that had been going on? Possibly it was because Josh was now with Emilia—which was not how he had planned to celebrate his recent release from jail. Regardless, Josh said, Heather explained over the phone that the kids were at the house alone with James Acome, who was watching them.

(To Detective Donald Buie in one interview, Josh claimed Heather "told me the whole deal that was going on with James at home and I told her . . . go on and do what you were going to do with putting him out and she told me she was gonna put him out . . . and I said go on and do that and call me back." Thus, from what Josh told Buie, that first phone call was centered on Heather telling Josh she was kicking James out of the house.)

Hearing and sensing the resentment and sheer disgust in Heather's voice at his asking where the children were, Josh explained to me later, "I saw nothing but red when she told me that because allegedly [James had had a relationship with an underage girl]." According to how Josh later told it, Heather was throwing it in his face that James was alone with the kids because she knew it would twist and turn the knife already in Josh's back.

"Josh, if you do not give me that car back," Heather supposedly said next, "I am taking the kids *back* to Mississippi— and you know what happened to me when I was a young girl staying with my mom."

(Josh did not mention this to Buie during any of his interviews. But in a letter to me, he explained that Heather was allegedly saying that she was going to put the kids in harm's way because she had been sexually assaulted by someone in her family back when she was a teen. To Josh, this was the proverbial final nail—something had to be done to protect those kids.)

While on the phone with Heather, Josh thought back to when they lived in Mississippi with Heather's mother and what was going on inside Carolyn's house. Lots of alleged perverted acts were taking place, according to Josh. He did not want his children subjected to this.

Those thoughts, he told me, made him rage—but still, Josh thought of something other than yelling and screaming and threatening his wife.

"You're bluffing, Heather. You wouldn't do that."

"I am not. I've already called the station to see when the bus leaves."

"You are really going to take them away from me again?"

"Yes!"

Josh hung up the phone. He paced. He rubbed the back of his neck. That rage he'd felt in the past—whenever Heather pissed him off and he would strike her—brewed. He was a pressure cooker. He needed a release. Quickly. He needed to do something. Act on that internal rage. He couldn't allow Heather to have the last word, no less take the kids, leave town and bring them into what he viewed as a devil's lair.

After hanging up with Heather, Josh said later, he called Emilia—and claimed to have said: "Do you remember what you was trying to get me to do in December?"

Josh recalled Emilia responding "yes," on that night.

"Well, it's time," Josh said, "because she is about to take the kids to Mississippi, and, on top of that, she has gone and left them with [James Acome] alone, all day long."

"Get her over here tonight," Emilia told him—at least according to Josh's later claims.

They hung up.

Josh immediately called Heather back and, acting as though he was giving in, agreed to allow her to have the car back. He said, "Call me when you get off work so you can come and pick it up. I'd bring it over to you now, but I need help with something." Josh never said what he told Heather he needed help with, but she bought into his scenario, if we are to believe him.

(This alleged agreement Josh managed to facilitate seems highly suspicious. It is odd that Heather would, without asking what was up, agree to help a guy she was bickering with and, at this point, absolutely despised. On top of that, the idea that Emilia first came up with this plan to kill Heather, as Josh suggested to me, also has some problems—because during that one recorded phone call from inside the jail weeks before, Josh floated "that thing" for Emilia over the phone and she came across as legitimately not having any clue as to what he was talking about until she figured it out and then went along with it. In addition, in Josh's first statement to Detective Buie about his role in Heather's murder, he never mentioned that Emilia had said *anything* in December about a plan to kill Heather.)

Josh called Emilia back and they "concocted," according to what Josh told me, a plan revolving around some money to get Heather into that trailer in the back of Maria Zayas's house.

With that part of the plan decided, Josh set things in motion by calling his mother to tell her that he was upset because Heather was going back to Mississippi, but there wasn't much he could do about it. Josh said Heather was

Heather Strong
was born and raised
in Mississippi.
She dreamed of a
white-picket-fence life,
a beautiful home
and children.

While working as a waitress, Heather met Joshua Fulgham. They moved to Florida to find work and raise a family.

Joshua and Heather lived in this trailer home in Citra, Florida, outside of Tampa. *(Courtesy Marion County Sheriff's Office)*

Joshua Fulgham, with his son and daughter on his son's first birthday.

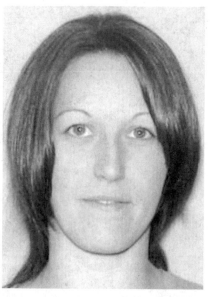

On February 15, 2009, Heather Strong left this Petro Travel Plaza in Florida, and was never seen alive again. *(Courtesy Marion County Sheriff's Office)*

This house in Boardman, Florida, where Joshua Fulgham's mistress lived with her mother, became the focus of the search for Heather Strong. *(Courtesy Marion County Sheriff's Office)*

About fifty yards in back of the home, an abandoned trailer contained evidence that suggested something very violent and bloody took place inside.
(Courtesy Marion County Sheriff's Office)

Joshua's mistress, Emilia Carr, later told police that this broken window led her to search inside the trailer. *(Courtesy Marion County Sheriff's Office)*

According to Emilia, this chair was used to restrain Heather as she was tortured. *(Courtesy Marion County Sheriff's Office)*

The trailer was used as a storage shed and was full of unwanted articles. *(Courtesy Marion County Sheriff's Office)*

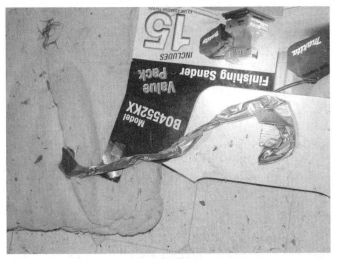

A piece of silver duct tape, recovered from the abandoned trailer, was thought to have been used during Heather's murder.
(Courtesy Marion County Sheriff's Office)

Several yards from the corner of the trailer was a small clearing of land with a pile of debris that appeared to be "staged."
(Courtesy Marion County Sheriff's Office)

Joshua Fulgham had a long history of arrests, including violent assaults and drug charges.
(Courtesy Marion County Sheriff's Office)

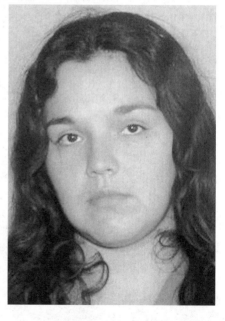

Baby-faced Emilia "Lily" Carr became obsessed with Joshua Fulgham.
(Courtesy Marion County Sheriff's Office)

Marion County Sheriff's Office investigators excavated the area near the trailer after Joshua Fulgham told them where he believed Heather Strong was buried. *(Courtesy Marion County Sheriff's Office)*

Underneath this overturned chair, crime scene investigators found
a board buried about sixteen inches underground.
(Courtesy Marion County Sheriff's Office)

After digging underneath the board, investigators uncovered
a suitcase that contained the body of Heather Strong.
(Courtesy Marion County Sheriff's Office)

The suitcase held the body of a young adult female.
(Courtesy Marion County Sheriff's Office)

It was soon confirmed that the body in the suitcase wearing this T-shirt, which was saturated with dried blood, was that of Heather Strong. *(Courtesy Marion County Sheriff's Office)*

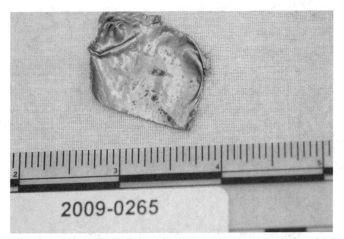

2009-0265

This piece of silver duct tape matched other pieces of tape found inside the trailer. *(Courtesy Marion County Sheriff's Office)*

Joshua Fulgham was charged with the murder of his wife, Heather Strong, and was later convicted of participating in her abduction and premeditated slaying. *(Courtesy Marion County Sheriff's Office)*

Convicted of first-degree murder, Emilia Carr was the second female to be sentenced to the death penalty in Florida after serial killer Aileen "Monster" Wuornos. *(Courtesy Marion County Sheriff's Office)*

Heather Strong is deeply missed by all who knew and loved her.

going to leave the kids with him because she needed some time to straighten her head out.

This gave a reason for Heather turning up missing in the coming days and the kids being left at Judy's house. Josh involved his mother—without her knowing—in a conspiracy to kill Heather. He laid these details out for me in a letter he sent me.

"If that is the case, Josh," his mother told him, "you need to draw up some type of an agreement with Heather over the kids being left with you."

"Can you do that, Momma?"

Judy said she would.

CHAPTER 56

"LISTEN, HEATHER, I want you to meet me at Emilia's house," Josh told me he explained to his wife over the phone later on that night. "I know where Emilia has fifteen hundred dollars stashed inside a trailer and I want to steal it. You'll be the lookout while I get it. I'll give you a cut."

Insinuating that she was greedy, Josh said, "Heather jumped all over the deal because she wanted" some of that money.

In the next breath, "I'll be by to pick you and the kids up soon," Josh said he told Heather, contradicting his earlier statement for her to meet him there.

Heather said she'd be expecting him.

Josh never told me where he picked Heather and the kids up. But James Acome later told police that Heather took off that night with the kids and it was the last time he ever saw her. According to that first interview Josh gave Detective Buie (postadmission), Josh said he met Heather at a local Subway grinder shop in Sparr, Florida, which is about a twenty-minute, seventeen-mile drive south of Boardman, where Emilia's mother lived.

"I pulled over there and backed in front of the store and . . . her and the kids came over," Josh told Buie.

They talked, Josh explained to the detective. His son sat in front; his daughter and Heather were in the back.

"And we were just talking, and . . . she told me, 'James hadn't got his shit, but he just left, and he left all his shit in the house.'"

Josh further stated that he and Heather—again, totally out of character when put into the context of the situation—were "just talking about spending some time together . . . and let's see where we go at that point."

Right then, Josh claimed, with Heather and the kids in the car, he had no intention of killing her. In a letter to me, however, Josh said he told Heather how he believed the fifteen hundred dollars was inside the trailer and that all Heather had to do was make sure no one saw him going in or coming out. Heather was to act as his wingman, in other words. But he claimed she had no idea where they were going, other than to a trailer somewhere.

"Okay," Heather said after Josh explained, with their children looking on.

"Let's go ahead and take the kids out to Momma's. . . ."

They pulled up to Judy Chandler's house and Josh brought the kids in to stay with their grandma. He didn't say it, but Josh must have reiterated to his mother that he was bringing Heather to the bus depot so she could head back home to Mississippi to get her mind together. That was the supposed ruse he had scripted with Emilia.

Everything seemed to coalesce as it unfolded.

From there, Josh drove toward Boardman. During the ride over to Emilia's, Josh told Heather, "If you help, I'll give you this car. I got a new title filled out and everything— I'll sign it over to you."

"Where?" Heather asked. She wanted to know where they were going.

"Emilia's."

"Josh, I'm not going over there. She's a freaking psycho."

Heather became nervous. She didn't want anything to do with showing up at Emilia's with him.

"Heather, listen, Emilia's not at home. She's done gone and seen her brother in Dunnellon. Her mom and them done left, too. If they're back when we get there, they'll be asleep."

Heather stared out the window. She was thinking about the request. Then she supposedly said: "Okay, I'll do it. But I don't want any bullshit, Josh."

"There ain't gonna be. Don't worry about it."

As they pulled into Emilia's driveway somewhere near eight at night (Josh later told Buie), Emilia was waiting inside the house, watching stealthily from behind a curtain.

AT SOME POINT while he was alone on that night (probably while inside his mother's house), Josh called Emilia, he later told Detective Buie.

"You remember [what] we talked about?" Josh claimed he asked Emilia during that phone call.

"Yeah."

"You still think about that?"

"We can do it," Emilia told him. (Josh shared this with Detective Buie, but not with me.) "I told you, I done got a place for her. Got all this yard back there. It's in the woods."

(This, of course, went against the phone call Josh had made to Emilia where he had asked her about the trailer and the backyard and all that land, and if the neighbor could see and if she knew what his plans for the land were. At that time, Emilia sounded as if the subject had been new to her and had never been brought up between them. But then, when explaining to Buie, Josh gave the impression that killing Heather in the trailer and getting rid of her body somewhere on the property was all Emilia's idea and they discussed it on the night he drove Heather over there.)

What Josh meant by "what we talked about," he further clarified for Buie, was something Emilia had initiated during Josh's stint in jail. There was one night when Emilia was with Heather, Josh told Buie. The women were at Josh and Heather's place. James Acome was there, too. Emilia came up behind Heather and put a knife to her throat; she threatened to slash her neck if she didn't drop the charges against Josh. James stepped in and stopped it, but Heather soon after signed the papers to have the charges dropped.

Josh told Buie his mother "printed up a paper for me on the computer . . . saying that we're gonna keep the kids until she gets her stuff straightened out. . . ."

They never had Heather sign it. Instead, Emilia filled it out, Josh said.

AFTER DROPPING OFF the kids at his mother's, driving and then parking near Emilia's house and heading into the backyard toward the trailer, Josh asked Heather, "You hungry?"

"No, I ate already. . . . Let's just get this over with."

Josh thought Heather wanted to get back home as soon as possible. He also claimed to have asked her about Ben and what was going on with that relationship.

Heather became impatient. She didn't want to engage in small talk. According to Josh, our only source for this conversation, all she wanted to know was where that money was located so she could help him steal it.

Josh never said why it never occurred to Heather that he could have gotten just about anybody else to help him. Why her? Why would she fall for this? They had been at odds, fighting and arguing about the kids for weeks. He'd threatened her and Ben. He made it clear he was going to the Department of Children Services to report her and James. Why would

Heather agree to go, especially alone, with this man whom she knew to be violent and volatile? Just for a few bucks?

Josh's story doesn't make much sense.

Nonetheless, we do know that Josh and Heather entered that trailer at some point shortly after 8:00 P.M. on February 15, 2009—and that only one of them, not long after, would leave alive.

CHAPTER 57

IT WAS DARK by the time they got out to the trailer in the backyard of Maria Zayas's house.

"You got a flashlight?" Heather asked.

"No," Josh said.

("So we . . . both went in with cigarette lighters," Josh told Detective Buie.)

Josh had Heather walk in first.

He looked around to make certain no one else was watching—except maybe Emilia peeking at them from a window—and then followed behind.

They looked around inside the trailer after entering.

"Damn, it was on these tables somewhere," Josh said, referring to the money. They were in the living-room portion of the trailer, which was hampered down with garbage and household items, like a hoarder's home. "I know it was here. She showed it to me just this weekend."

When Josh explained this scene to Detective Buie, he put the entire idea and crime on Emilia. "I said, 'Where do I take [Heather] to?'" Josh explained. "[Emilia] said, 'Bring her back there in the back trailer.' And I said all right. I said, 'What's the best way to get her back there?' She said, 'Well, she knows I had money, Josh.' I said, 'Well, I'll tell her we're coming over there, you showed me money, and I'm gonna

come over there and get it. . . .' That's exactly what I told
Emilia."

In a letter to me explaining this night, Josh never mentioned that Emilia had come up with this plan. Further, again
going back to that one phone call from jail where Josh
seemed to devise this plan, it all pointed to Josh being the
driving force behind this murder, Emilia the subordinate
minion, going along and coming up with ideas of her own as
the crime unfolded, but not before.

Josh pleaded with Heather to search the trailer for the
money. As Heather began to flip over cushions in couches
and to dig through boxes, Josh approached her.

That black chair was in the center of a small room.

"Sit down," Josh said, swinging the chair around to face
Heather. The look on Josh's face had changed by now. He
meant what he said. He wasn't in a hurry anymore to find
money that was never there to begin with.

Heather looked at him. She knew this guy well enough to
understand that when his expression changed, Josh Fulgham
meant business.

"What?" Heather asked, seemingly confused.

"Sit *down,* Heather. I need to talk to you."

"No way. Not a chance, Josh. Take me from here."

"I'm not doing that. We need to talk. I have some questions
I want to ask you."

Heather took a look at her husband. He was serious.

Then, after a pause, without warning, she made a break
for the door.

Josh reached out to grab her.

Heather broke loose. "Let me go. . . ."

"No!"

As Heather went to open the door to leave, Josh told me,
Emilia walked in.

"You need to get quiet," Emilia told Heather.

"I'm out of here—fuck this!" Heather said before booking
down the narrow hallway toward the back of the trailer.

("And that was when Emilia hit her . . . hit her with that flashlight," Josh told Detective Buie, blaming Emilia for striking Heather first, perhaps not recalling that he had already told Buie he didn't have a flashlight with him on that night—but, in fact, he did, and he actually struck Heather with the flashlight as she went for the door and Emilia walked in.)

Emilia's blow with the flashlight to Heather's head (though he was likely referring to his own assault) was not enough to "knock her out," Josh recalled. But Heather fell back and used her hand to break the fall and landed on the window as she went down, smashing it into shards.

On the ground now, Heather was dazed. Josh grabbed her. Then he dragged Heather over to the chair and made her sit down. When Heather resisted, being much bigger than her, Josh held her down in the chair with his body weight.

"We went back to an old mobile home that was used for storage and after a few moments Emilia came out," Josh stated, recalling for me these moments leading up to the end of Heather's life in rather plainspoken, common language. "Heather knew about what time it was, so she tried to run out. I told her to sit down, that we were going to talk about some things."

"Sit!" Josh screamed at Heather. "I need to tell you some things and then you can leave."

Emilia walked over, Josh explained to Detective Buie, as he held Heather down. Then "Emilia taped her up. She got her hands taped up. I did her feet down at the bottom. I did them with tape. Emilia wrapped tape around her mouth before she even put the bag over her. Well, somehow Heather got the tape loose from her mouth and got it down around her neck. So Emilia used more. She used a whole roll of duct tape. . . ."

"You have sex with James?" Josh asked Heather after she was secured in the chair. He mentioned to me that Emilia had taped Heather to the chair and tried to tape her mouth shut *after* he asked these questions. Josh never shared this with Buie, however.

Heather denied having sex with James, Josh told me, adding—again trivializing the situation with pedestrian language—that he "made Heather sit down in a chair."

This becomes hard to believe, because Heather was living with James at this point. Of course she was sleeping with the guy.

Anyway . . . Josh said he then began asking Heather about other guys she'd possibly cheated on him with. Not only men from recent years, but from past years as well. Josh wanted to know all of their names. Each one.

Heather didn't respond immediately, so Josh started screaming at her, with the hope of scaring her.

That was when, he said, she "came clean."

"Yes. Yes. Yes," Heather snapped.

"Three days after I was put in jail, did you or did you not sleep with James?"

"Yes," Heather said.

"Did you and Ben plan that bullshit [about the shotgun] the day that both of you made that report?"

"Yes," Heather answered here, according to Josh, though he failed to tell Buie.

"Had you been sleeping with Ben *after* you came back to me?"

"Yes."

Heather tried standing, Josh explained, so "I slammed her back down into the chair."

Josh stood directly in front of his wife now. He bent down and looked her square in the eyes. The way he told it, it came across as a scene out of Quentin Tarantino's *Reservoir Dogs:* "Tell me about that mark I saw on [our child's eye]. . . ."

"She admitted to slapping him when he would not stop crying . . . ," Josh explained to me. "I lost it and told Emilia . . . , 'Do what you have to do.'" The way he explained this was as if Emilia was Josh's muscle; he left it up to her what to do next and how far to take the situation.

Josh then sat down on Heather, he said, because he was afraid she "would push back into Emilia and hurt the baby."

Indeed, kidnapping, terrorizing and ultimately murdering Heather Strong all went on, mind you, while Emilia was eight months pregnant with Josh's (supposed) baby. Emilia, a mother-to-be, was involved in the beating and murder of a mother of two—all of this brutality occurred as Emilia carried a child (her fourth) who had been fathered by the same guy as her victim's children, making her child-to-be the half-sibling to Josh and Heather's.

Some would call that more than cold-blooded.

Maybe even downright evil at its core.

CHAPTER 58

JOSH'S VERSION OF killing his wife changed over the course of his interviews with MCSO and his later letters to me. Not major details, but with subtleties. All murderers who confess their crimes minimize their roles, either by design or unconscious regret and guilt. When two or more are involved in a murder, that minimization becomes even greater because the opportunity exists to put things on your codefendant.

"He said/she said."

Josh wrote to me how, at first: *Emilia tryed [sic] to break [Heather's] neck but that did not work out so she took a plastic bag from Dollar General and held it over her head until she suffocated her to death.*

In one swooping, run-on sentence, with a common word misspelled, Josh placed the entire onus of the murder on Emilia.

Josh added: *[I don't want to make it] sound like Emilia did it all by herself because I am just as guilty, but I am* not *the one that actually took her life.*

And there we have the minimization effect. Josh was involved, but he was trying to say, maybe without even realizing it, that he was a better human being than Emilia and had more morals, all because he did not commit the act of murder itself.

Josh explained that he could "never do this" on his own without "coaching from Emilia."

The version Josh tried selling to Detective Buie went like this: As Heather loosened that tape and it slipped down to her neck, Emilia used an entire roll of duct tape to secure Heather to the chair so she could not move.

"That's when she put the bag over her head," Josh told Buie. "She taped it around to where it was solid around her, and she had her arm around her neck, she was trying to snap her neck. . . ."

Buie asked Josh about the claustrophobic comment he had made during one interview, before admitting to the crime, when Josh claimed that Heather was scared of being confined in small spaces. Buie wanted to know when that came up.

"Please, Josh . . . you know I am claustrophobic," Heather said, according to what Josh told Buie.

"Yeah, bitch," Josh said back, "you know I am, too, but you put me in jail for thirty-one days."

Josh said Emilia and Heather didn't say much to each other during the entire process from life to death, which took no longer than thirty minutes.

At one point while that bag was over Heather's head, her body stopped convulsing and went still. She couldn't breathe. Some claim that there's a point before death when the body and brain experience a state of euphoria—hence, the auto-erotic asphyxiation deaths that sometimes occur. But Heather, we can be certain, was not in any position to be "high" at all while desperately trying to inhale her final breaths. This was a violent, callous, cold way to kill a human being. It takes time. The body becomes weak and defenseless and disoriented from the lack of oxygen and the victim suffers greatly as the body shuts down.

"She was out," Josh explained. "I knew 'cause she done

got still, she wasn't, um, like that no more, trying to, when the tape was over her mouth, trying to say something."

Emilia then walked over to Heather once again. Placing her arms around Heather's neck, she was determined to snap it like a cracker, Josh said. However, as Heather struggled for and ran out of oxygen, gasping for life's vital source, her legs jutted out in front of her. Josh described it as "I heard her make, like, a gurgling noise in her throat or something."

Josh reached down and loosened the tape around Heather's feet after he heard her make that gurgling noise.

Emilia had brought a flashlight with her, Josh said after the fact, and the batteries wore down and cut out. So it was dark inside the trailer now. They couldn't see anything.

Josh struck his cigarette lighter.

And that's when he noticed something.

"[Heather] wasn't dead yet."

CHAPTER 59

IN HIS LETTERS to me, Josh skipped over the narrative of him and Emilia killing Heather, which he gave to Detective Buie. He, instead, provided a rant—or excuse, really—for killing the mother of his children. According to one of Josh's letters, the main reason why Heather had to die could be blamed on the justice and family court system that does not listen to a father's plea regarding the custody of his children. Furthermore, not only would he have never killed Heather without Emilia's consistent pushing and perseverance, but: *I am easily convinced, especially when it comes to a woman doing the talking,* Josh wrote, meaning that he was a sucker for a pretty woman and what she wanted, so he gave in.

I also want it to be known that I tryed [sic] to go about this in a legal way, Josh wrote. He had "contacted" the "proper authorities," but they just wouldn't listen to him. In any event, in Josh's skewed way of looking at the world, these organizations would blame all fathers for bringing allegations against the mothers of their children so they could get out of paying child support.

Josh talked of how he spoke to "a few people" about taking Heather to court, but he was told, over and over, that a judge would never side with him.

He left out the part about being an admitted drug abuser, a violent person with no steady job, as well as a man with a record who liked to fight with everybody.

When he felt all of his legal options were never going to amount to anything (even though he had never pursued any one of them in a courtroom), *I turned to the one thing I knew: violence,* Josh wrote.

Indeed, not only violence, but Josh became judge and jury himself, taking Heather's life in place of having a court sort it out—which was the one thing, besides Emilia's constant harping, he said tipped him over the edge and into the realm of killing her.

A little push from Emilia so me and my kids could live together, he wrote.

Why?

Because Heather was always going to use the children as "pawns," Josh concluded.

CHAPTER 60

EMILIA LIT A candle after their lighters stopped firing. They needed light. Heather was still breathing. They had to finish the job.

Looking for a place to put the candle where they could garner the most light, Emilia found the top of the refrigerator to be the best spot.

As they did this, Josh told Detective Buie, Heather must have breathed her last. When they went back to check on her, she was not moving anymore. Her hair was tousled over her face.

Heather Strong was finally dead, both Josh and Emilia believed.

They unstrapped her from the chair and laid her out on the floor. Then Josh walked up, knelt down and reached toward her face.

"And I pulled . . . her hair back out of her face and I seen her eyes."

They were "halfway open," Josh explained, crying as he described this part of the murder to Detective Buie. And in a rare moment of feeling some remorse for his role, Josh added under his breath: "I fucked around on her—she didn't kill me."

Looking at Heather lying there on the floor, her eyes half

open, her body still as concrete, Josh said he then knew "she was gone."

Josh placed his hand over her nose to make sure. He didn't feel Heather breathing anymore.

He looked around the room and realized something else, however.

Emilia was gone.

Standing, Josh saw Heather's sneakers; they must have come off during the scuffle or when they strapped her to the chair. Either way, he needed to get rid of them. But even more than that, what was he going to do with Heather's body?

CHAPTER 61

JOSH CLAIMED THAT after they murdered Heather, he was afraid of Emilia. He had witnessed firsthand "what she was capable of," and he knew then that he could never double-cross Emilia, trust her with his kids or treat her the way he had in the past.

I was afraid she would get jealous of me and the kids and end up hurting them, Josh wrote.

Moreover, in that same missive, Josh talked about Detective Buie, a man he spent a considerable amount of time with during his arrest and confession. Josh even stayed in contact with him afterward. Buie, Josh said, was a man he respected: *Very honest . . . He had a job to do and he done a fair and honest job with it all.*

As bizarre as this would later come across, one of the most difficult moments of having murdered Heather, Josh claimed, was realizing how her death would ultimately upset and disappoint his mother, Judy Chandler.

My mom raised Heather from her teen years up until things started to get crazy between me and Heather. My mom is the one who took Heather to get her driver's license and my mom was the one who put designer clothes and shoes on the girl, he wrote.

Josh went on to talk about Heather's life almost as if it was not going anywhere, and that maybe she'd be better off meeting her Maker. The way it came out—though it's unclear if Josh meant it this way—was as if Josh believed he was doing Heather a favor by killing her. He said (quite strangely, I might add, while writing about Heather in both the past and present tenses) *[Heather] does not even have a GED . . . [and] I am not putting her down or talking about her because Heather cannot help who or what she came from. I miss her every day and regret that any of this shit had even took place. . . .*

Beyond that, Josh made sure to tell me that his sorrow and remorse wasn't based in the fact that he wound up in prison, but because, he wrote, *Heather went through a lot of shit on the night of this murder.*

Being strapped to a chair, beaten, tortured, a bag placed over her head and oxygen taken away from her as she slowly died a horrible death, likely as she thought about her children and never seeing them again—all of this had been boiled down to "a lot of shit."

CHAPTER 62

JOSH EXPLAINED TO Detective Donald Buie that at the moment when he realized Heather was actually dead, Emilia came back into the trailer, but he never said where she had gone, why she had left or how long she was gone. Together, Josh said, he and Emilia placed Heather inside a "bag" and dragged her body over to a table in the room, before shoving her underneath so as to hide her until they decided what to do next. Of course, like most murderers, Josh and Emilia never made a plan for afterward. They (premeditatedly) planned Heather's murder, right up until the point of her death, but not a damn thing after.

"I totally covered her face up," Josh said. "I didn't want to look at her no more."

With Heather underneath the table, Josh pulled a big bag of garbage from inside the trailer over and placed it in front of Heather's body so anybody walking in would not see her. The last thing they needed now was Emilia's mother, sister or some neighborhood kid stumbling upon the body.

What Josh meant by placing Heather in a "bag" was made clear later in the interview when he talked about how he "zipped" the bag up, so he must have been referring to that suitcase she was later found in.

Staring at Heather's body lodged underneath the table,

garbage shielding it from view, Josh told Emilia, "Come on. Let's get out of here." The plan was now to come back at some point and move Heather's body, getting rid of her for good. They just didn't know where yet.

They walked out of the trailer and headed to the car, where Heather had left her purse.

Emilia had an idea.

"I'll have everything you need tomorrow," she told Josh, grabbing Heather's purse and taking it with her. "When you come back tomorrow, you just bury her."

CHAPTER 63

THAT NEXT DAY Josh worked a little later than usual. But by 3:00 P.M. (he usually got off near two o'clock), he was "hauling ass" over to Emilia's house.

"Listen, listen," Josh said to Emilia when he arrived, "she needs to stay there again—one more day—because I gotta get home right now and cannot bury her. I can't let my mom know that something is up." Josh didn't want to change his behavior at all. He feared by doing so, it might make him look suspicious, once word got out that Heather was missing.

Emilia said okay. "But wait here a minute." She walked over to a storage area in the house and came back with Heather's purse. "Here," she said, handing Josh several personal items of Heather's: the kids' birth certificates, Social Security cards, medical cards, the food stamp card and the ATM card that Josh would later use to withdraw money from Heather's account.

Inside Heather's purse, Josh said, was "a pack of cigarettes," which he took, "a red lighter and a shitload of change, like seventy dollars' worth."

It appeared that Heather had carried her entire life inside that purse, and here were two people she despised more than most—two people who had caused her so much grief and anguish and problems over the past year or more, two people who had conspired to kill her—going through her things like a couple of common street thieves robbing a handbag and rifling through it in a back alley somewhere.

Josh took off, telling Emilia he was coming back the following day, hopefully, to finish the job.

BEN WAS AT the petrol station near his shop, gassing up his airboat later on that same afternoon, when Josh speedily pulled into the parking lot.

Josh had the kids with him.

That's odd, Ben thought. *Why does he have both of the kids?* Ben knew Heather would never willingly hand the kids over to Josh, especially both at the same time.

"Heather wasn't one just to let her kids go off with that bastard," Ben recalled. "She was always pretty protective of her young'uns. Always wanted to be around them."

Josh was causing a ruckus in the parking lot, messing with someone.

Ben walked over. "You better get your ass out of here, man. Now!"

Josh took off.

CHAPTER 64

JOSH GOT UP the next day and, after making sure nobody was watching, put a shovel in the trunk of his car. He told Detective Buie he took it from his mother's house (a subtle fact that did not jibe with what Emilia's mother later told Buie about Josh borrowing a shovel). And again, while telling this part of the murder tale to Buie, Josh relayed a simple fact that seemed to put things into perspective and explained a little bit about the kind of heartless person Josh had become: The shovel, he made clear, was Heather's. She'd bought it when they were together.

Josh drove to his job.

At the end of the day, he drove directly to Emilia's.

"Where is the best place to bury her?" Josh asked his girlfriend. He had stewed about this the entire day. He needed to find the right location to dig a hole and put Heather inside it. They needed to be done with this murder.

There was an old railroad track on the west side of Emilia's house. Emilia talked about carrying Heather's corpse down those tracks and picking a spot away from everything, adding, "There's an old tunnel or cave down there."

It seemed perfect.

Josh thought about it.

"No way," he told Emilia. "Somebody is liable to be down there looking around one day for things and run into *it*. I'd rather not do that. I want to put *it* where I know where *it's* at, and it will be safe until I do what I want to do with *it*."

That word choice—"it"—as Josh explained this awkward situation he and Emilia were in, postmurder, was a revealing sign to Buie of how Josh had placed Heather into a degrading lexicon of imagery that made *him* feel better about what he had done, quite brazenly demoralizing Heather in the process. Josh had boiled her life down to her being an *it*. She was not even a person, a human being, anymore.

"Let's walk out here by the trailer and look," Emilia suggested.

The reason they chose that spot in the back of the trailer, Josh explained, was "because we were gonna come out that front door with *it*," but they couldn't get the front door open. The hole was already dug (by Josh), so they had to carry Heather in the bag out into that space in the northeast corner of the trailer by the door they couldn't open.

Josh said he placed that barn board over the bag and Heather's head, which had been wrapped in (or covered by) a blue blanket, anyway, after digging the grave: "So I wouldn't throw dirt in her face . . ."

Throughout those two days when Josh had gone to work after killing his wife, he said, he mainly thought about how much he "regretted" killing her. It was digging the hole, he claimed, that set off a round of remorse inside him. The impetus for killing Heather, Josh was now saying, clearly lying to Buie, took place when Heather admitted to having slept with James Acome three days after Josh was put in jail.

That hurt like hell, Josh said. Once Heather had admitted to this infidelity (as he saw it), there was no turning back.

"It really hit me hard."

"Let me ask you something," Buie floated as he interviewed Josh in late March 2009, several days after Josh had admitted killing Heather with Emilia (who was still a free woman then). "So if she didn't tell you that, do you think you would have went as far as you went?"

"I don't. I don't think I would have been able to," Josh responded.

As they talked more about Josh not being able to kill Heather, had she not slept with James, Josh admitted something he perhaps didn't realize.

"Emilia told me she didn't think I'd even go through with it," Josh told Buie. "She kept calling me on the phone at my mom's. . . . She'd be like, 'What are you doing?' . . ."

The fact that Josh asked Heather about her alleged infidelity—not that he wasn't sleeping with Emilia any chance he got—which she denied routinely, saying, "I would never do that," enraged him to the point of violence when he finally realized she was lying. And it was at that moment of betrayal, Josh was now saying, when he decided enough was enough—he *had* to kill her.

And yet the question left hanging at this point became: How deep was Emilia involved? And would the MCSO ever have enough to arrest her?

Little did Detectives Buie or Spivey know then that there was an unlikely witness about to step courageously forward and blow their entire investigation up, giving them all they needed to take down Emilia Carr.

CHAPTER 65

INDEED, AFTER GETTING Josh to admit his role in Heather's murder, there was one important job left to do for Detective Donald Buie and the MCSO: get Emilia to cave, or catch Emilia in that one fabrication that would bury her. Thus far, Buie had spoken to the prosecutor's office and they said he needed more. What the MCSO had on Emilia right now was weak.

Emilia was no Josh Fulgham. Some claimed she had above-average intelligence. But the one thing the MCSO had going for its case was Emilia's own narcissism, which she had a hard time keeping in check. Emilia just couldn't keep her nose out of the investigation, nor could she keep her mouth shut. Plus, there was that little issue of a human being growing inside her belly. The child was now just weeks away from being born, and the baby's daddy was facing felony murder and kidnapping charges, which could land him on death row.

Still, Detective Buie faced an impasse. He was unsure where to take the investigation. Yet, as he thought about it, Buie had one important thought regarding this case, which would ultimately impact everything Emilia did and said: "She loved Josh and hated Heather with the same breath—

she knew that Josh would always go back to Heather, and for that reason, Heather had to die."

That simplified situation told Buie that Emilia had to be involved on a much broader scale and deeper level than any of them imagined. In fact, Buie and Spivey believed Emilia was as involved as Josh, maybe even more. The problem they faced was that they had no evidence against Emilia to prove their theory.

Listening to the tapes from those jailhouse phone calls that Josh had made to Emilia, Buie could hear an underlying theme of a plan to murder Heather. It was bubbling there, Buie believed. For Buie, Emilia was driving (and devising) that plan.

"I think that when Josh was in jail, he was maybe saying those things about Heather out of anger," Buie commented later. "But I think when he got out, Emilia was persistent and wanted to make sure he kept his word."

Emilia was not about to allow Josh to back down once again from what he had promised her. The stakes were too high this time around—she was pregnant.

"Because once she got Heather out of the picture," Buie added, "she could continue with Josh the way she had always wanted."

Another interesting aside that Buie uncovered was that the engagement ring Josh gave to Heather, and she wore after they got married, had actually been on Emilia's finger before that. Josh had given the ring to Emilia and asked *her* to marry him, only to take it back one day and give it to Heather. Buie believed that once Emilia realized she had been replaced for good by Heather, and Josh had even given Heather the same ring, that sealed Heather's fate in Emilia's eyes. All Emilia saw then when she looked at Heather was one solution: erasing her completely from the picture. No other solution would work for her.

Still, all of this, Buie knew, was conjecture and speculation of intent to murder. It was his theory. It had no foundation in evidentiary resolve at this time, not to mention the drawbacks to dragging Emilia in and accusing her of it all. They had talked to Emilia a total of nine times since the MCSO had brought her and Josh in for questioning back on March 18. Emilia had always seemed to begin explaining a potential role in the murder, but she would then back off, placing the bag, motive and means in Josh's hands. She never entirely fingered herself. On top of that, as Buie kept taking the case against Emilia to the prosecutor's office, they repeatedly told him no. There was not enough.

"Go back and get more."

Equally complicating things was all the physical and forensic evidence the MCSO was pulling together from the crime scene and Josh's house, and it all pointed back at Josh.

So Buie sat down one afternoon and thought about a plan to get Emilia to crack. What could he do? He wasn't about to let it go.

Then an idea hit him.

Buie walked over to his supervisor, sat down in Brian Spivey's office, and began discussing the case against Emilia and the course Buie wanted to take.

"Nothing short of a confession," Spivey indicated.

That's what the MCSO needed from Emilia.

"She's not going to talk much more," Buie said. "And the prosecution wants more."

As they sat talking about a way to charge Emilia, wouldn't you know, as these things go, luck walked in through the door. Or, rather, it called on the telephone.

Spivey's phone rang. "Hold it a minute," he said to Buie, who was talking at the time.

Buie sat and waited.

On the other end of the line was a name out of the blue, a person connected to Josh who had a plan to bury Emilia herself—only she didn't know it.

CHAPTER 66

JOSH'S SISTER, MICHELLE Gustafson, was on the phone with Detective Brian Spivey, asking him for advice. Donald Buie sat in Spivey's office, excitedly listening to Spivey's end of this conversation.

"I don't know what to do," Michelle told Spivey.

"How can I help?"

"Well, Emilia is reaching out to me."

Spivey looked at Buie. He smiled.

Opportunity was knocking.

Big-time.

What the MCSO had done to facilitate this call—without even realizing it—was shut down all of Josh's contact with everyone on the outside, mainly his family and Emilia. The goal was to make Emilia sweat it out. Force her hand. In not being able to talk to Josh, and also knowing that if she did communicate with Josh what she said had to be limited, Emilia called Michelle and asked to meet and talk. Basically, Emilia wanted to use Michelle to gauge what Josh was saying about her to the police and also to slip him private messages via Michelle.

Spivey explained to Michelle that Josh was in jail and he had admitted responsibility in Heather's murder, and there was no changing those facts. He was going away for a long,

long time. There wasn't anything anyone could do for him at this point but show him support and encourage him to be truthful in everything he did from this moment on.

Michelle was a down-to-earth, compassionate and understanding person. She lived in the real world. She understood morality. She knew that she could be of great help to the MCSO, not necessarily only to help her brother, but also to honor her sister-in-law, a dead woman with no voice left in anything.

"What we're asking is that you listen to Emilia, allow her to speak," Spivey explained to Michelle, "and help us out at the same time."

Michelle didn't really think about it before saying yes. Sure, she was scared and anxious, but also willing to do whatever it took to help.

They decided to set up a meeting for the following day. Michelle met with Buie and Spivey at the MCSO beforehand. It was March 24, 2009, early afternoon. Buie wired Michelle up with a recorder and they had her make a phone call to Emilia asking if the two of them could meet. It wouldn't seem suspicious, because Emilia had been the one to reach out to Michelle the previous day.

Michelle told Emilia she'd pick her up. They could take a ride and have a chat.

Emilia said okay.

What Michelle didn't tell Emilia, obviously, was that Buie and Spivey would be listening to the entire conversation. Michelle's goal was to get Emilia to admit her role—if any—in the murder of Heather Strong.

It was 4:03 P.M. when Spivey and Buie met with Michelle by the park where they planned to have her bring Emilia. They wanted to go through what would happen, step-by-step, to make sure Michelle was good with all of it.

Spivey encouraged Michelle to keep Emilia in the car, and to keep her engaged in conversation as long as she could. He coached her on a few things she could say to get Emilia to admit to any crimes.

"We're going to be inside that building . . . ," Spivey explained, pointing to a warehouse-type building nearby.

"I'll pull right up there, under that tree," Michelle suggested.

"Yes."

"Any questions?" Spivey asked.

"When this is done, can I go home and puke?"

"You can stick your head out the door and puke whenever you need to."

"Okay."

"By the way, what will you say if you have an emergency?" Spivey wanted to be clear on this.

"Bo, bo, bo, bo, bo, bo . . ."

"Okay, good. And we'll be right there."

Michelle had a plan—something very specific to bring up in order to get a reaction out of Emilia. And that was it. Michelle got into her car and away she went, on her own, to pick up Emilia.

CHAPTER 67

NINE MINUTES LATER, Emilia and Michelle took off from Emilia's house in Boardman en route to that park. Along the way, Michelle started the conversation off talking about the kids. She shed tears as she shared with Emilia her thoughts about them having both no mother and now no father. What future did the kids have? Their father had murdered their mother. That was their legacy.

Emilia responded by saying her kids were in foster care. Once social services found out Emilia was being investigated and questioned as part of a murder investigation, her kids were taken out of the home.

"He shouldn't even be there, I'm telling you right now," Emilia said, referring to Josh in lockup.

"Emilia, I've already spoken to Josh," Michelle said, letting Emilia know in a subtle way that she had been told that Josh had admitted to everything. There were no secrets here, Michelle suggested.

Emilia was interested in Michelle having spoken with Josh. "When?" she asked.

Michelle could almost hear the gears grinding inside Emilia's head as she thought about everything.

Fast on her feet, ignoring the "when" question, Michelle

changed the subject: "You know he tried to kill himself, right?"

"When?"

"Saturday."

Emilia was shocked by this. She hadn't heard.

Michelle shrugged.

"Go this way," Emilia suggested, as if on cue, pointing out the way Michelle already had wanted to go. "There's a little park about a mile . . ."

Michelle pulled off to the side of the road near that park where Buie and Spivey were stationed nearby in a warehouse building just around the block, listening. She found a nice spot, with not a lot of people around, and parked. Michelle was definitely nervous, but it didn't show. Emilia seemed on edge, as if looking over her shoulder. Buie and Spivey were concerned, of course, because they had a suspect who was alleged to have pulled a knife on Heather and threatened to slash her throat and then tried to snap her neck. What would Emilia try to do if she realized Michelle was baiting and recording her?

After a brief moment of silence between them, Emilia initiated a rant about how bad the cops wanted Josh. Emilia said she tried to tell Josh to keep his mouth shut and everything would be okay, but he just couldn't listen. The worst thing Josh could do, Emilia said, was to talk, adding, "His story keeps changing—when I know for a fact what happened and who did what."

Michelle listened carefully, looking for any opportunity to set the hook.

It didn't take long before Emilia blamed James and his buddy once again, saying how she and Josh needed to stick to that narrative.

Michelle thought on her feet, found a soft opening and decided to take a crack, saying, "Hang on, Emilia! I'm *not* the cops. I'm not here to hurt you or Josh. I'm just . . . I'm here for those kids and that baby, because I'm its blood aunt, too."

"Yeah, I know."

Michelle told Emilia she wanted the truth. "I already heard it from Josh." She cried more dynamically and it came off as genuine, because it was. Michelle was all at once scared, confused, worried, fearful and unsure of what kind of future her niece and nephew were going to have. "You got to tell me the truth so I can help you and Josh. Don't tell me James and [his buddy did this]. *Don't* lie."

Emilia stared out the window. Then: "What did he tell you, Michelle?"

"Emilia," Michelle said through a barrage of tears, "tell me *your* side."

"What did *he* tell you? Did he tell you over a recorded phone?"

Michelle said no, Josh had sat her down the day before they took him in and told her *everything*. She said she knew about his and Emilia's role in Heather's murder. There was no chance Emilia could sit there and bullshit Michelle about anything, because Michelle claimed to know it all. What Michelle demanded from Emilia was the truth in order to help both of them, she explained more than once. Michelle pleaded with Emilia to take her seriously and listen to her. Michelle wanted to hear from Emilia's mouth that same truth Josh had related, because Michelle was sick to her stomach about all of this and hadn't eaten for days.

"What do you think, Michelle?" Emilia asked, no doubt testing Michelle to see how much she knew.

"That you tried to break Heather's neck and you couldn't do it, so then you-all . . . suffocated her and buried her."

It couldn't be put any more simple than that.

"Does your mom know?" Emilia asked.

Michelle said no, Judy wasn't aware of anything yet.

"What made him tell you?" Emilia asked, seemingly agreeing with Michelle about what had happened.

"It's killing him."

"So what is he gonna do now?" Emilia wondered. Michelle could tell Emilia was beginning to feel comfortable with the conversation. "'Cause if he confesses to this," Emilia added, "we both go down and we both lose our kids. And right now, the people they want is *not* me and Josh."

"Will you tell me so I know what Josh said is true? I'm not here to hurt you."

"I know," Emilia said before saying she wanted to get out of the car. Suddenly she was beginning to feel funny about talking inside the car. She looked around and became a bit anxious.

Michelle said she'd roll down the windows, but she wanted to stay put.

"He didn't lie, Michelle," Emilia confessed.

Listening inside the building just down the block, Buie and Spivey looked at each other. A hole had just opened up in Emilia's boat.

"He didn't lie, Michelle."

"'He didn't lie'?" Michelle asked. "What happened?"

"Pretty much what he told you," Emilia admitted.

There it was: *"Pretty much what he told you."*

Michelle asked Emilia to explain. She wanted her version. Michelle explained how much she needed to hear it from Emilia's mouth to her ears. This was all too much to take in—so unreal, so unnerving, so disturbing. Michelle wanted Emilia to fess up. It would only make sense to her, she suggested, if Emilia explained what had actually taken place inside the trailer.

So Emilia began to speak. She said Josh didn't want Heather to leave again with the kids. That was how it all started. Then she insisted that Heather actually signed that letter, handing over custody of the children to Josh. But the reason why her handwriting might not have looked like her own was because signing the letter, Emilia said, "was not by choice! But she signed it."

Michelle gasped. Here was Emilia admitting to killing her sister-in-law, and Michelle was recording it for law enforcement. This could all backfire horribly without warning. Emilia was not some passive waif. She was streetwise and street-smart. Michelle understood that if Emilia had killed once, she'd have no trouble getting violent again.

"I don't know if you want to know in detail what happened or not . . . ," Emilia stated.

"I do," Michelle said through her own reluctance. "I can't sleep. I can't eat . . . so I want *detail*."

"I don't know if you can *handle* it, Michelle," Emilia warned.

Michelle insisted that Emilia continue.

Emilia talked about how the cops still thought it was James and his buddy, and even though it wasn't right for Josh and her to blame two people who had nothing to do with it, Emilia said James deserved it. So she had no trouble throwing him and his friend into the fire and continuing with the ruse, as long as it kept her and Josh from being charged.

They went back and forth for a few minutes. Michelle did most of the talking, imploring Emilia to come clean and tell her everything she could recall. It was classic the way Michelle sold it all to Emilia, telling her "three heads" were better than two in order to figure out what they could do next, and that the only way Michelle could be of any help to either Josh or Emilia was to know all of the facts, however troubling and chilling they were. Michelle was cool and calm now, realizing that Emilia was confessing.

Emilia took a deep breath, which Buie and Spivey could hear on their end.

That's it, Buie thought. *She's ready.* He could picture Emilia dropping her shoulders, looking down at the ground, telling herself, *What the hell—why not?*

After a great big sigh, Emilia mentioned how she was never clear how Josh was able to convince Heather to come over to her house that night. Heather's arrival with

Josh baffled Emilia at first, she said. She thought it was conniving and brilliant when she found out that Josh had come up with that subterfuge of the stashed money. But nevertheless, Emilia added, Heather and Josh showed up, and Josh had it all planned from there. Josh told Emilia to walk into the trailer at a specific time and to shock Heather. The two of them would then gang up on her.

Smartly, Michelle interrupted Emilia, asking if they had planned the murder together.

Emilia could be heard taking another deep breath, but then she spoke. "When he called me . . . he said . . . he was on his way. He pulled up. I stayed inside for a few minutes, like I was told. When I got out there, he was talking to her and he was telling her, 'I want the truth.' She said, 'The truth about what?' He said, 'Why did you lie? Why did you have me arrested?' She said, 'Because me and Ben told you we was gonna put you in prison!'"

From there, Emilia explained how Josh and Heather talked about Heather's plan to take off to Mississippi with the kids, leaving Josh for good.

"Every time he heard something he didn't like," Emilia told Michelle, "he hit her. He hit her upside the head and broke a flashlight. . . . She tried to run for the door"—Emilia took another one of those deep breaths—"and she knocked me down, so I had bruises on my knee . . . and when she was running for the door, she knocked the window out."

Emilia said Josh dragged Heather back to the area of the trailer where he had that chair set up for her; then he taped her to the chair before screaming in her face, letting her know she had hurt him for the last time.

"So, what happened next?" Michelle asked when Emilia stopped.

"We put a bag over her head," Emilia admitted. "We tried to snap her neck. That didn't work."

"We, we, we" was about all Buie and Spivey heard. If they were gambling men watching a horse race, this would

be that fist-pumping moment as their horse crossed the finish line.

They had her.

Michelle wanted more. Specifically, she asked, why did Emilia want to break Heather's neck? Josh had told Buie and Spivey, and also restated in a letter to me, that Emilia came up with the neck-breaking idea because she had taken those massage therapy classes and had trained in how to crack someone's neck without hurting him. So Emilia figured she was qualified in the neck-breaking area and could handle that part of the murder collaboration.

"I figured it would be quick and painless," Emilia said in response to Michelle's question regarding breaking Heather's neck.

But then Emilia abruptly stopped talking. Something had startled her.

Michelle stared at her.

Emilia had a serious look on her face.

After a few seconds of looking around, then staring back at Michelle, Emilia said: "You're not recording this conversation, are you, Michelle? Please?"

CHAPTER 68

DETECTIVES DONALD BUIE and Brian Spivey were now greatly concerned for their undercover confidential informant (CI) after hearing Emilia ask if she was being recorded. A touch of paranoia had crept into Emilia's voice. She sounded worried, greatly troubled and concerned. She was giving Michelle the goods here. What was Michelle's purpose again? Just to know the facts? Maybe Emilia wasn't buying that any longer?

"I'm not . . . I'm . . . no . . . huh," Michelle said nervously in response to Emilia's questioning her about wearing a wire.

Spivey and Buie stared at the listening device.

"I'm just trying to understand," Michelle said. "Now, I mean, it's about . . . kids in the middle."

That was smart: Michelle was bringing the kids into it and making it personal for Emilia. She might react emotionally to that.

"Yeah, I know . . . ," Emilia said as Michelle, Buie and Spivey took a breath of their own and felt a bit better.

Michelle explained that Josh had taken his pants and had tied them around his neck, after Emilia pressed her for details about his supposed suicide attempt. Then Emilia went back to her "James and his buddy" argument, insisting how they needed to stick to that. From where Emilia viewed things, the MCSO was about to sign off on it and believe them.

"Yeah . . . if he can keep his mouth shut," Emilia said.

Michelle wanted to clarify something. She said she heard Josh talking to Emilia one day before the murder and that she figured out later, after Josh explained to her what they had done, that the conversation she heard was part of them planning the murder. It was a brilliant move on Michelle's part. Murder was one thing—however, premeditated, planned murder was entirely different. In the state of Florida, premeditated murder was not taken lightly. If a jury convicted you of premeditated murder in the first degree, you could be staring down the barrel of a death sentence.

"We had joked about it," Emilia said. "We were not really serious. I thought he was full of shit. . . . He never really follows through with nothing."

Emilia spoke about the baby she was carrying and how it would ultimately be "connected" by blood to her kids and Josh's other children; and that once the baby was born, Michelle could step in and possibly get Emilia's kids out of foster care because she would be a "blood aunt."

Michelle ignored that comment and asked, "When you-all talked, did you plan on just confronting her?"

Emilia said she didn't think Josh was serious. Then she talked about how the MCSO could not connect Josh or her to the crime because their DNA was supposed to be inside "that shed" anyway, and there were "strips of duct tape hanging out there all the time. . . ."

The more she talked, the deeper the hole Emilia dug herself into by alluding to pieces of evidence in the case never yet discussed publicly or with her or Josh during their interviews. She kept returning to James and his buddy, but Michelle tweaked the focus of the conversation back to Emilia's role and what she knew.

The feeling here was that Emilia believed she was safe-guarded from arrest and prosecution because she had talked her way out of it all by submitting to those interviews with the MCSO. Josh might have mentioned her name, she said, but there was no way the MCSO was going to believe him.

They soon got on the subject of the backyard behind Emilia's mother's house. Michelle wanted to know why they chose the backyard, of all places, to kill and then bury Heather.

Emilia actually yawned, then answered: "Because your brother just wanted her in there for a little while and he was gonna move her. I cannot believe he led them back there. Had he not led them back there, they could have questioned him all they wanted—without a body, they cannot do nothing."

Family came up and discussions of their situation ended things for several minutes: Who knew what? Where were all the kids living? Who said what to whom? Michelle was impressed by how strong and unyielding Emilia came across, as if none of this bothered her. The fact that she could talk about life and death with such a stoic, straight face—no tears, zero emotions and no worries—said something to Michelle about who Emilia was on the inside. Through her manner of speaking and demeanor, Emilia came across as cold and callous, as if she didn't care about anything or anyone else but herself.

By this point, Michelle was unable to control her raw emotions. She was shaking and crying. She said, "You're like a rock. I need a nerve pill [and] I want to puke, and you're—"

"It's because," Emilia said, interrupting, "I've already cried. . . ." Then Emilia said how she didn't want to send her body into early labor by becoming emotional.

"I hate to ask this question," Michelle said a bit later, "but I *need* to know, 'cause this has been the thing that's kept me up. . . . Did—did Heather go peacefully, or did she—"

Emilia interrupted again: "Did she fight him?"

"Yeah."

"She *fought* him," Emilia said proudly.

"Did you help at any point during all that, or just . . ."

Emilia breathed deeply. "Yeah . . . I helped him tape her to the chair. . . ."

The conversation digressed back to James and his buddy. Emilia kept beating that drum, over and over. If only they could all stick to that story, the end result would be in their favor.

Without being prompted, Emilia talked about how angry Josh had been with Heather, before mentioning (again) that James Acome was the perfect scapegoat. The cops would buy it eventually.

Then Emilia gave Michelle some insight into Josh's mind-set on the night of the murder. She said he wasn't "of his right mind . . . not emotionally there. He had gone to another place . . . because when he went to bury the body, he couldn't even look at it. He would cry . . . [and] he almost threw up."

But not Emilia. She looked on as they packaged, dragged and then buried Heather. Emilia had no feelings whatsoever.

Nothing.

"Really?" Michelle asked.

Emilia said she thought Josh felt remorse later, but when it was going on, he "was glazed over . . . and it wasn't Josh—he *wasn't* there."

Emilia was under the belief that had the MCSO developed any significant evidence against her, they'd have her in handcuffs already. She wasn't worried because they had not arrested her yet. She also believed Josh was going to be, at some point, released. They couldn't hold him.

It was close to 4:30 P.M., and Michelle wondered if she should head back home. Near the end of the conversation, Michelle asked Emilia if she "strangled" Heather, adding, "You just tried to snap her neck. . . ?"

"Uh-huh," Emilia said, agreeing.

"And then you-all put a bag over her head? So there's no marks around . . ."

"I don't think so."

As Michelle began to say something else, she spotted a person, a man, walking toward the vehicle. "Uh . . . who is that? Emilia, who is that?" Michelle asked hurriedly.

The guy walked closer.

Michelle didn't recognize him.

Emilia looked, but she couldn't get a clear view. "I don't know," she said. Then, as he stepped into view, Emilia said, "Holy shit!"

CHAPTER 69

INSIDE THAT WAREHOUSE, listening to the conversation, Buie and Spivey decided that they'd heard enough. As it stood, it seemed they had nothing short of a confession from Emilia on tape. There was no reason to put Michelle in any more danger. Before they had wired Michelle up, Buie and Spivey devised a plan to approach the car when the time called for it. But their tactic wasn't to roll in with lights blaring, gold badges out, accusations and Miranda warnings flying. It was to continue the dance with Emilia.

Take things one step at a time.

And not blow Michelle's cover now.

"It's a freaking detective!" Michelle squawked, staring at Spivey as he got closer to the window. Buie was right behind him.

"Oh, crap," Emilia said.

"Uh-oh," Michelle added, sounding scared—yet actually quite relieved to see these two guys.

Emilia whispered, "Tell them we are talking about the baby."

Michelle rolled down her window.

Buie addressed Emilia: "Hey, your momma told us you were up here."

"Okay," Emilia said.

"Can we talk to you for a sec?" Buie asked.

Buie and Spivey wanted to get Emilia downtown and question her once again based on what they had just learned.

Emilia opened the car door and stepped away from the vehicle with Buie so they could talk on their own. Spivey stayed with Michelle, who was beginning to flip out a bit.

Buie asked Emilia, "Can you come down and talk to us some more? We just have a few more follow-up questions."

Emilia wasn't thrilled. She said she had to go to the toilet, but she said she would go.

Buie walked back to the car with Emilia and addressed Michelle, who was still sitting in the car. "She's gonna ride with you back to her house so she can use the restroom."

"Okay."

"And then she's gonna come talk with us."

Buie said a few things to Michelle to throw off any scent that Emilia might have picked up on. He asked Michelle if she had been drinking and if she had a valid driver's license.

Everyone seemed content for right now. Michelle started the car and she and Emilia took off. The wire was still on; Buie and Spivey, following behind, were still monitoring the conversation.

Emilia explained again as they drove that Michelle needed to make a point to tell them they were discussing the baby, nothing else. Sounding defeated, Emilia then explained how, when she got to her house, she was going to change into "gray sweats in case they arrest me."

Instinct doesn't lie. Emilia could sense something was up.

Michelle panicked. She started to breathe heavily, sweat and hyperventilate.

"You okay?" Emilia asked, staring at her.

"I feel like I'm having a heart attack." Michelle was crying.

"For what?" Emilia wondered. "Your license is good, right?"

Michelle couldn't talk. She had difficulty catching her breath. Her chest felt tight, heavy. It felt as if it would explode.

"Michelle!" Emilia said. "Calm down!"

"I'm trying. . . ."

Buie hit the lights, indicating that he wanted to pull them over. This was by design. When Emilia and Michelle were talking back at the park, they were actually in another county. Sensing Michelle needed to be relieved here, Buie wanted to wait until they entered Marion County before actually grabbing Emilia and taking her to her house and then downtown by himself.

Michelle stopped her car. Looked down at the floorboard. Took several deep breaths and continued to cry.

Emilia stared at her.

Buie walked up to the window. "You okay?"

Emilia had a worried look about her. She sensed trouble.

"I'm just taking her home . . . ," Michelle said to Buie. "And then I'm gonna go home."

Buie told Michelle to sit tight while he went and spoke to Spivey.

"It's nothing. . . . It's nothing she done," Michelle said, looking at Emilia, who had gone church silent. "I just think I'm having a heart attack."

Buie returned quickly. He asked Emilia to step out of the car, indicating that he and Spivey would take her to her mom's and then downtown.

Emilia did not resist.

CHAPTER 70

JOSH EXPLAINED TO me what happened on the day of his arrest on charges of threatening Heather with a gun. That day seemed to be a turning point for Josh Fulgham—a line in the sand that Heather had crossed. They had just been married in December. And here it was, a few weeks later, and Heather was having him tossed in jail for something he didn't do.

Josh was waiting at work for Heather to come and pick him up. As he stood by the roadside, "two cops pulled up," Josh revealed. One asked if he was Joshua Fulgham.

"What's up?" Josh wondered.

The cop explained that his wife had reported him pulling a gun on her, and Ben McCollum had reported witnessing the same thing. But it was a day after Josh had done this, allegedly, so Josh was curious as to why they had waited.

Josh said the cop agreed; the charges were likely bogus, but Josh needed to answer to them, nonetheless.

It was at that exact moment that Josh realized there would never be a relationship between him and Heather again. It was over—for good. He never had any intention to kill her, Josh insisted. But while in jail, once he started talking to Emilia, and then when he got out, he discovered that the thought to get rid of Heather was something they could not let go of. It was as though once they put the plan out into the universe, it needed to take place. At least that was how they felt.

Three people knew what happened inside that trailer when Heather was murdered—one of them is dead. According to Josh, he and Emilia were equally responsible. He claimed the situation escalated while they were inside the trailer. When Heather went for the door to get out, Josh, Emilia and Heather "wrestled around on the floor," Josh informed me. And it was at that time when Josh told himself, *Screw it.* He got up off the ground and decided to let Heather go.

But Emilia said, "Hell no!" So I made Heather get in that chair. She kept trying to get up, so I [sat] down on her and let Emilia tape her to the chair so she could not get up, Josh wrote.

Josh was clear that it was at this moment that he began to question Heather about her alleged infidelities. Heather didn't want to answer at first, Josh said. She was terrified.

Josh recalled Heather saying, "You'll kill me," as she sat there, strapped to the chair. Emilia was right in her face, screaming at her to come clean, and Josh was behind Emilia, doing the same.

"Tell him what you told me while he was in jail," Emilia said to Heather.

"Answer the damn questions, Heather!" Josh yelled.

"No, no . . . you will kill me."

"Tell him!" Emilia yelled.

And then Heather mentioned sleeping with Josh's "best friend," which sent him off into a place of frenzy and rage to the point where he began striking her.

"I hit her," Josh told me. He didn't know how many times he hit her, "but it was a lot."

Heather would not stop pleading with them to stop. She was scared for her life. The situation became chaotic and seemed to build on its own. Josh became angrier as each moment passed and each blow struck Heather somewhere on her body. And because Heather would not stop talking, Josh said, he had "Emilia tape her mouth up. . . ."

What happened next, Josh wrote: *Emilia tryed* [sic] *to break her neck and that did not work so she decided to suffocate her with a bag over her face.*

What's troubling and terrifying about this scenario is that Heather Strong, for perhaps as long as twenty minutes or more, knew she was going to die. In that context, Heather suffered twice: the emotional agony of thinking about leaving her children motherless, missing their smiles, their sweet smells, their laughter; and second, the actual pain of being tortured and then executed by two people who she knew and thought would never take things as far as they did.

And therein lies the greatest tragedy: The same man Heather loved and married—and to whom she'd borne three children—stood in front of her playing God, promising her that she was not leaving that trailer alive.

CHAPTER 71

EMILIA CARR WAS not the type to roll over and play nice with the police. In this situation, ever since she and Josh had been brought in, Emilia believed she'd had the upper hand all along. And, in many ways, she actually had—until she went and opened her mouth and put herself at the scene of a brutal murder, not only watching it unfold, but participating. If Emilia would have just kept her mouth shut—the same as she was asking Michelle to get across to Josh—she'd never be sitting back inside the MCSO answering questions.

This time, Buie had Emilia brought into the hard room. The conversation wasn't going to be as cordial as those others. Buie was ready to confront Emilia and tell her what he had developed over the course of his investigation.

Emilia asked if Michelle was okay.

After they got situated and Buie re-read Emilia her Miranda rights, he said, "Michelle is fine." He added how he appreciated that Emilia was concerned about Michelle "'cause she is going through a lot."

Emilia brought up the baby and they discussed this for a brief period of time. Then Buie got right into it, asking Emilia to explain once again what she found when she went out to the trailer on that day and saw Heather sitting in the chair, dead.

"We've already done this," Emilia said rather impatiently.

Buie pressed her on a few specific issues related to that same topic, indicating that he wanted her to share it all again.

"Okay, is this off the record?" Emilia asked. "Just you and me talking?"

It was not, Buie made clear. They were completely on the record.

Emilia had no choice. She explained the entire scene again—as she had painted it during other interviews—putting the burden of the crime on Josh, making the claim once again that she was not inside the trailer when Heather was killed.

This, Buie knew (and purposely had aimed to set up in his questioning today), was in total contradiction to what Emilia had just told Michelle on tape.

Now they had her contradicting herself.

Buie said the way in which Emilia had explained the scene inside the trailer sounded an awful lot like it was coming from someone witnessing the scene, not hearing about it secondhand. He was giving Emilia one more chance to come clean.

"Now you see why I want to talk to the state attorney's office," Emilia mentioned.

"'Cause you saw it, *didn't* you?" Buie pressed.

Emilia told Buie there was "so much more to this" and that she wanted to talk, but she needed to make sure certain things were in her favor before she said anything more—hence her bringing up the state attorney's office (SAO).

Buie tried to appeal to whatever morsel of morality might have existed within Emilia, or maybe he was fishing to see if she even had one, hoping to build a rapport with her so she would feel comfortable and open up.

But Emilia kept saying she couldn't talk openly on the record. Then, in the next breath, she announced that there were "two other people" involved "that are huge parts of this case . . . and I mean *huge*. . . ."

Not getting anywhere honorably, Buie then told Emilia to stop kidding herself. He said Josh had told them *everything*. It was time to fess up. "You were right there, darling, and I'm not sitting here playing a game with you," Buie added.

"I know. I know."

"I know you were there on the night she took her last breath. . . . I need you to be honest with yourself and get this burden off you. Show me something as a *person,* that you have some compassion in you."

"I do."

"People make mistakes."

"I do."

"Love is blinding, and I know you love Josh. . . ."

"Don't love him enough to kill somebody for."

They went back and forth: Emilia, not yet ready to admit her role; Buie, thinking for a minute that perhaps he'd cracked her. But she repeatedly insisted that she wasn't involved on any level other than knowing about the murder *after* the fact.

Watching things from another room, Brian Spivey decided to go in and have a seat. Emilia had always felt more comfortable around Spivey. Yet, Spivey made it clear almost immediately that he was not there as her listening friend anymore, same as he had played Mr. Neutral in those other interviews. Now he wanted answers, same as Buie.

Spivey first talked about the concern they had for Emilia not showing any remorse. This was alarming and troubling to them. The idea that she was not sorry for anything that had happened, murder aside, was shocking, especially seeing that she was an expectant mother.

Emilia said that not everyone shows remorse in the same way. Then she brought up James Acome and his buddy again.

Spivey and Buie mentioned how they didn't want to go down that road anymore.

Buie looked at Spivey. It was time. They were running in circles. So Buie put it out there to see what kind of reaction they'd get.

"Today you had a conversation with Josh's sister," Buie said slowly. "That conversation was recorded totally."

The blood drained from Emilia's face. She looked at Spivey, then at Buie.

"You, out of your own mouth, admitted to being there," Buie explained.

"We just didn't stumble across that car sitting in the park . . . ," Spivey added.

"Yeah, I know," Emilia answered.

"So far, you have shown me that you're acting like a coldhearted, hateful person who killed the mother of [your] children," Spivey said.

"Because I don't cry?" Emilia wondered. This was the first time she had heard Spivey speak to her with that sort of tone.

"No," he said. It was, more or less, because of all the lying. "You told that girl today that you tried to break her neck, and it didn't work!"

Now, faced with these new facts, Emilia changed her role dramatically: "I did what I was *told* to do," she claimed.

Buie asked Emilia to explain what she meant by that.

She said it again: "I did what I was told to do."

Spivey said Josh was claiming that Emilia had suffocated and killed Heather, not him.

"I did not kill her."

Buie became impatient. He was more direct with Emilia, demanding that she respect the both of them and the badge itself. Emilia had started to nod "yes" and "no" to their questions, and Buie wasn't going to have that in his interview suite. He asked Emilia if she understood what he meant by giving them the respect they deserved.

Softly she answered yes.

"I can't *hear* you!" Buie demanded.

"Yes!"

"What did you guys do *after* she took her last breath?" Buie wanted to know.

"Can I ask you something?" Emilia countered.

"Can you answer that for me?"

Emilia said it didn't matter what her answers were: If she talked or didn't, weren't they going to arrest her, anyway? So, what did she have to lose by not saying anything else at this point?

Buie and Spivey didn't know how to respond to that. They knew Emilia's game was to try and talk her way out of things and she would continue doing that.

And they were right: Over and over, Emilia said, "I did not kill her."

Spivey and Buie humored Emilia and said they wanted to know how had Heather died—if Emilia had not killed her?

"He held a bag over her face," Emilia said.

He taped Heather's face and hands and neck.

He hit her.

He cleaned everything up.

He saved Heather's shoes.

He. He. He.

And because of Josh's anger issues and the way he acted on that day in front of her, Emilia said, she was "scared shitless" throughout the entire murder and after, worried Josh would hurt her if she ever talked about it.

They confronted Emilia with everything she had told Michelle.

Her reaction was quite baffling. Not exactly agreeing with the totality of what she had said, Emilia eased her way into admitting her role, the entire time still placing the blame on Josh. She maintained that she never thought he was serious; that is, up until the moment he struck Heather that first time. Emilia might have been there and watched it, but she did not plan or participate in Heather's murder until Josh made her do so.

Buie explained that she was going to be charged with first-degree murder. He said he was sorry for how it all turned out. However, Emilia could have made it a lot easier on herself and others if she had been forthcoming with true information from the start, instead of telling all those lies they had listened to for the past week.

Emilia wasn't happy with that. She claimed others had put her in a position to lie. It wasn't her fault.

"*You* did it, baby," Buie clarified, patronizing Emilia.

"I didn't kill that girl," she repeated.

"You did!"

"I didn't kill her."

"Yes. You. Did."

Spivey asked Emilia to tell them what happened, then, if she hadn't done what Josh claimed she had done (and so did she, by her own admission to Michelle).

"He held her down, because he was stronger," she said, before finally admitting to taping Heather's hands and feet.

Buie asked what Heather was saying specifically to Emilia at that moment.

"She was just crying."

Realizing they were perhaps getting some of the truth out of her, Buie listened as Emilia then talked about Heather telling Josh she was claustrophobic, and Josh saying to her that he felt the same as he sat in the jail for all those sleepless nights. This, of course, was something Josh had said, too.

The one point Emilia seemed to make several times—and it was clear that this was something she believed to be true—was that Josh had become this other person with "glazed-over eyes," which she had never seen before, as he stepped into the role of killer. She said that once he reached that place inside himself, there was no turning back and no stopping him. It was a look, Emilia could tell, that Heather had recognized, too, on that day. When she had, Heather urinated on herself, knowing that she was not going to leave the trailer alive. Josh had turned into a monster. He was going to kill Heather, and there was nothing Emilia could say to change the outcome of this.

Nothing.

For twenty additional minutes, they talked details: the glass breaking, the door jamming, the burial site, whether Emilia ever pulled a knife on Heather (she said she didn't), where they got the blanket to cover her head inside the hole Josh had dumped her body in (a storage shed).

Josh had "dragged" Heather around the trailer to that grave he had dug, while Emilia stayed inside the trailer, she said. The only time she went out to the grave site was when Josh asked her to see if she thought it was deep enough. Emilia also said Josh "disposed" of Heather's purse in a Dumpster. She had no idea where it was located.

She admitted to bringing a candle out there for light.

She admitted to watching Josh break a flashlight over Heather's head.

She admitted to walking into the trailer with the flashlight.

She admitted to "standing back" after taping Heather up so Josh could yell at her.

She admitted to "a lot of it" being a "blur."

She admitted to trying to snap Heather's neck—not because she wanted Heather's death to be quick and painless, but because she "was scared" of *not* doing what Josh told her to do and the ramifications that would ensue from not following his orders.

Like Josh, Emilia tried to minimize her role in the entire plan, execution and cleanup afterward, but Buie and Spivey were not allowing her that excuse. Every time Emilia tried to play down her role in a specific moment of the murder, Spivey or Buie reminded her of the fact that she stood by, watched it all, helped Josh all the way through the process, even spoke to him over the phone about it and then never said anything to anyone afterward. She even knew that there was a corpse in her backyard all that time. Emilia slept comfortably inside the house yards away from it, and she had never mentioned it to anyone—never shared how scared she was of Josh. In other words, Emilia had plenty of opportunity after the murder to run to police for help, explaining how frightened she was of this madman, but she never did. Even after he was locked away and could certainly not hurt her, she didn't reach out.

"Tell me what you think you're guilty of?" Buie asked.

"Helping a monster."

"I'm sorry, of *being* a monster?"

"*Helping* a monster!"

Emilia took a few steps back and claimed that what she had told Michelle amounted to nothing, and they were never going to be able to use it against her. All she was guilty of was "trying to comfort" Michelle during a time of need.

Laughable. Buie stopped himself from busting up right there inside the interview suite.

"She didn't need comfort. She knew her brother did it," Buie finally said, explaining Michelle's position.

Emilia said that at one point while she was in the trailer watching Josh commit murder, she was "standing up against the table, shaking."

They ignored that comment.

It deserved to be.

The remainder of the interview was simple law enforcement mechanics: questions of what, when, where? Emilia stumbled her way through most of it. She was completely stuck on the personal attack that the detectives had waged because she failed to show any remorse or emotion. It bothered Emilia that they thought this about her, so she tried to explain that she was someone who didn't wear her heart on her sleeve. She felt she was being judged for that.

Buie agreed to disagree and then explained that she was being booked on first-degree murder charges, same as Josh.

For Emilia Carr, the dance was over.

If she needed to explain herself from this point forward, she could speak to her lawyer.

CHAPTER 72

JOSH AND EMILIA were indicted on murder charges by the end of April 2009. Emilia was twenty-four-years old, pregnant, and now facing life behind bars or worse, the possibility of a death sentence. Florida was one state where you didn't want to muck around with killing people in cold blood during the course of a kidnapping or other mitigating and aggravating circumstances—that is, unless you were interested in potentially staring down a tube, with a syringe at the end of it, strapped to a gurney. In Florida, like in some other states, such as Texas, juries sentenced people to death. Many of those perpetrators actually saw the needle within a reasonable amount of time after all their appeals had been exhausted.

Special Prosecutor (SP) Rock Hooker came out swinging, stating the facts of the state attorney's (SA's) case as he talked about the indictments to the media: "It is evident from the physical evidence and from the statements taken in this case that Heather Strong suffered tremendously before she died. And because of that, both defendants will pay."

Less than a month after she was indicted, Emilia went into labor and was rushed from the jail to a local hospital, where she gave birth to a baby girl—a child who might or might not be Josh's, some said. There were rumors flying that Emilia had slept with a friend of Josh's while the two were fighting and that she had become pregnant to either spite Josh or trick him into thinking he was the dad so he would stay with her.

In any event, the baby was quickly whisked out of Emilia's arms and into state custody after she was born.

Department of Children and Families (DCF) spokeswoman Elizabeth Arenas told reporters that Emilia's healthy baby was released from Munroe Regional Medical Center and placed in foster care the same day she had been born. DCF was trying to find "possible relatives" to place the child with.

"I don't think the baby is mine," Josh said when asked.

CHAPTER 73

ON JUNE 11, 2009, Detective Donald Buie received a copy of a letter Josh had written to Heather's mother. In that letter, Josh apologized for killing Heather. He said he was sorry. He mentioned how he wished he could take it all back. And when his final judgment in a court of law came down the road, Josh hoped liked hell that the jury would see it fit within their hearts to sentence him to death. In Josh's mind, that was the just sentence he deserved.

A week later, Emilia's mother called Brian Spivey and Donald Buie and said she had information about Emilia's case. On that voice mail, Maria Zayas told a story of having spoken to her daughter just recently, and Emilia wanted to meet with Spivey and Buie right away to share what she knew.

They sent a car to the jail to pick up Emilia.

The effusive "other woman" in Josh Fulgham's life had changed a bit since the last time Buie and Spivey had seen her. Emilia had her baby and had not yet lost the baby weight and, of course, was rather heavier than usual. Still, Emilia had always carried a bit of weight and it had never stopped her from being attractive. However, on this day, there was something else about her. Emilia had that weathered prison look to her already: braided hair, lighter skin, a certain swag in her walk, a touch of that prison slang in her voice, a terribly bitter chip on her shoulder.

Emilia was now saying she was being railroaded. Once the facts of her case were made public, she would be released from prison.

Buie and Spivey sat down with Emilia and caught up a bit. Then they got into it.

Emilia said she didn't need her attorney present to say what she wanted; she waived her rights in that regard.

Buie read Emilia her Miranda rights and she formally agreed to speak to them without her lawyer present.

This is never a good idea for someone facing felony first-degree murder charges.

The gist of what Emilia wanted to get across came straightaway: "I lied," she said.

There was a bit of a lull among the detectives.

Lied?

"Lied."

Emilia went on to say she "lied about her involvement in the death of Heather Strong and that, in fact, she had *no* involvement and . . . she was not even present during [Heather's] death."

Once again, Emilia Carr was changing her story.

Buie and Spivey, not really surprised by this, terminated the interview.

Emilia was driven back to her jail cell.

CHAPTER 74

ON JUNE 17, 2009, Josh Fulgham and Emilia Carr waived their right to a speedy trial, which meant that a year, at least, would have to pass before either saw the inside of a courtroom, a jury, and were allowed to present a defense. Yet, one thing was made clear by SA Brad King from the SAO: Joshua and Emilia would be facing a jury of their peers and fighting for their lives, because there was a good indication that the SAO was going to seek the death penalty in both cases.

CHAPTER 75

MURDER IS A vile, evil part of society. Most everyone agrees on that point. Each murder is vastly different from another, despite motive, modus operandi, method or means. The death penalty does not deter potential murderers, most will agree, whereas opponents of capital punishment will say there have always been and will continue to be innocent people put to death. Death penalty trials are an unpredictable and extremely tenuous facet of our judicial system. Just the two words strung together can rile some people up enough to hurl insults and make threats. Heated arguments ensue. Debates turn into shouting matches. Advocates believe strongly, same as gun supporters, in their cause; while opponents picket and use bullhorns and hold candlelight vigils at the scene of prison executions. It's all very polarizing and split down the middle, as far as public opinion. The death penalty debate ranks right up there with the big ones, like abortion and euthanasia. These are taboo social issues that we, as a society, often don't confront with any sort of educated or worthy discourse. Perhaps famed author J. R. R. Tolkien best put the challenge and weight of those choosing life or death in his wildly successful book *The Fellowship of the Ring*, when he wrote, "Many that live deserve death. And some die that deserve life. Can you give it to them? Then be not too eager to deal out death in the name of justice, fearing for your own safety. Even the wise cannot see all ends."

Without any doubt, Josh Fulgham was guilty of planning, plotting and carrying out the murder of his wife, Heather Strong. In fact, just two days after Emilia was arrested and charged with Heather's murder, Josh summoned Detective Buie for yet another chat. Buie went. Josh, who had spent several days in solitary confinement staring at the walls by then, possibly contemplating his life and what he had done, sat down and explained to Buie that he was finished lying. He couldn't do it anymore. It was time to speak the absolute truth.

"I'm all ears," Buie said.

Josh proceeded to go through the lead-up to, and the actual moments of, the murder one more time, leaving no detail out and pleading with Buie to believe that everything he was now telling him was the truth, as best as he could recall it.

Buie took it all down. He believed Josh. He also believed that Josh had shown some remorse and sorrow for what he had done.

Emilia Carr's role, on the other hand, with the kidnapping and potential assault charge aside, was questionable where the burden of first-degree murder stemmed. Had Emilia participated in the planning and murder itself—or was Emilia only there as a witness, as a bystander to help? Her story had changed so many times. Josh was sticking to his story of Emilia trying to snap Heather's neck and placing the garbage bag, which ultimately suffocated her, over Heather's head. But Emilia was now trying to proclaim that she was not even inside the trailer.

Near the end of November 2010, Emilia was summoned from her cell and led into a room where her attorney waited.

Emilia was now twenty-six years old. She had spent the better part of nineteen months in jail. She was a little more beaten down by the system; her baby face was rounder and further filled out. She was certainly a bit harder around the edges, more resolved to fight on and be proven not guilty, and a bit more apprehensive when it came to anything having to do with the justice system and cutting deals.

"No," Emilia said to her lawyer after listening to the proposal from the SAO.

The state was offering life in prison for a guilty plea. Emilia could take her case to jury trial, which was scheduled to start in a few days, and open herself up to a possible death sentence—or she could give in, admit her role and responsibility and walk away with what many were saying was a sweet offer: life for a life.

"The state told the court that if Miss Carr wanted to sign an agreement for life, they would go to the victim's family and see if they approved," Candace Hawthorne, Emilia's court-appointed attorney, told reporters on Monday, November 29, 2010.

After being turned down, SA Brad King and SP Rock Hooker went forward with the state's plan to pursue the death penalty.

It took days to sit the perfect jury for what was a rare female death penalty trial (even rarer would be for that same jury to sentence a female to death if/when she was found guilty). But by December 1, 2010, inside Judge Willard Pope's Fifth Circuit Marion County courtroom, a twelve-member panel of seven male and five female jurors was seated by 3:00 P.M., paving the way for opening statements to begin.

CHAPTER 76

FIFTY-THREE-YEAR-OLD Brad King sported the look of a hard-nosed, seasoned prosecutor. He had the chiseled, handsome, albeit tough, appearance and solid build of a professional baseball player, with his thick mane of black hair against mahogany-tanned Florida skin. Born in Terre Haute, Indiana, King had majored in finance and banking at the University of Florida, graduating with high honors in 1978, before applying his sights toward law at the same college. King was that perfect mixture of politician and civil servant; he knew how to handle the public side of being a prosecutor, but also the bureaucratic red tape that can sometimes come from dealing with cops. Most everyone he dealt with respected King, who had a reputation for demanding perhaps more evidence than necessary in order to take on certain cases. When agreeing to prosecute a case, however, King was prepared to wage a courtroom war he rarely lost. With regard to Emilia's case, King was firm in his belief that Heather Strong had been singled out, chosen, kidnapped, tortured and then cruelly murdered in such a heinous and premeditated fashion that those responsible deserved to die. What is more, King also believed that a key participant in that crime—from the beginning planning stages to the later

execution itself and cover-up that followed—was Emilia
Carr. Here was a woman who, incidentally, throughout all of
her denials and accusations, interviews with police and
public appeals to be heard, had never, ever said anything remotely remorseful pertaining to any part of the crime. Nor
had she ever said she was sorry that Heather had been killed,
regardless of who it turned out the perpetrator(s) had been.

For Brad King, who had seen scores of sociopaths and
psychopaths pass through the hallways of justice he kept
guard over, this alone said something important about Emilia
as a human.

King began with what had called them all to this house
of justice on this particular day: the evidence. As he began
his opening statement, King promised anecdotal, forensic,
DNA, fingerprint, photographic, documentation, recordings and admissions, among other staple pieces of law
enforcement, all proving that this woman was guilty of the
crimes charged herein. He said the state was going to present twenty-two witnesses. He used heavy words when
describing what the two defendants—Emilia in particular, seeing that Josh's trial would take place after Emilia's
case had been fully adjudicated—had done to Heather
Strong: "confined," "terrorized," "abducted," "constrained"
and, of course, "murdered."

The well-rehearsed SA then painted a picture of a love
triangle—Heather, Josh, Emilia—but he also brought James
Acome into that mix, telling jurors James's story would be
an important element of this trial, too. From there, he talked
about how he was planning on presenting his case chrono-
logically because it would help jurors better understand what
would be, at times, a seemingly confusing mishmash of
narratives. Yet, the "genesis" of the state's case, King pointed
out, as well as the apex of the law enforcement account, the
single most compelling portion of this murder case jurors
would soon hear, would be centered on the fact that Josh

was living with Emilia back in early December 2008—a time when the seed of this malicious crime was planted.

"Sometime shortly before Christmas," King told jurors, "he kicks [Emilia] out and has Heather Strong come back and they reunite again."

And bang! That was the beginning of the end for Heather Strong, King snapped.

According to the state, one piece of information summed up this case—that romantic situation, as it presented itself to Emilia, was the impetus for her to begin putting a bug in Josh's ear to get rid of Heather for good. It wasn't the fact that Heather had set Josh up for an arrest on gun charges later on. What had started the ball rolling for Emilia, King suggested, was the day she was booted out of Josh's house and her romantic rival moved in, taking her place.

SA King talked about how Emilia then finagled her way into Heather's life after Josh was put in jail: how Emilia offered to babysit Heather's kids, and, thus, Emilia confronted Heather and threatened her. Not to mention how Emilia then solicited two men to kill Heather—and, when none of that worked, Emilia Carr then devised a plan to do away with Heather for good.

What King did perfectly in his opening was to work James Acome into the lover-swapping narrative, explaining to jurors that Emilia and James had a child together. After Josh went to jail in January 2008, Heather hooked up with James, leaving Emilia all alone. Connected to both James and Josh, Heather was the common denominator in Emilia's life that caused her the most grief and personal pain—and here Emilia was pregnant (so she claimed) with Josh's child. Emilia had no one. Heather always seemed to be in the way of Emilia's happiness.

Judge Willard Pope—with his silvery gray hair, groomed like a politician's (tightly around the ears, short in the back, perfectly parted to one side)—looked on, listening very carefully to the prosecutor. For judges, death penalty cases are an added stressor. They need to be handled with kid gloves, and lawyers don't get as much leeway in talking through their cases and questioning witnesses as they might in a non–death penalty trial. No trial judge wants his or her case to come back on appeal based on something that could have been avoided in the courtroom with a bit more attention to detail. Judge Pope, appointed to his position in 2003 by then-Governor Jeb Bush, had just been retained that August for a six-year term after running an unopposed reelection campaign. There was no better judge in the state of Florida to sit watch over a trial of this magnitude than Willard Pope.

Brad King went through his case, point by point, using the technology available in the room, a PowerPoint-like presentation, to explain what each juror should expect to see and hear over the course of the trial. One important point King brought up during this portion of his opening was how, at any time during what had been nine different interviews Emilia gave to Detective Donald Buie, she could have come clean and told him where Heather was buried—and still stick to her initial tale of being there, but not participating. But Emilia never said anything about it. She allowed Heather's body to decompose in a hole in the back of her mother's yard, knowing full well it was there, while she tried slithering her way out from beneath mounting evidence against her.

The constant bell King rang was that Emilia, whenever she had been presented with additional evidence against the story she was trying to sell at the time, would call Spivey and say, *"Oh yeah, now that I think of it, I need to tell you something I might have overlooked. . . ."*

"And you can . . . see she's whispering," Brad King said of the numerous recorded interviews Emilia gave to Buie and Spivey, "like, you know, *'I don't want anybody to hear this, but here is all I know now.'"*

Time and again, when faced with the facts of the case,

Emilia Carr opened up just a bit more. When they told her, for instance, they had located Heather's body in her mother's backyard, after Josh had led them to the grave, Emilia changed her story again and asked for immunity.

Each and every time they looked at the evidence, King continued, the MCSO was more and more certain Emilia was involved.

She mentioned duct tape.

They found duct tape.

She mentioned a black garbage bag.

They found the bag.

She mentioned a broken window.

There was shattered glass on the ground.

The more she talked, the more they felt she knew these things because she had been there when the crime happened. It wasn't hard for Brad King to place the defendant at the scene of this murder. But then Emilia called Michelle Gustafson, Josh's sister, and the case broke wide open.

"And [Michelle] goes to Emilia Carr's house, her mother's house, picks her up," King said in his sometimes-thunderous tone, hammering a point home, "and they have a conversation. . . . They drive up to a park . . . and while they're still there in the park, talking, Donald Buie and Brian Spivey are *listening*."

He next explained how Buie got "fed up" with Emilia's lies and confronted her after she had that conversation with Michelle.

"We weren't there by chance," Buie told Emilia on that day, letting her know they had been recording her and Michelle's conversation, King told the courtroom.

One indelible comment, which turned out to be extremely incriminating, which Emilia had made inside the car, King told jurors to listen for when they heard the tape. This turned out to be when Michelle asked: "'Well, did she go peacefully, or did she'—and you can hear Emilia Carr break in and say, 'Did she fight him? Yeah. Yeah. She fought him.'"

For this prosecutor, that one statement put Emilia at the scene. Yet, the next comment out of Emilia's mouth to Michelle was even more detrimental to any later story Emilia would tell of not being at the scene: "Did you help at any point during all of that?" Michelle asked, and Emilia subsequently replied, "Yeah, I helped him tape her to the chair," King recounted.

At this very early stage of the trial, jurors had to be asking themselves: *Why would an innocent woman, not inside the trailer when a kidnapping, torture and murder took place, ever admit to such a thing to the sister of the man who purportedly acted alone in killing his wife, if she didn't do it?* On face value, with common sense employed, the insinuation seemed ludicrous. Her later story of not being at the scene was, simply, King repeated more than once, Emilia Carr changing her story again to fit the new circumstances.

For a little under a half hour, King talked jurors through his case, concluding, as prosecutors often do, on a persuasive note, imploring jurors to follow the evidence, same as law enforcement had done.

"Listen to all of it," King said, especially the tape of the Michelle/Emilia conversation. "Watch her reactions on the videotapes," he added, referring to the interviews Buie and Spivey had conducted. "Listen to the inflection in her voice, and *you* decide." He paused brilliantly here, allowing the power of suggestion its rightful place. Then, softly, "You decide," he said again. "Thank you."

CHAPTER 77

CANDACE HAWTHORNE HAD her work cut out for her as Emilia's appointed defense counsel. With long, flowing, curly blond hair and large-framed tortoise-shell glasses, Hawthorne looked the part of the experienced death penalty lawyer she had become. She'd been involved in capital cases as far back as 1998 as an assistant public defender and several in between. In May 2008, however, Hawthorne represented then-twenty-year-old Renaldo McGirth, the "primary actor," according to the court that tried and convicted him, in the brutal execution-style murder of sixty-three-year-old Diana Miller inside her retirement community home. In that case, Hawthorne went face-to-face with Brad King, too—and lost big-time. McGirth actually made history during the course of the trial after becoming the youngest inmate in Florida to be sent to death row.

On the flip side of that loss, in December 2009, Hawthorne successfully negotiated a deal for a Brooksville, Florida, man after helping him avoid trial and a potential death sentence. Regarding her client in that case, Hawthorne said after the deal was finalized and signed, "It would have been difficult to humanize him [to a jury]. He wasn't a Boy Scout."

Hawthorne knew these capital murder waters well. She

understood that each death penalty case was dependent upon the circumstances and individual on trial, and how he or she fared in the eyes of public opinion and the evidence. Yet, she also knew that, in their favor, death row in any state using capital punishment was not brimming with females. Still, the cards were stacked against Emilia when the numbers were taken as a whole. With California having the most inmates on death row at 741 (as of 2013), Florida was second with 412. Even more discouraging was the overall size of death row between 1968 and 2010: 517 to 3,158. Death row had grown considerably over the course of forty years by a tad over six times.

The one number Emilia had on her side among those same stats, however, was her race. In Florida, out of those 410 inmates on death row, as Emilia sat in the courtroom on December 1, 2010, watching Candace Hawthorne prepare her notes for her opening statement, 223 were white, 153 black, and only 34 Latino.

Dressed in a business suit, with a beige blouse, Emilia sat with her head held high as Hawthorne began. There can be no doubt Emilia was certain that once a jury heard her side of the story, numbers and stats and opinions would not matter. Because when the facts presented themselves to the jurors, each would understand that Emilia had no choice but to listen to Josh. She had feared that if she had told the truth at any time, Josh would do to her and their unborn child what he had done to Heather. You put a woman in fear for her life and the lives of her children and she will do anything in her power to survive, Emilia was now saying with this new defense she was mounting—even lie through her teeth in spite of herself and the incredibly expanding evidence against her.

"As to the theory of what happened," Hawthorne said a few moments into her opening, "that is going to be for you to decide after you hear the evidence from the witnesses and look at the documents. . . ."

On a board in the courtroom, Hawthorne wrote out a date: *September 2008.*

"That's one of the things I disagree with," she said. "I think this case started back then. And it probably started many years before that, because Josh and Heather were like oil and water."

So Hawthorne's case, as many suspected, was going to be built on a foundation of Josh and Heather's volatile and violent relationship, and how motive in this case centered on Josh, not Emilia.

Hawthorne explained how Jamie Carr, Emilia's ex-husband, had custody of Emilia's fourth baby, a child supposedly fathered by Josh. Hawthorne was smart to work in "high-risk pregnancy" when talking about this child and how Emilia was pregnant during the course of being questioned, which just might help later on when all of those statements came back to bite her.

The bare essential of this murder, Hawthorne maintained, was in that month of September when Heather was arrested on battery charges after Josh made a complaint against her.

"Emilia was a witness to that," Hawthorne pointed out.

Then Ben McCollum's name came up, Hawthorne saying how Heather moved in with Ben as a nanny, only to begin a romantic relationship with him.

"Josh was very possessive of Heather," Hawthorne announced. "And when Heather had other men in her life or other people in her life, he would do whatever he could to chase them away, to remove them, because he didn't want Heather having a relationship with anybody but *him*."

It was a strong argument for motive, devoid of Emilia, of course. Josh had acted all on his own, Hawthorne seemed to suggest. He was a man who hated Heather for what she had done to him. When Ben and Heather hooked up, well, that was a last-straw scenario for Josh. He couldn't handle the rejection.

Josh was "afraid that Heather was going back to Mississippi and [would] take the kids, like she had before," Hawthorne outlined.

It must have all looked good on paper and then sounded feasible when spoken by such a prestigious, competent attorney. But where was Emilia in all of this? She couldn't just be the "other woman" sitting on the sidelines innocently. Emilia had done and said things she needed to explain.

James Acome was next. Heather had moved in with James, Hawthorne said, pleading with jurors to focus on this important detail, because Emilia needed "financial support and somebody else in her life to take care of her kids."

This was something Josh, in jail at the time, could not fathom, could not handle and could not process emotionally. That rage Josh had harbored all his life bubbled to the surface, as it had so many times before.

Josh, Josh, Josh.

Hawthorne banged on and on. *Josh* wanted Heather to himself. *Josh* wanted to be with his kids. *Josh* was not in control of any of this while in jail. *Josh* was afraid Heather would disappear with the kids.

Again, it sounded good. A finger had been pointed. But the facts of the case dictated that while Josh was on the telephone with Emilia during this same period, he was wooing Emilia, telling her how great she was, how much he loved her and how he was finished with Heather entirely. The facts, in other words, did not support Emilia's argument.

"But did Emilia Carr really want to kill Heather?" Hawthorne asked. She allowed the statement to resonate with jurors.

"No!" she answered. "Probably got mad at her, probably threw some words around, but there is no evidence to support any *real* anger or violence. It's just, you know, tit for tat, and it went back and forth."

Sounded great.

Tit for tat.

Blow for blow.

Word for word.

Only problem here was that Emilia's tat included pulling a knife on Heather, holding it to her throat, threatening Heather and—from her own mouth—trying to snap Heather's neck.

Where did that fit in?

Hawthorne argued that Emilia was in no position to hurt Heather because she was pregnant. Any "dispute" (or issue between them) that Emilia and Heather had, Hawthorne said, was "over at the house, babysitting her children."

There was no choice in the matter for Hawthorne but to address all of those interviews Emilia had voluntarily given to the police. She needed to talk about how Emilia held back info—and there was only one way she could get her client out of it.

Blame the police.

Hawthorne claimed Emilia was kept at the MCSO longer than she should have been. The detectives had promised to take her home "real soon," but they never did. They shifted her around to different rooms in order to unnerve her. Rooms that both had a camera and didn't, as if it was an intentional part of getting Emilia to admit things she didn't say. She also suggested that the police did not give Emilia much food or drink. Emilia's pregnancy was "high-risk" and she was under a lot of stress. Emilia had wanted to help, but they scared her when they said they'd found a body on her mother's property.

Hawthorne illuminated this: "Because Josh [had] told her, 'You don't want to say anything because you'll wind up in the same place. And don't worry about Heather, she's closer than you think.'"

The documentation and recordings of these interviews, however, would tell a different story for jurors—and contradict most of what Emilia was claiming here.

There was also a suggestion that DCF acted in concert with the MCSO when they took Emilia's children into custody on March 24, the day the ball dropped on Emilia and she found herself facing a crisis of needing to find out more about the case in order to get her children back.

"So that morning," Hawthorne said, ". . . at [a probate] hearing, Emilia Carr sees Michelle Gustafson . . . and they talk. And Michelle starts up a conversation and they make a plan to get together later. And then Emilia calls her later."

Nowhere in there did Hawthorne mention that Michelle initiated the meeting *after* Emilia called her on the phone wanting to know what Josh was saying.

As for that recorded conversation in the car between Michelle and Emilia, something that Hawthorne had no choice but to try and explain away, she put it all on Buie and Spivey for coaxing Michelle into asking the right questions to get the answers they wanted.

Hawthorne spent all of three sentences talking about that recorded conversation and then, perhaps smartly, moved on.

Moments later, after collecting her thoughts, Hawthorne looked up from her notes and concluded by stating that Emilia was a victim of an overzealous investigation that needed a scapegoat beyond Josh. She asked jurors to pay attention to this theory during the course of the trial: "And the trickery used by law enforcement, did that compel Emilia Carr to give a false statement to the police to try to help prosecute Josh and allow her to become a witness?"

The problem with an argument like this was that Josh had admitted his role—completely. He was ready to accept death; they had that admission in his own handwriting. They did not need Emilia to convict Josh.

"It's not going to be easy," Hawthorne said in the end. ". . . I wish you Godspeed in your task."

CHAPTER 78

THE STATE PROMISED a chronological version of its case from the moment Heather went missing to the arrests of Josh and Emilia and all of the evidence it gathered afterward. And that was exactly how Brad King began on the morning of December 1, 2010, after opening statements concluded.

Brenda Smith, Heather's boss, a twenty-five-year employee of the Iron Skillet at the Petro, came in and told her story of that February 15, 2009, afternoon when Heather seemed so agitated and nervous after talking on the phone to a man Smith believed to be Josh Fulgham. Heather, Brenda Smith said, completed her shift at 3:00 P.M. and left; Brenda never saw her again.

Brenda's testimony was quick and to the point. She set up the disappearance and connected Josh to calling the Petro and being one of the last people to have communicated with Heather.

Candace Hawthorne was gentle with Heather's friend and boss. As a defense attorney, you have to choose your battles wisely; you can't attack everyone. Less is always more, especially when you're fighting for the life of your client. And defense attorneys know going into any trial that, despite what the law says (innocent until proven guilty), you are always coming from behind.

For the most part, Hawthorne used Brenda Smith to make sure jurors understood that Heather was dating Ben McCollum in late 2008 and that Heather broke it off with him to marry Josh, but Josh was arrested one month after the wedding.

Hawthorne asked Brenda about a meeting Heather had with "two men" in business suits during the first week of February. They had "some papers" they wanted Heather to sign. Brenda spoke with Heather after the men left the restaurant.

"And did you give her advice?" Hawthorne asked.

"Yes, ma'am, I did."

"Okay, and did you advise her that she shouldn't sign those papers?"

They did not discuss what papers they were, but it was clear that it had something to do with dropping charges against Josh.

"Yes, ma'am, I did."

"And did you tell her that 'When he gets out, he's really going to kill you'?"

"Yes, I did."

Hawthorne did a fair job with Brenda Smith, being sure to point a finger directly at Josh. If she was to be successful, Hawthorne had to build a case against Josh as a monster— a vicious, violent sociopath—a man who had made a decision to murder Heather on his own and drag Emilia into it against her will.

CHAPTER 79

OVER THE COURSE of the morning, Ben McCollum told his version of knowing Heather, offering no surprises. Ben set up a timeline for the state, telling jurors how he had entered the picture in early 2008, only to be booted from Heather's life after she decided to marry Josh. And once again, Ben gave Hawthorne the opportunity to paint Josh as a thug—a yelling and screaming soon-to-be ex-spouse who threatened Ben and Heather on numerous occasions.

After Ben, twenty-seven-year-old James Acome filed into the courtroom. James had a terrible overbite to contend with, which made him a bit hard to understand at times. He had piercing blue eyes and short-cropped black hair, along with a bit of a criminal record to explain. At first, James talked of how he had gone to school with Emilia, which was how they first met. And when Josh and Heather moved into town from Mississippi, James said, he and one of his buddies became friends with them.

Emilia sat, staring at James Acome, a bit of a self-righteous smile on her face.

As he explained his life in Citra and McIntosh, James said he had an on-again, off-again relationship with Emilia and they sometimes slept together.

"And as a result of that relationship, have you been told that one of her children is yours?" Brad King asked.

"Yes, sir."

"Who told you that?"

"She did."

The subject of James Acome's buddy came up next—that same friend Emilia had allegedly asked, along with James, to lure Heather so she could snap her neck. James said they all hung out together, even while Josh was in jail during that January through February 2009 window of time.

King wanted to know if, during that period, James Acome had ever seen Emilia put her hands on Heather.

"Yes, sir," James testified.

They discussed the circumstances surrounding the attack. Heather and Emilia were hanging out at Josh and Heather's trailer, James explained. They had been drinking. Emilia was ready to leave and had started packing her things. She told Heather she had a letter Josh's mother had dictated to her over the phone that she needed Heather to sign. Emilia wanted Heather not only to sign it, James testified, but to write something to the effect of Emilia giving the letter to Josh's lawyers so they could rewrite it the way they wanted and use Heather's signature.

"She said she wasn't writing that," James testified that Heather told Emilia.

"And what was Emilia Carr's response to that?" Brad King asked.

"That's when Emilia Carr walked up behind her and wrapped her hand around her . . . and pulled a knife and put it to her throat."

James said he jumped up and "grabbed Emilia in a choke hold and she dropped the knife."

Both girls made up, James said, and actually apologized to each other.

King made sure to get James Acome's felonies on record, for James had no trouble admitting to "three [arrests] dealing in stolen properties," and then King passed the witness to Hawthorne.

Hawthorne wanted to know when James began seeing Heather.

He said he moved in with her on January 26, 2009.

James then said he knew Josh "very well." Josh had never threatened him, and he had never seen Josh threaten or strike Heather.

Then Hawthorne got into that knife incident James had described for King. By the time she was done, James Acome had said they were drinking a lot and continued to maintain a relationship in the days after the altercation. So the implication was that it couldn't have been all that bad if Heather continued to allow Emilia in her life after the alleged knife incident.

After that and several inconsequential questions, James Acome was cut loose.

Next in the witness chair was James Acome's friend.

Out of the box, he said he had known James for ten years. They hung out a lot together. He also knew Josh. And Emilia.

"And what do you actually call Emilia?"

"Lily."

Then the questioning turned to that day in the car when Emilia and James and his buddy were taking a ride to the store. He recalled it being a time when Josh was still in jail, shortly before Heather went missing. The exact date had eluded him.

"She needed a ride to the store to get some diapers and things," he said.

"All right. During this trip to the store, did an unusual conversation take place between you and Emilia?"

"Yes."

SP Rock Hooker asked the witness to elaborate.

"Basically, she offered me—said she was fixing to get her income tax, and offered me money to help her lure

Heather Strong, get her drunk, so that she could snap her neck."

"In other words, *kill* Heather?"

"Yes."

"And how much did she offer you?"

"Five hundred dollars."

"Okay, and you said *what* in your deposition?" Hooker asked, making a point to clarify this amount, seeing that there had been a discrepancy.

"I said . . . I think I said seven hundred."

Hooker wanted to know, in this witness's opinion, did he believe Emilia to be horsing around when she asked him to lure Heather into a death trap? He and James knew Emilia and had been friends with her since high school. They both understood when she was serious and when she was playing around.

"She was serious," he said.

"And how do you know that?"

"Because I've known her for over ten years. I *know*!"

Hooker had additional questions and Hawthorne came in with her cross-examination, but nothing could put a damper on what this guy had said about Emilia wanting to hire him and James to "lure" Heather so she could kill her— something Emilia had tried to do, it had been well documented, but she wasn't able to because she wasn't strong enough.

Concluding this first morning of testimony, the state brought in several additional witnesses to put a bow on that narrative surrounding the early days of Heather's disappearance, including Misty Strong, the cousin who had reported Heather missing, and Beth Billings, the MCSO officer who had a gut feeling something wasn't right and opened the investigation. Likewise, Josh's mother, Judy Chandler, testified near the end of the morning, telling jurors all she could recall about the events that had led up to, and then following, her daughter-in-law's disappearance.

CHAPTER 80

HE WALKED WITH a careful and reserved stride. He dressed nicely in a finely tailored and firmly pressed suit and tie, his gold badge prominently displayed by his belt, his gun holster strapped to his hip, his black shoes sporting a military shine. Detective Donald Buie, at that moment celebrating eleven years behind the badge at the MCSO, was the key figure in law enforcement for Brad King. Buie had put it all together and had managed to get Josh to show him where the body was buried.

Buie spoke professionally, with respect: "yes, sir" or "no, sir." He answered questions in an articulate manner that spoke to his precision and expertise. The man was a cop, through and through—no doubt about it. He lived and breathed this stuff. The last thing this cop would do would be to stick his neck out for a perp like Emilia Carr and make things up to put her behind bars. It just wasn't in Buie's DNA to go that route. And with all the evidence the man had accumulated and collected with the help of his MCSO colleagues, Buie didn't need any outside assistance with this one. Emilia had sunk herself. She didn't need Buie's help. So if Hawthorne was going to go down that road after Rock Hooker got done with direct testimony, she had better listen closely to Buie's answers and try to find another hole to fill. Buie's reputation and his integrity were rock solid.

Unbreakable.

Off the bat, Buie talked Hooker through the early part of his investigation into a missing person case. He dotted *i*'s and crossed *t*'s. And it was through those initial days of the investigation, when Buie interviewed Josh and Heather's oldest child, that several red flags popped up for this cop, indicating to him that Josh Fulgham was the last person to be with Heather. And no sooner had he gotten Josh and Emilia into the MCSO than Buie began to see holes in their stories and developed a sense of the case in the form of: *They're hiding something.* Buie wasn't trying to say he was Columbo or Matlock; he was saying that the evidence and what Josh and Emilia were saying didn't gel. He knew they were lying to him because the facts of the case and what his two main suspects were telling him did not add up.

With all of that laid out plainly, Hooker brought up the fact that Buie and Spivey recorded some of those interviews, which allowed the state the opportunity to enter those tapes into evidence and to play some of that material for the courtroom. The jury was also furnished with transcripts of the interviews.

They all sat and listened to that first interview Emilia gave to Buie.

After it played, Hooker asked Buie to "go back" and "talk about" that day when he and Spivey went to Emilia's house with Josh.

Buie explained that the trip took place just before that interview they had all just heard. He said Josh was in custody at that time for fraud, for using Heather's credit card. And when they brought Josh over to Emilia's to search for the body, Emilia could have left the house (she was there), but she chose to stay and watch what was going on.

"He was released on February 6, 2009," Buie told Hooker

after being asked when Josh got out of jail on those assault charges.

"And that would be how many days before we know that Heather Strong was killed?"

"Nine days."

"Thank you."

Hawthorne walked through the various interviews with Buie and, in the end, after about a half hour of trying to find a way to explain why Emilia lied so often, she gave up because there was no other way to end what was damaging testimony to her client other than getting Buie off the stand as fast as she could.

CHAPTER 81

THE FOLLOWING MORNING, December 2, 2010, began as the state's technical experts arrived to set the stage for manner of death, where the body had been found, how Heather had likely been placed in that hole and what forensic evidence CSIs had uncovered. These experts would show how it all tied into what both Josh *and* Emilia had said about the murder, when they were interviewed back at the MCSO.

Susan Livoti was the manager of the MCSO's property room. She played a pivotal role in the evidence-gathering portion of the state's case, as well as keeping the integrity of that evidence in check. Livoti and two colleagues, she explained to Brad King, took care of all the evidence and made sure it was cataloged, packaged properly and stored from the moment it left the scene of a crime. These types of experts are often the unsung heroes of any successful prosecution and investigation. Without dedicated cops like Susan Livoti and her colleagues, evidence would lose its rightful place in the courtroom. Could anyone forget the fiasco of the OJ Simpson case when the blood evidence from Nicole's condo was transported improperly from that scene to the police department and was ultimately contaminated? One trip-up like that in a case and the entire investigation can crumble into a verdict of not guilty.

At the time the MCSO uncovered Heather's remains in that makeshift grave in back of Emilia's house, Livoti was a crime scene tech. She had gone out to the scene herself, she testified.

Maybe more important than what Livoti had to say was what the state entered as evidence through Livoti's testimony: a videotape of that day when they all went out to the scene after Josh pointed out where Heather was buried. This shaky video, taken by a cop and not a photographer, was eerie and poignant all at once. For those watching it, it displayed the sheer darkness and evil surrounding this case, reminding everyone that a human being had been kidnapped, tortured, murdered and then buried in a shallow grave. That horror, which can sometimes get lost during a trial, was implicit in each frame of this video.

What made the video even more intense when played inside the courtroom was the fact that there was no sound: just the shots of the camera from the POV of Livoti capturing the magnitude and sadness of the crime scene.

Next, King and Livoti talked about the blanket they found covering Heather's face and neck area. It still smelled so bad from decomposing flesh, and was in such bad condition, that King and Livoti had made the decision not to bring it into the courtroom.

They discussed the black chair that was used as a fixture to bind and contain Heather. That, too, would be a biohazard if brought into the room, so they chose, instead, to show the jury photos of it.

If there was one gold-standard trial rule Brad King followed quite obviously during the first two days of this trial, it was that he never kept a witness on the stand longer than necessary. That might sound obvious, but many attorneys, both defense and prosecution alike, do not follow this simple canon, especially where scientific experts are concerned. And not following it can make the difference between giving jurors just enough information and completely boring them to sleep, where they then forget most of what you intended to get across.

After talking about those pieces of evidence, King said he had nothing further for Susan Livoti and that Hawthorne was free to take a crack.

The only possible chance Candace Hawthorne had here was to chip away at the integrity of the paperwork surrounding bagging and tagging the evidence. Yet, as they talked through it, the idea that Susan Livoti was anything other than the ultimate professional was ludicrous. Hawthorne's cross-examination proved (if nothing else) that the woman had followed procedure better than most. She took her job very seriously.

After trying her best to get Livoti to admit to any mistakes—however minor—with no such luck, Hawthorne indicated she was finished.

Dr. Barbara Wolf walked in next, sat down inside the witness stand, and prepared to talk about her findings in examining Heather Strong's corpse inside the medical examiner's office.

CHAPTER 82

THE SINGLE MOST clear fact SA Brad King was able to establish with Barbara Wolf's direct testimony was that Heather Strong suffered and died a horribly violent death at the hands of her killer(s). In the end, Wolf's assertion was that asphyxia killed Heather, a manner of death she had determined by examining Heather's body and consulting later on with investigators in the case. Beyond that, Wolf offered a complete narrative of the crime scene as Heather's body was carefully removed from that grave in back of Emilia's house.

For Candace Hawthorne, she made clear in her brief cross-examination of Wolf that the doctor had taken "swabbings" (as she called them) of fluid from Heather's mouth, anus and vagina. Wolf could not obtain much in the form of forensic evidence from Heather's fingernails, she testified, because decomposition had just about consumed Heather's body to the point where, Wolf explained, Heather's fingernails actually slipped off like fake nails when touched.

The notion Hawthorne was going for here was a return to her mantra: *Josh, Josh, Josh.* Because when all was said and done, it was Josh's DNA that was tied to Heather's murder—not Hawthorne's client, Emilia Carr.

Brad King brought in Shannon Woodward next as his case was set to cruise control. Again digressing back to the refrain he had followed from his first witness, King was allowing the facts to speak for themselves, nothing more. Woodward had been a forensic DNA scientist for the MCSO during the course of the investigation. She was no longer with the office, but that did not impede any of her technical testimony as Woodward connected Heather through blood and hair samples to the duct tape found inside the trailer. And, once again, King followed his own lead in that after about a dozen questions, he passed the scientist along to Hawthorne, who then continued with her point that all of the evidence led back to one perp.

Josh Fulgham.

Next up were the lab techs responsible for analyzing the DNA and blood evidence. There were no surprises on either side here. They were on and off the stand quickly, keeping the trial not only moving along, but also focused on the bare facts and what those facts said about the defendant.

Over the course of December 2 and 3, Mike Mongeluzzo was called by King to talk about his role in the investigation, as were Brian Spivey and Donald Buie, both for a second time.

Mainly, King called Mongeluzzo and Spivey to reiterate for the jury the idea that Emilia's rights were never violated. They testified under oath that she spoke to them by her own free will, waiving her right to an attorney both orally and in writing. Additionally, as their interviews progressed and Detective Donald Buie took over, it appeared more likely that Emilia was changing her story to fit any mounting evidence coming in against her.

The weekend of December 4 and 5 came and went. On Monday, December 6, 2010, Donald Buie was back on the stand, Spivey following him. Each cop talked in more detail about the MCSO's investigation while allowing the state to enter additional transcripts of their interviews with Emilia, as well as several videotapes of those same interviews.

Several pivotal pieces of information that Brian Spivey

provided jurors included the fact that it was Emilia who had initiated most of the contact with the MCSO. Buie and Spivey were not badgering her to come in and talk. They didn't really need her. It had been Emilia calling them and asking if she could share additional information.

During one of these conversations, according to what Spivey told the jurors, Emilia said, "I can put the nail in the coffin, as long as I don't go to jail or prison."

That comment was made, Spivey testified, during a phone call a few days before Emilia's arrest. During all of these phone calls, and again in person as they interviewed her, Spivey explained, Emilia continuously asked detectives for immunity in exchange for information about Heather's murder.

Tit for tat.

As Spivey testified, several jurors were clearly shifting in their chairs as they heard him describe Emilia's two-faced actions and reactions, which came across as a guilty woman trying to save her own skin by turning over more rocks, exposing herself as the second half of a conspiracy to murder Heather Strong.

"I need to know I'm protected," jurors heard Emilia tell Spivey during one recorded phone conversation that was played during his direct testimony. "I'm not going to say anything without immunity, because I'm going to go down with him [if I don't have it]. I didn't kill the girl."

Emilia sounded desperate.

Anxious.

Nervous.

Guilty.

And then, after Candace Hawthorne finished her very brief, inconsequential cross-examination of Buie and Spivey, as quickly as the state had begun to lay out its case against Emilia Carr just days before, SA Brad King announced the state was resting.

They were finished.

CHAPTER 83

CANDACE HAWTHORNE WASTED little time. No sooner had the state rested did she motion the judge for an acquittal, for which Judge Willard Pope allowed a few minutes' argument from each side for and against before quashing the motion like the irritating mosquito it was.

It was a formality, essentially. Thus far, there had been nothing out of line during the trial to warrant any such request, but Candace Hawthorne had to try any avenue she could to get the jury to find her client not guilty.

As Emilia's defense unfolded, Hawthorne started at the beginning, calling her first defense witness, Milagro Yera, Emilia's younger sister.

Milagro meant "miracle" in English, Emilia's sister explained. Before noting that Miracle was how she referred to Milagro since they'd known each other, Candace Hawthorne asked if it was okay to address the witness as such while she answered questions on the stand.

"Yes," Milagro "Miracle" Yera responded enthusiastically.

Miracle was twenty-three at the time of her testimony. She was just a tiny little thing, four feet nine inches tall, which made her about five inches shorter than Emilia, she explained. They were friends, as well as sisters.

Family.

Tight-knit.

They had always looked out for each other.

As they chatted back and forth, Hawthorne walked Miracle down a path of explaining how her sister had a difficult, high-risk pregnancy that last time Emilia was carrying a child, which one might guess was the reason for Miracle's testimony. So dangerous was that pregnancy, Hawthorne insisted in her questioning, "Did she have to restrict her movement or other things around the house?"

"I believe so, yes," Miracle said. "She couldn't really lift a lot of weight at that time."

And there it was: the subtle reason smacking jurors across the face, explaining why Emilia was perhaps not involved at the level the prosecution had argued. How could she manhandle Heather, crack her in the head with a flashlight, chase her inside that trailer, help Josh drag her body, if she was experiencing a difficult pregnancy?

Hawthorne merged that disagreement into the date in question, February 15, 2009. She asked Miracle if she was home that day.

Miracle said she was.

Prompted by Hawthorne, Miracle recalled this fact because she remembered that she was "watching the kids, helping my sister watch the kids."

The way they discussed this night made it sound as though it was one more in a line of family nights at home with the kids, planning future events, having old-fashioned family fun and bonding—just two sisters at home, loving and caring for the kids in their house.

Hawthorne continued with that night, asking Miracle if she could recall anyone stopping by.

James Acome and his friend showed up, Miracle testified, adding, "She went outside," after Hawthorne wanted to know if Emilia invited the two men inside. "I stayed inside." Emilia spent about thirty minutes with them and then came back into the house. Miracle believed they sat on the porch and talked.

After they left, Emilia stayed up for another half hour and went to bed, Miracle explained.

"And was she there in the morning when you woke up?" Hawthorne asked.

"Yes."

"Miracle, thank you very much."

King asked one question, wanting to know if the Yera house had a phone back in February 2009, and if Miracle recalled getting any phone calls for her sister that night.

"No, not that I can recall," she told jurors.

Maria Zayas, Emilia's mother, was called next. Maria talked briefly about how she did not have had a complete, formal education, but she managed to learn how to read and write.

Not far into her testimony, Maria mentioned how Emilia was living with her back in February 2009. That night, February 15, Maria said, she could recall vividly because they were celebrating a birthday and James and his friend had stopped by the house.

Then, echoing Miracle's testimony in responding to Brad King, Maria said she did not recall Emilia receiving any phone calls that night.

Ending Maria's very brief direct testimony, Hawthorne asked Emilia's mother if the MCSO had ever asked her who was at her house on that night.

"No, ma'am," she said.

Hawthorne then wanted to know if Maria ever saw Josh that night.

"No, ma'am," she said again.

Under his cross-examination, King established the phone number Maria had back in February 2009. The reason he did this was because phone records would prove that Josh did call the house that night, despite what Miracle and her mother had recalled. All of this business about none of them remembering if Emilia had received any calls was purely conjecture and a waste of time, especially when the phone records proved Josh had called Emilia.

After Maria walked off the witness stand, there was some discussion about Hawthorne's next witness. Lunchtime was quickly approaching and Hawthorne did not want to get into it, only to have to break for lunch shortly thereafter. So she wanted to know if it pleased the court that they recessed at this point.

The judge agreed.

Gavel.

Chowtime.

CHAPTER 84

SHE HAD TO do it. Emilia believed she had no choice in the matter. The one witness that could tell Emilia Carr's story best was, of course, Emilia. She had to take the stand and explain to these jurors that she was forced to watch this horrible act of deadly violence. She had feared for her life and that of her unborn child if she spoke about any of it to the police. It was her only chance to make all of the evidence against her fizzle into that gorgeous Florida orange-and-yellow sunset that would take place later that day just outside of the courtroom windows. Rare, indeed, is the day that a murder defendant testifies in her own defense, only because it opens her up to cross-examination. Still, Emilia Carr was someone who believed she could explain anything away if given the opportunity. Her taking the stand fell right in line with her continually contacting the MCSO during the investigation to divulge bits and pieces of information piecemeal.

"Miss Carr," Judge Pope asked Emilia before the lunch break, "your attorney has indicated that you intend . . . to take the stand and testify. Have you discussed with your lawyer the advantages and disadvantages of you taking the stand to testify in your own defense?"

"Yes, sir," Emilia said.

Judge Pope asked several additional questions, alerting

Emilia to her right to remain silent and it being her choice, and her choice alone, to give up that right. He reminded her that the state had the right to impeach her testimony on cross-examination and wanted to know if Emilia understood that.

"Yes, sir," she said.

Emilia explained that she was ready. She wanted to talk. She wanted jurors to hear from her what happened.

What wasn't discussed, however, as the court sorted out how Emilia felt regarding testifying on her own behalf, was the unspoken fact that Emilia had to answer two vital questions jurors would be asking themselves after hearing the testimony: Why did she admit to Michelle Gustafson that she had participated in the murder with Josh if she hadn't been involved? What purpose would that admission serve?

CHAPTER 85

JOSH FULGHAM SAT in jail waiting for the outcome of his former lover's trial. For Josh, he hoped the jury did not fall for Emilia's charm and wit. He thought he knew Emilia better than anyone—especially how manipulative and conning and convincing she could be when needed. He knew that had he been given the opportunity to testify against her—which he wasn't going to be—how he viewed his culpability would be overshadowed by his actions.

As Josh sat and waited for Emilia's trial to conclude, few things were more impregnated in his mind than those moments when he and Emilia murdered his wife. Some of the details, which Josh remembered later, included what he thought about in the hours after they had killed Heather and had begun to contemplate the notion of now having to bury her body.

"A lot of things went through my mind in those twenty-four hours after we killed her," Josh explained to me. Thinking about what to do with Heather's body, Josh said, his mind "went blank."

One of the more disturbing parts of it all, Josh said, was when he finally decided to bury Heather in the back of the trailer. He dug that hole, he explained. But when it came time to "drag" Heather out there and put her in the hole, he was horrified of the notion of seeing Heather's face.

"I pulled the bag out there and made Emilia keep a cover on the face so I did not have to see it because it was sticking out of the bag. I put the bag in the hole and Emilia pulled the cover over the whole bag. . . ."

As many suspected later, Josh placed that board over Heather because, as he told me, "I did not want to throw dirt in Heather's face." That blanket he had put over her head was more of a shield, so he didn't have to look at her face.

He claimed he was a "nervous wreck for the next thirty days."

Josh said he gave Buie "his confession" on Heather's birthday because he was tired of lying and believed he "owed it to her to tell the truth and get closure on the case."

Josh called Buie his "buddy" and said he had "a lot of respect for him."

As for Heather, Josh said, he asked her one day why "she got me so mad and caused me to abuse her."

This is your classic abuser blaming the victim. It was Heather's fault, according to Josh's own admission, that he *had* to hit her. Heather, he said, responded to him on that day that the only way she could get his attention was by making him furious.

"After she told me that, I tried to change, and for a while, I . . . got calm about the stuff and did everything I could to make her happy."

Josh blamed the birth of his second child with Heather for ruining their sex life—which, in turn, made him go out and start "screwing around." Everything, he said, went downhill from there.

As Josh later explained, Emilia was a woman who provided him with that sex he was missing at home. Nothing else. She was a mere sexual partner. He had no feelings of love for her. Emilia was just . . . well . . . there. He spoke of that time when he met Emilia and she was the perfect remedy for what he was missing at home.

"I am not proud of any of this stuff," Josh said. "I will regret the rest of my life how I treated Heather, for being involved in murdering her, not because I am in prison, but because she gave me beautiful babies. . . ."

Josh realized Emilia would ultimately blame him and accepted that there are "people that will feed into her bullshit."

In the end, Josh said, Emilia, he "and God all know what happened out there that night." Then, in a strange choice of words, Josh said, "I take full credit for my part in this. . . ."

Maybe he meant "responsibility," not so much "credit."

He believed Emilia should do the same.

"She got in that car with my sister and made that confession. . . ."

In his mind, Josh concluded, he blamed Emilia for Heather's murder.

On December 6, 2010, like everyone else connected to this case, Josh was waiting for one thing: *What would Emilia say on the stand?*

CHAPTER 86

EMILIA WORE HER hair up in a French twist, with one corkscrew lock hanging down over her forehead, curling along her eye line, brushing up against her cheek and flowing down below her neck like a perfect black ribbon. She dressed conservatively in a gray blazer, dark pants and a white shirt—an older Catholic school student was likely the look they were going for. She came across as relaxed and calm. Emilia looked good, actually, all considering. Many believed the next day or more on the stand for Emilia was going to be the performance of her life—literally. Taking things this far and not agreeing to a plea, Emilia was fighting for not only her freedom, but also trying to avoid a place on death row.

As soon as Candace Hawthorne started, a well inside Emilia opened up and she seemed to be forever on the verge of tears. Did this show of emotion come across as Emilia being sympathetic? Was Emilia showing legitimate sorrow for the entire mess she was involved in? Or was Emilia simply sorry for herself?

Jurors gave no indication that any of it mattered at this stage. They sat stoically, for the most part, holding their cards close; some were taking notes, and others listening carefully, not reacting one way or another.

Emilia, of course, was an expert at hiding her true emotion, so any waterworks here was out of character for the twenty-six-year-old.

Candace Hawthorne threw several softballs out of the gate: Where were you born? How did you get the name of Carr? Where were you living in 2009? How many children do you have? Yet, after giving jurors the opportunity to hear Emilia's vitals, Hawthorne dove right into those murky waters with Emilia, asking her why the MCSO contacted her in March 2009.

What was interesting about this exchange, particularly, was a revelation from Emilia that she did not know a missing person report had been filed on Heather until she spoke to the police. According to Emilia's testimony, she had no idea Heather had been considered missing. It was a good explanation, if jurors believed it, of why she never thought Josh might be responsible.

Emilia talked about those early interviews she gave to Buie and Spivey, explaining how she was allowed to go home in between many of the interviews. Contrary to what King had argued, however, Emilia then said Buie and Spivey were constantly calling and asking her questions and wanting to know if she would come back down to the station house. The way Emilia spun this, it sounded as though she had been badgered continually by the police. She said she didn't sleep much that first night or after because they kept demanding more information from her.

"Okay," Hawthorne said, "now, you have sat here with us listening to the video recordings of your interviews, right?"

"Yes."

"And you have listened to the audio recordings of your interviews?"

"Yes."

"Okay, did you lie to the police, Miss Carr?"

Emilia paused. "Repeatedly," she said with a straight face.

"Why?" Hawthorne asked.

And here came the overall argument Emilia wanted to get across: "Because they kept threatening I wouldn't see my kids. In the very first interview, Buie said, 'You want to see that baby born, don't you?' I love my kids." She began to cry. "I would have said *anything*."

And thus began a back-and-forth exchange between the defense attorney and the defendant detailing how Emilia believed that when she lied to the police, she would be telling them what they wanted to hear. After she told those lies, she believed, they would let her go, and then she would be able to see (and keep) her kids. Emilia talked about being frightened of the state swooping in and taking her children away from her for good, because she was a suspect in a murder case. This was the main reason why she had lied to the police of her involvement: If she gave them specific information about the murder, they would consider her a witness—not a suspect—and, hopefully, would leave her alone.

"Why did you talk to Michelle Gustafson?" Hawthorne wanted to know. This was the other high-pitched ringing in jurors' ears. Why would Emilia admit to precise details of the murder if she hadn't been involved?

"Because the detectives kept telling me for immunity I had to know what I was talking about," Emilia explained. "I needed more details, more details. So I figured if I can meet with Michelle . . . and act like I was on her brother's side, she would feed me more information."

Once she got that additional information about the murder, Emilia added, she could then go back and feed it to Buie and Spivey to prove she knew what she was talking about, thus taking the heat off her.

This was extraordinarily important to the totality of her situation, Emilia insisted. Because if DCF ever found out she was involved in this case—on any level—they would take her children away from her for good (which they ultimately did). So, in educating herself about the details of the murder (or finding out what Josh had told Michelle),

Emilia said she could give the MCSO what they were looking for. All of it would make her look good in the eyes of DCF.

The other aspect of the investigation Emilia had to explain—if what she was now saying held *any* water—had been that walk-through of the trailer with Detective Brian Spivey. Why in the hell would she do that if she had no idea what happened? Why would she give Spivey all those details about Heather being strapped to the chair, a bag over her head, Josh running around the trailer like a madman, Emilia finding her body?

"They wanted me to cooperate," Emilia told jurors. "That's what they wanted." She said Josh had been telling them she knew about the murder, so she tried to placate that notion of being at the scene Josh had described. It was all part of her so-called elaborate plan to seem like she knew more than she did. She added how the MCSO felt she was involved. "I knew I [wasn't]. I didn't see the harm in [telling them I was]."

Emilia kept hitting on this idea of involving herself, telling Michelle and the MCSO she was more involved than she was because she knew Josh was telling lies about her and she needed to get hold of the right information so she could work toward helping the MCSO. Throughout this entire time, she said, Emilia believed the MCSO was trying to convince the SAO that she should be given immunity in the case in order to testify against Josh.

That call to Emilia's house on the night Heather was murdered, the one the MCSO proved with phone records, Emilia explained: "[Josh] wanted me to put my baby up for adoption."

That was the purpose of him calling the house that night.

"Did he tell you he was bringing Heather over [during that same call]?" Hawthorne asked.

"No."

"Did you know Heather was coming over to your home?"

"No."

"Did you ever go out to that trailer the next day?"

"No."

"Did you go out there that night?"

"No."

"When was the first time you knew Heather was buried on your mom's property?"

"When Detective Buie told me."

Candace Hawthorne finished. Emilia's direct testimony took all of about fifteen minutes. They never discussed the proposition Emilia had made to James and his friend—the payout of five hundred to seven hundred dollars to lure Heather over so she could snap her neck. The jury had to be thinking that since they never discussed it, there was either some truth to it or Emilia did not have an answer.

Either way, there were unanswered questions that Emilia and her attorney did not go near. But one could bet that SA Brad King would as he stepped up and prepared to mount his cross-examination.

CHAPTER 87

WHEN IT CAME to questioning defendants, Brad King had the experience, the savoir faire, the tenacity and the nerve. He possessed the careful nature not to overstep his boundaries and allow his personal feelings to get in the way of what can be the most difficult job a trial attorney faced. After all, like the American Bar Association says in its general standards: *The prosecutor . . . must exercise sound discretion in the performance of his or her functions.* Juries don't want to be patronized and smacked upside the head with pompous, over-the-top lectures by prosecutors simply looking to move up the political chain toward a cushy position. They don't want to squirm in their chairs while a prosecutor rips a defendant to shreds in what might seem like a steamroll. Members of the public chosen to sit on murder trials are smarter than that. They'll reject it on merit alone. Juries want facts, fair questions and a prosecutor who knows his case inside out—despite what Hollywood versions of this important part of our judicial process depicts.

Brad King began exactly where he believed the jury would most likely want him to: "Miss Carr, you told this jury that you lied to Marion County detectives . . . a number of times—is that right?"

"Yes."

"And did those lies begin on the first night, March 18, 2009?"

Emilia wanted to know which interview King was referring to.

"The very first one."

"I don't believe so."

"So your testimony is that you were telling them the truth when you said that the last time you saw Heather was on January the tenth?"

"No, that was a lie, sorry."

Emilia then explained that the last time she recalled seeing Heather was "mid to late January." SA King got the defendant to admit that it was near the time Emilia had grabbed Heather by the hair and threatened her.

The SA and his defendant next got into a bit of a verbal sparring match when King mentioned how Emilia watched the video of her interview. On this video, one could clearly see that she did not react passionately or lash out at all when they told her to stop lying if she wanted to see her child born. More than that, Emilia had displayed a striking lack of empathy. Why didn't she break down, in other words, if she had felt so threatened by all of this?

Emilia did not have an answer.

They discussed how Emilia had told Michelle that she wanted to kill Heather.

Emilia agreed. She had, in fact, said those words. (What else could she do? They had her on tape.)

"Okay," King continued, "did you go to [James's friend] and offer him money to help you kill her?"

"No, sir."

"No?"

"No."

"Did you go to [James] Acome?"

"No."

"So your testimony is that you were *lying* to the detectives on March 24, 2009—"

"Yes," Emilia said, not allowing King to finish.

King continued his train of thought: ". . . when you told them that you were there with Joshua Fulgham and Heather Strong in your trailer?"

"Yes. Yes, I lied."

The gallery was quiet and tense. This was the apex of the SAO's case. One of Heather's killers was totally denying any role in this crime.

"And you lied to them when you said you tried to break her neck?"

"Yes."

King went through a litany of other "facts" Emilia had provided investigators, all of which Emilia now said she had lied about.

Taping Heather to the chair.

Lie.

Placing the garbage bag over her head.

Lie.

That she spoke to Josh about killing Heather.

Lie.

That she knew Heather had been murdered inside the trailer in her mother's backyard.

Lie.

She saw Heather in the trailer, alive and dead.

Lie.

On and on and on, this went. Emilia claimed to have lied about everything.

Then the obvious question: "So you don't even know *who* actually killed her?"

"No, I don't."

"That's your testimony here today?"

"Yes."

Actually, Emilia held her ground quite well on the stand.

She came across as poised and confident, although there was a touch of sarcasm in her voice at times, some tears at others, but she remained unbreakable.

As King and Emilia traded barbs back and forth for the next five minutes, King and the jury heard nothing more than: *"I lied, I lied, I lied."*

Not at all frustrated, because he knew the facts and evidence proved Emilia was telling the biggest lie of all right there on the witness stand, King posed a question he was certain jurors were asking themselves: "So, is your testimony today also that Josh . . . never said *anything* to you about having killed Heather Strong?"

"No, he didn't."

What about that conversation with Michelle? Was all of that untrue? King wanted to know.

"No," she said, meaning that some of what they discussed was factual.

Shortly thereafter, King checked his notes and looked up at the defendant. He asked, "Do you really, Miss Carr, have *any* idea how many lies you told so far in this case?"

"Quite a few," Emilia answered, and King thought that was the perfect note to end on, suffice it to say he was not going to get her to admit to anything that made her look in the least bit guilty of anything other than lying.

There was a redirect, a recross, both of which lasted about ten additional minutes—and that was the end of Emilia Carr's starring role in her trial. As these things go, she managed fairly well. There was no glorious moment by the prosecutor presenting a smoking gun, breaking her down on the stand. Emilia had an agenda and she stuck to it. Now it was up to a jury either to take her at her word, or believe she was still telling lies.

As the day drew to a close with a few minor motions and arguments by the attorneys, Candace Hawthorne said she was done.

The defense rested.

Outside the courtroom, as Candace Hawthorne walked toward her car, a reporter asked Emilia's attorney about all the "lies" Emilia had admitted telling in this case and how it would ultimately impact the jury's overall impression of her.

Hawthorne made a great point after she stopped walking, looked at the reporter, and fired back, "They haven't proven the body of the crime. There is no *physical* evidence to show Emilia Carr was there."

CHAPTER 88

TUESDAY, DECEMBER 7, 2010, started off on a rather chilly note, with temperatures hovering in the thirties. Pretty darn cold by Florida standards at any time of the year. It was quite windy, too, making it feel much colder than it actually was. But skies were clear and the warm weather was just around the corner. No one could stop that unbearable, tropical heat from invading the Sunshine State in the coming weeks.

SP Rock Hooker took to the floor to give the state's closing. As the closer in a trial of this magnitude, one did not want to belabor any issue, bore jurors with legal terms, laws and rules, or shower them with what he believed to be his clever writing skills, making jurors feel as if they didn't understand the case they had just sat through. A sassy lawyer, who thought he was smarter than everyone else, could easily alienate jurors during his final bow. The best closings stuck to the facts and remained short; they did not make anybody in the room feel like an idiot.

"'He was stronger, so he held her down,'" Hooker said thunderously, opening with a monumental, straightforward line from Emilia's mouth. "'I taped her hands and feet. . . .'"

Hooker then beseeched jurors to "decide . . . that this case" was simple when boiled down to the unassuming facts, because "[it was] about a husband and a girlfriend who decided to murder the wife and bury the wife in the . . . pregnant girlfriend's backyard."

For this prosecutor, it didn't get much more simple than that.

Hooker talked about the two counts Emilia faced, both of which the jury needed to focus on during deliberations. He asked jurors not to forget that murder in the first degree was only one side of the indictment coin; the second was kidnapping. Added together, these charges were as serious as things got inside a courtroom.

He said the state shouldered the burden of substantiating its case and the "evidence is how we prove the charges. . . ."

It was clear that the most important word here was "evidence." It was not "speculation" or "conjecture" or "opinion." *Evidence.*

As he continued, Hooker shared with jurors the notion that Heather being a mother and having two children should not enter into the jury's discussions, same as Emilia, the defendant, having four children should not be. Being mothers might be noble, it might be the most important job both women did in their lives, but it should not have anything to do with the facts of the case.

"This idea of not having sympathy for either of the parties," Hooker said, would be an instruction by the judge. "Your verdict," he then added smartly, "should not be influenced by feelings of sympathy that you may feel for either side."

Continuing, Hooker reminded jurors that they would better serve the community if they used their "collective memories" when trying to recall evidence, and, if needed, they should request to see or hear some or all of the interview tapes.

The SP next talked very briefly about each interview Emilia agreed to, before focusing on that trailer walk-through Emilia conducted with Brian Spivey. He said that interview Spivey did with Emilia inside the trailer was pivotal because Emilia, on the stand the previous day, had "recanted *all* of that as not being true."

Reminding jurors why they were all there, Hooker said, "Heather Strong is dead! . . . The death was caused by the criminal act of Emilia Lily Carr. . . ." He referred to what Josh and Emilia did as "premeditated murder."

The worst kind.

"Killing with premeditation is killing after consciously deciding to do so, continuously deciding to do so. The decision must be present in the mind at the time of the killing."

These were all poignant marks to hit upon. This type of bare-fact argument placed the burden of the crime, the viciousness and the brutality, where it belonged: Hooker was saying Emilia and Josh took the time to plan out the end of a life, and then carried that plan out in the most violent, cruelest ways imaginable. For up to thirty minutes, Heather Strong knew she was going to die. The agony and emotional torture she went through at the end of her life was unfathomable. During the entire time Emilia and Josh made this plan and set it into motion, either one could have walked away.

In the end, Rock Hooker told jurors to pay attention to the facts of the case, look at the *evidence,* study those interviews between Emilia and the MCSO and make sure not to be fooled by an admitted, compulsive, pathological liar.

CHAPTER 89

CANDACE HAWTHORNE OPENED by thanking jurors for their service, a classic way of establishing that all-important rapport and projecting humility and respect. But then, in a quite awkward and rather flowery way, Hawthorne quoted Sir Walter Scott: "'Oh, what a tangled web we weave, when first we practice to deceive.'"

Though she had good intentions with this memorable quote, it came off as insipid and fairly confusing, not to mention over-the-top rhetoric.

Hawthorne announced the main characters involved in that "tangled web" as Emilia, Buie and Spivey, among others, which set the stage for her primary argument: Emilia, a very pregnant woman, was intimidated, confused and worn down by two cops to the point that she believed she was going to lose her kids if she didn't come up with the answers that these MCSO detectives were looking for.

She said the case revolved around the "relationships be-tween the parties" and "statements, statements, statements."

Effectively, she brought up the physical evidence. "To sum it up, real short and sweet, there is *no* DNA evidence that has been testified about in this court that came back showing Miss Carr's bodily fluids on *anything*. . . . No saliva. Hair. Nothing!" She added that not one Florida

Department of Law Enforcement (FDLE) expert testified about the "duct tape, *any* roll from the duct tape, *anything*!" No hair "taken out of the trailer." She claimed they had no fingerprints.

Her argument sounded rock solid. Emilia wasn't being tied to this murder by any physical evidence whatsoever. As Hawthorne talked about it, the impact was generally felt. Juries love—and maybe expect today more than any other time in history—to see *CSI* TV show evidence putting the proverbial gun or knife or garbage bag in the perp's hand. They yearn to see that flashy, computerized super forensic evidence they see on crime dramas. It's been referred to as the "*CSI* effect," when juries sit, wanting and waiting for the forensic evidence to tell them definitively that the defendant is guilty. Yet, in this case, Hawthorne skillfully wove into her closing, they were not going to find any such thing.

Hawthorne told jurors about the trailer being on Emilia's mother's property as just about the only connection to her there; she talked about the medical examiner being unable to determine cause of death until she referred back to the MCSO reports; then she talked about what they did have: the body of Emilia's boyfriend's wife found buried on that same piece of property.

"Heather Strong . . . ," Hawthorne said, "God bless her."

Emilia's attorney banged on, always going back to the lack of any physical evidence pointing to her client. As the clock ticked over her shoulder, Hawthorne covered everything she could—or at least any part of the case that did not place Emilia under any guilty light. She even mentioned how the CSI team from the MCSO sifted through all of the dirt in the hole where Heather's body had been uncovered and around the immediate area, but they found nothing indicating Emilia was ever there. She asked jurors to "set aside all the other stuff, anything any witnesses said" for a few moments and just put the focus on that *lack* of physical evidence. What did it say? What did it explain to jurors about the case the state was charging?

Throughout it all, Hawthorne probably spent too much time sounding these chimes simply because the state had already explained that Emilia, being an accessory to the murder, sat by and *watched* Josh do most of the physical, hard work involved in suffocating Heather and handling the body.

For fifteen minutes, Hawthorne talked about the tape and how none of it contained any evidence that Emilia ever touched it. Even the rolls of tape and bits of tape inside the trailer that the CSI team took as evidence and had tested failed to yield any connection to Emilia.

"And [forensics] determined that the prints on that tape that was in a box on a table in that trailer in Boardman belonged to whom?"

She paused, then, answering her own question, said, "Josh Fulgham! Not Emilia Carr."

Ben McCollum came up next. Then Judy Chandler. A witness from the Fulgham kids' school. James Acome. She said their statements needed to be looked at closely and jurors should decide what was true and what was false. She didn't mention what she thought was true or false or who, she thought, might have lied, but she didn't need to do that. This type of closing was all about speculating and giving jurors an alternative way of thinking about the case.

Interestingly, Hawthorne then moved onto the flashlight and Heather's shoes. She had to talk about those two important pieces of evidence because it had been Emilia who brought them up while talking to police and Emilia who ultimately pointed out where they were located on the property. However, Hawthorne saw no significance in any of it because no prints or DNA leading back to Emilia had ever been found on the items.

"And what we have is . . . Emilia having said, 'Yeah, he

gave me those shoes and just wanted me to hold on to them.'
They swabbed them. Nothing came back on the swabs."

After quoting Franklin Delano Roosevelt by stating how
"repetition does not [transform] a lie into a truth," Hawthorne said she brought this up because her client had given
the MCSO not nine or ten interviews, but a total of eleven.
And as Hawthorne went through each interview briefly,
touching on bits and pieces from each one, she made the
point that Emilia was often repeating back to the detectives
what they had told her, lending more credence, in Hawthorne's view, of Emilia searching for information in what
they were telling her in order to parrot it back.

"I'm telling you, it flows," Hawthorne said at one point.
"She does start picking up the stuff and feeding it back to
them. She does. They are giving her information. She's
trying to get immunity. She's asking for immunity. They're
telling her, 'Trust us. . . . Trust us.' That's a lie."

Harkening back to Roosevelt's radio address, Hawthorne
said "the state" wanted jurors to "believe that repetition
becomes the truth."

As for that Michelle Gustafson conversation Emilia had
in which she gave gruesome details about the murder,
Hawthorne claimed Emilia was only repeating what Brian
Spivey had told her in order to find out what Josh had told
Michelle.

Over and over, Hawthorne blamed the police for lying to
Emilia in order to make a round peg fit into a square hole.
The way Hawthorne made it sound, and rightly so (because
with the death penalty on the table, this attorney had to do
whatever she could to save a life), the MCSO pushed and
pushed until they got Emilia to say what they wanted.

In the end, Candace Hawthorne asked jurors to pay
careful attention to *all* of the instructions the judge was
going to give them, because there would be additional ways
for them to find Emilia guilty of lesser crimes if there was

any doubt regarding that first-degree murder charge. After that, staying in line with quoting famous people, Hawthorne dusted off Sophocles, the ancient Greek tragedian playwright, and spoke of how he once said: "Truly, to tell lies is not honorable, but when the truth entails tremendous ruin, to speak dishonorably is pardonable."

CHAPTER 90

THIS VERDICT COULD go either way, Brad King and Candace Hawthorne knew, despite what had happened in court during the trial. Lawyers often stay away from trying to project what a jury is thinking as they file into a room and start deliberations. It becomes a slippery slope of emotion if a lawyer begins to feel too self-assured. Surprises always happen in jury rooms. Florida juries, especially, had a reputation for shocking people: the Trayvon Martin and Casey Anthony verdicts, to name only two, were decisions out of Florida that sent alarming ripples across the world.

That all being said, Brad King was confident he had put on the best case he could. After all, according to Detectives Donald Buie and Brian Spivey, King kept kicking the case against Emilia back to the MCSO, saying they did not have enough. That conversation inside Michelle Gustafson's car, however, turned into the game changer. It was going to be hard for a jury to overlook what was said inside that vehicle and, thus, buy into Emilia's claim that she was fishing for information. On that one recording, Emilia came across as too cocky and too worried about Josh and what he was saying about her to law enforcement. It would be a stretch, at best, to agree that she was trying to find out all Josh knew in order to give Buie and Spivey what they wanted.

Judge Willard Pope read what turned into long, tedious instructions for jurors and asked that they retire, take their time and deliberate. They should talk about the case, ask each other questions and review all of the evidence.

Late into the day on December 7, 2010, somewhere around four o'clock, two hours into the jury's deliberations, the foreman indicated they had a question for the court.

Emilia and the lawyers were summoned back into the courtroom.

The jury wanted to hear a taped interview between Emilia and Spivey as they drove back to the MCSO from Boardman. There was no indication particularly what interested the jury about this interview, but the judge saw no issue with allowing them to listen.

Once that was done, they went back into sequestration. There was some concern about the time of day and what to do: allow them to continue or call it a day and go back at it in the morning. However, only after two and a half hours— total—inside that deliberation room, the jury foreman gave word that they'd reached a verdict.

Tomorrow wasn't going to be necessary.

When Brad King heard, he looked over at Rock Hooker. They both knew guilt came quick; an innocent verdict took time to hash out among jurors. Here it would seem they went into that room, talked about the case a bit, then took a vote.

The clerk stood and read the questions on the jury's ticket, along with the penciled-in answers: "'Verdict, Count One. We the jury find as follows, as to the defendant in this case . . . is *guilty* of murder in the first degree. . . . Verdict, Count Two. We the jury find as follows, as to the defendant in this case . . . is *guilty* of kidnapping.'"

Emilia dropped her head. Hawthorne grimaced.

The judge polled each juror; all answered, "Yes."

Seven men and five women had found Emilia Lily Carr

guilty of both crimes. That same jury, after a break, would then sit and decide Emilia's punishment after hearing evidence in the penalty phase.

Reporters tracked down Heather's mother outside the court afterward. She had traveled from Mississippi with other family members to be there for the trial (they ended up staying with Ben McCollum, actually). Now that Emilia had been found guilty, everyone was curious to hear what Carolyn Spence had to say about one of her daughter's killers.

"I'm relieved," Carolyn said, indicating that it was a just verdict. The woman was guilty and the jury did not believe her lies. Carolyn was satisfied.

Neither Brad King nor Candace Hawthorne was willing to comment. The jury had spoken, sure; but they needed to gear up now and go back to the drawing board to begin preparations for the next phase. For Candace Hawthorne, she had one thought on her mind: saving Emilia's life.

CHAPTER 91

THE MIND LIVES inside a bubble of past events, continuously calling up history, trying either not to repeat it or somehow to change it. While the heart, in a struggle of consciousness, thrives on the present, its focus strictly on the now, thus living for the moment. If Emilia Carr and her character witnesses were going save Emilia's life with their testimony during the sentencing phase of this trial, now would be the time to stick to a plan that included the latter. There was nothing to be gained by talking about the past and the fact that Emilia did not agree with the jury's verdict. Now was the time to concentrate entirely on the present and maybe—if Emilia was as smart as she claimed—even think about throwing herself on the mercy of the court, perhaps admitting her role in this murder and begging for forgiveness. If she did that, there was at least the *chance* of her walking away with a life sentence. The alternative, on the other hand, was not a good one.

Up first for Emilia on December 9, 2010, after a day of opening arguments and the state's one witness, was Sue Zayas, Emilia's aunt, who talked mostly about the family and how often she and her husband (Emilia's uncle, who had since passed away) would visit. This allowed Hawthorne to enter into evidence several family photographs depicting what seemed to be a close bunch of people that laughed, cried and did things together.

Hawthorne asked Sue if she had ever talked to Emilia about her niece's "aspirations" in life.

"Emilia always had a plan," Sue told jurors. "She was always looking for something to better herself," adding how for Emilia, if one particular plan did not work, "always had a backup." (Right: If not the snap of a neck, then a plastic bag would do!)

Everything Emilia did, Sue insisted, she did for the sake of her children.

Brad King had a few questions for Emilia's aunt, most of which focused on Emilia's above-average intelligence, thus leaving the jury with the impression that Emilia Carr was no dummy and should have known better.

Emilia's mother, Maria Zayas, walked slowly into the courtroom, with her stride a bit slower than normal. Her shoulders were a bit slouched; her expression was a bit sadder and more solemn. Maria was certainly feeling the burden of the verdict. Her daughter had been found guilty of the most monstrous crime imaginable. What could this mother, in all of her humility, say to these jurors to try and help save her daughter's life, especially when Emilia was not yet ready to take responsibility?

Maria began by saying she was born in Miami, but the family moved around a lot. They lived as "migrants . . . so we really didn't have a steady place when I was growing up." Anyone in the family old enough to put in a solid day's work picked grapefruits, cherries, corn, tomatoes and cucumbers. "We did it all," Maria added.

Maria had completed only the sixth grade in school. She learned to read or write on her own, but not much more than "simple words." Throughout her childhood and into her young adult life, Maria explained, her family chased work, wherever picking fruits took them: Ohio, Michigan, Texas and North Carolina. Still, they always wound up in Florida.

At fourteen years old, Maria got pregnant with her first child, a daughter. Soon, Maria had a boy; then she met a man, married him and, two years later, had Emilia. Two years after that, Milagro arrived.

Years went by and Maria's husband, in 1988, was charged with an unfathomable crime and DCF took Maria's children out of the home. They were placed in foster care.

"Were you able to have unsupervised visits?" Hawthorne asked, trying to get Maria to point out what Emilia's father had been charged with.

"No, they were always supervised."

"And were the children allowed to visit with their father?"

"No, he could have no contact."

"And why was that?"

"He sexually molested Emilia."

Some time passed, Maria explained. She accepted her husband back into the home after he completed a court-ordered program and they soon got their children back.

According to Emilia, the abuse continued. However, she excelled in school, Maria explained. She was always bringing home A's and B's and routinely made the honor roll. Emilia was a model student, never got into any trouble and never cut classes.

After she graduated from high school, Emilia wanted to become a photographer, Maria said. She also got into modeling and went to Barbizon, a modeling school in Tampa. At fourteen or fifteen years old, Emilia was stunning, Maria told jurors. She had everything going for her. Maria was certain that Emilia was going to be the one in the family to make it out of poverty and avoid working the farms. She had a chance. She had even gone into the ROTC (Reserve Officer Training Corps), a college-based program and first step into enlistment in the military.

Throughout her line of questioning, Hawthorne stopped periodically and admitted photos of Emilia, a line of memories, essentially, detailing her life with her family. Through those photos, it became clear that Emilia was the center of attention, the one family member everyone seemed to look toward for hope and promise of the future.

After discussing family history, Hawthorne moved on to a deposition Maria had given in 2001 regarding her husband, Emilia's father. Hawthorne asked Maria about it, setting the tone of the testimony with a rather pointed question: "Do you remember why your husband was in jail [back then]?"

"He molested my daughter Emilia."

"And did something else happen . . . while he was in jail?"

Maria seemed confused about the question, maybe conflicted. She became emotional. The weight of the trial, the guilty verdict, the idea in the back of her mind that each answer she gave had the potential to save her daughter's life, it was implicit in her cracking voice. As any mother in the same position would have done, Maria wanted to say the right thing.

Hawthorne rephrased her question. "Were you ever made aware of [a second] charge against him?"

"It was me, my mom and my daughter [Emilia]," Maria said before stopping to collect her composure. This was so hard, so personal, so final.

Emilia looked stunned. She could feel the pain from her mother, a woman who had always stood by Emilia's side, no matter the circumstance. Maria had always helped Emilia when she could . . . for forever, it seemed. But this . . . Maria was helpless. How much could she do with only her words?

Maria took a deep breath. Then she explained what happened, beginning with how her husband knew that she and Emilia and Emilia's grandmother were going to be in court testifying against him in the sexual molestation case. They would each sit and describe explicit, graphic details based on their knowledge of "what he did to Emilia," Maria said. But when Emilia's father found out that they had planned to bury him in the courtroom with testimony, "he hired somebody on the outside." Maria described how he had even given the person "directions to my bedroom . . . to my baby's bedroom [and my] momma's. He wanted to get rid of us because we were going to go and testify. He was going to prison for the rest of his life."

Emilia's own father was going to have three women—one of whom was his own child, the other his wife—murdered because they had become a problem in his deviant life of molesting children. This type of direct testimony—revealing those deep, dark family secrets—gave jurors, without Candace Hawthorne having even to try, a vivid picture of how Emilia might have learned to deal with problematic people herself.

Maria went on to note that "the guy he hired to kill us, it was an undercover cop."

Now Emilia's father had two problems.

When her father went to jail for what he did, Maria told jurors, Emilia blamed herself. She and her dad had been close, like a father and his son, Maria used as an analogy. They did everything together. So when Emilia's words sent the old man to prison, she took on the burden of putting him there and it weighed heavily on her.

"She even felt like she destroyed the family," Maria said of Emilia's courage to come forward and not only admit she was abused, but to testify against her father.

Emilia went to see various counselors, Maria said, to talk about the abuse and the feelings she was having surrounding blaming herself.

"But nobody [could] seem to help her. I mean, she would just keep it all inside."

Some might argue that pain turned into rage.

The cycle seemed to continue when Emilia met a man and became pregnant at sixteen. All her hopes of modeling and the ROTC suddenly disappeared and she was now a mother.

The state stepped in at one time and removed her child.

She'd always get her children back after the state took them, but it was forever a struggle for Emilia, Maria said.

Brad King had nothing more than to ask Maria a few questions that cleared up some timeline issues he had a problem with. Maria was confused about a few dates. But other than that, King was confident in allowing this part of the trial to be focused on the defendant. It was Emilia's show here. King didn't need to prove that Emilia was a bad person; the jury already had agreed to that in finding her guilty. This was about Candace Hawthorne providing the jury with the information that could save Emilia's life.

CHAPTER 92

EMILIA'S OLDER SISTER and grandmother testified on that same day, December 9. Each woman sat in the witness stand and gave similar testimony, telling jurors that the family had problems, lived a hard life of moving around all the time, working their fingers to the bone in the fruit fields, endured a host of medical issues and never had enough money to live even a simple, humble life. Throughout all of this testimony, the message Candace Hawthorne wanted to get across became clear: Emilia was a beacon of hope. She was the golden child with the smarts, the looks and the know-how to pull the family out of the societal doldrums they routinely found themselves in. Only it didn't happen that way. Emilia, forever the healthiest and smartest of the bunch, had fallen into early marriage and early divorce, given birth at a young age, and was forced to place her dreams on hold and then finally abandon them altogether.

What any of this had to do with Emilia killing Heather was a guess. If anything, the testimony spoke of a young woman growing up in poverty, developing an increasing bitterness at society and anybody who had it better than she did. Abused and frustrated, with a multitude of failed relationships in her wake by the time she hit her twenties,

Emilia developed a reputation for becoming angry whenever someone crossed her.

Candace Hawthorne rested her case after Miracle came in and said a few cheerful words about her sister; then Dr. Ava Land, a psychologist, talked for a few moments about Emilia's state of mind and what sexual abuse in early childhood had the potential to do to a young girl.

Closing arguments took place the following morning, December 10. Both lawyers kept their comments brief and followed a pattern one might expect at this stage of a death penalty sentencing phase. The central themes that attorney Candace Hawthorne focused on became utterly implicit throughout the testimony of character witnesses she had presented: Emilia was so young; this was her first and only felonious act; she'd had such a deprived and abusive childhood, she deserved a pass here in the form of life without parole. Part of Hawthorne's argument was somewhat substantiated by Dr. Land, who had testified that Emilia might appear to be cool, calm and social—on the outside. "But I believe there is a good deal of anxiety and distress under the surface," Land told jurors. In all she did, the psychologist then pointed out, Emilia perpetually felt the need to "protect herself." Through that, she grew increasingly antisocial and disgusted with people who did not feed into her narcissism.

Brad King had, perhaps, the most profound comments of the day. During his closing, while bringing the totality of the state's case back down to reality—putting the victim up front and center (where she belonged)—the SA explained why the state had sought the death penalty. King said it was because of the brutal manner in which Heather was kidnapped, held hostage, emotionally and physically tortured, then murdered: "Those evils go to the very heart of our independence and dignity," King passionately stated, adding that, at its core, *that* was "the evil" the state of Florida was "looking to punish" in seeking death over life behind bars. Jurors could never forget, King reiterated, regardless of what Emilia Carr had gone through as a child, how deplorably and heartlessly Heather had been treated before she was murdered in such a heinous and cruel manner.

In her most memorable statement of the defense's closing (maybe during the entire trial), Candace Hawthorne said Emilia deserved a second chance at life because the molestation she suffered as a child until she was a teen stifled any progress and promise her life might have shown early on. In effect, that repeated sexual abuse by someone who was supposed to protect her took away her dignity and care for other human beings.

"For a small child to keep that secret," Hawthorne said of the sexual abuse, "she had to engage in fantasy to take her away." Hawthorne stopped there, pausing for a brief instant. Anyone who was listening could tell Hawthorne believed this about her client and truly was fighting here to save a life: "She learned to fantasize."

A bit of drama unfolded before Hawthorne rested, when Brad King indicated during a sidebar conversation that he wanted to play a videotape of a recent prison visit from Emilia's sisters and grandmother, in which Emilia and said family members were giggly as they reminisced about the testimony Dr. Land had given. They were actually having a laugh about it.

Brad King believed this one moment of behind-the-scenes video portrayed the "real" Emilia Carr—the woman who thought a fight for her life was nothing more than a joke. It showed how cold Emilia had become, in King's view, and that she hadn't taken the court, the charges or the penalty phase seriously.

In the end, King never argued further for the tape to be shown to jurors because Hawthorne soon rested and Emilia never testified during the penalty phase.

CHAPTER 93

THE JUDGE ORDERED a short recess after King and Hawthorne closed their cases, brought everyone back, and gave the penalty phase of this trial over to the jury for its review and vote.

It was important to Judge Pope how the jury felt about life or death. In the end, though, it was not up to the jury to decide Emilia's ultimate fate; all they were doing here was giving the judge a recommendation. Pope would be the final judge, literally, deciding at a later date whether Emilia lived or died. Legally, he could agree or disagree with the jury's recommendation.

It took two hours for the jury to come back. Shocking everyone in the courtroom, they had voted to put Emilia Carr on death row, by a margin of seven to five.

Effectively, one vote had decided the jury's recommendation of death.

Judge Pope announced that it would be some time before he made his concluding voice heard in the matter of the *State of Florida* v. *Emilia Carr*. The jury's opinion was important, Emilia and her attorney knew. By law, however, Candace Hawthorne explained to Emilia and her family, the judge was bound to give the jury's recommendation "great weight." He could decide either way, however. And in

Florida, judges were known to impose life without parole sentences instead of death. With the vote being so close here, many assumed, Emilia had a good chance—unlike Heather Strong—of escaping death.

The judge set a hearing date for February 22, 2011.

CHAPTER 94

FROM BEHIND BARS, after the penalty phase of her trial was over, Emilia Carr spoke. Local reporter Natalia Martinez, who had covered the trial for WCJB-TV, the northern Florida affiliate of ABC News, interviewed Emilia on December 13, 2010. Emilia was waiting in Marion County Jail for her orders to be shipped off to one of Florida's maximum-security prisons for women.

The fact that the jury had recommended death for Emilia had perhaps sobered her thinking. Looking dumpy and deprived of sleep, Emilia wore white-and-red candy-cane-striped prison jumpers. Her hair was a bit disheveled and noticeably dry; there was a strange, obvious gap between her two front, upper teeth.

"I thought when people saw the trial they would know that I had nothing to do with this," Emilia proclaimed to Martinez.

Here she was facing the hour of death and Emilia was still shouting from behind a bullhorn the notion that she was never inside that trailer while Josh was murdering Heather. Detectives Buie and Spivey, Emilia added, as soon as they started "questioning me, first thing they started doing was threatening me with my kids."

It was an old, tired argument—one that Emilia had tried

already and failed. But she bantered on and on. The entire time she spoke to the police, Emilia explained to Martinez, she was making things up. Emilia had been totally convinced Josh was "trying to put it all on me from the beginning."

Most everyone had heard this all before. Emilia sounded desperate. What did she think would happen if she continued? The jury had spoken. All she was doing now was adding additional shovels full of dirt on a grave Judge Pope was perhaps preparing.

Moments into the interview, Emilia started to cry. She talked about how she was the "only one" who could take care of her and her sister's children, because within her "family . . . I'm the only one that's educated—and I'm in here because of a man."

"She is damn good at lying and making people believe her," Josh Fulgham said. He was behind bars, awaiting a date with the SA. Josh had sat back and watched Emilia's trial unfold. He was satisfied that Emilia had been unable to manipulate the system to her benefit. That's what had worried Josh the most, he said, that Emilia would be able to talk her way out of it all.

According to Josh, Emilia had once written to him and asked that he write a letter to the governor of Florida, asking for her "emergency rush release" because she was an "innocent mother of four." Josh said that he was "supposed to tell [the governor] if he didn't set her free that I was going to go public and tell on television that he has left [an] innocent woman [heading for] . . . death row, after I had done told him she was innocent."

The bottom line within all of this was that it didn't matter. Emilia's fate was in the hands of a judge, who was just about to make his final decision.

CHAPTER 95

ANY PLAN SHE might have had from behind bars to escape final justice, if Emilia had one at all, did not work. As promised, on February 22, 2011, after assembling all of the parties involved once again, Judge Willard Pope sat behind his bench. With a dreadful look about his face, he announced to the courtroom how much thought he had put into his decision. In the end, though, the judge said it wasn't a tough decision to make after all—that is, legally speaking. Once he sat down and took everything into account, Judge Willard Pope realized there was only one result he could come to.

Death.

With utter silence inside the courtroom, Emilia faced Judge Pope. Her expression was bleak and defiant. Pope looked at Emilia and said, "'This court is compelled to conclude that the actions of Emilia Carr in this case, and the manner, means and circumstances by which those actions were taken, require the imposition of the ultimate penalty.'"

Death.

Pope was reading aloud from what was a detailed, passionate, well-written, well-thought-out, twenty-nine-page order.

Emilia dropped her head when she realized her fight was

over. She was heading to death row. But then, suddenly, she looked up and seemed to face the judge's conclusion with a modicum of acceptance.

Judge Pope allowed Emilia to speak. In a short statement, Emilia gave the impression that she was not going to back down from the story she had been trying to sell everyone. She viewed the entire process as unfair and biased. She said she had been erroneously "convicted of telling a lie." Nothing more. She was heading to death row, essentially, for lying to the police.

It was outrageous. It was wrong. It was unjust.

Emilia's case would be filed under automatic review. An appeal was due process in all death penalty cases. That would be the place from this point on where Emilia could argue through her attorneys against the judge's sentence and the jury's decision.

Pope continued, explaining to the court how he "assigned great weight" to "three aggravating circumstances" in the case where his decision to affirm the jury's recommended sentence was concerned. Legally, this fact was vital to his decision. Heather Strong, Pope said, had been brutally murdered during the commission of the "separate felony offense of kidnapping." He explained the crimes were "especially heinous, atrocious and cruel." He referred to the murder as "cold, calculated and premeditated."

Alternatively, Pope had given Emilia's "lack of criminal history" the most weight out of much of what he looked at. The argument that she'd had a tough upbringing, was sexually assaulted and didn't have many chances in life played zero part in the judge's decision, he explained. He said he placed "little or no weight" on those sad, mitigating factors. In addition, Pope said there was "no evidence" presented to him that Emilia was ever manipulated by Joshua Fulgham. Plus, effectively, testimony from a clinical psychologist proved that she was, and still is, "in control of her own faculties."

Lastly, in the case he listened to inside his courtroom,

Pope agreed with just about everyone else besides Emilia and her attorneys that the state presented "overwhelming evidence" of Emilia's guilt.

There was a brief moment of pause and reflection from the well-liked judge. It was clear he took this matter seriously; deciding to send a young mother of four young children to death row was not easy. Then, in carefully chosen language, as he had throughout the entire trial, Judge Pope ended with a word of hope (depending on which way one looked at things) while staring directly at Emilia: "May God have mercy on your soul."

In confirming the jury's decision, sending Emilia Carr to death row, Judge Willard Pope made a bit of history as Emilia Carr became the first woman to receive the death penalty in Marion County since famed serial killer Aileen Wuornos, convicted in the same county and executed in October 2002. Emilia would join one other woman, Tiffany Cole, on Florida's death row. Cole, also in her late twenties, was sentenced in March 2008 for her role in the vicious and cruel double murder of a Jacksonville, Florida, couple.

This case was far from over, however. The way Candace Hawthorne felt after the latest decision indicated anything but finality. Outside the courtroom, Hawthorne spoke to various reporters hovering around her. "I'd be interested to see if the Florida Supreme Court affirms the judge's decision," Hawthorne said with a bit of tailored cynicism in her voice. "I don't think they will."

Brad King was not celebrating. One did not jump for joy at the prospect of placing a young woman on death row in a state where the punishment, after all the appeals were exhausted, was often carried out . Even if Emilia spent twenty years on death row, it would still make her a young woman at forty-plus when the state of Florida summoned her to the death chamber for execution. King, instead, took the high road and called Pope's affirmation of the jury's recommendation an "appropriate" decision to make from the bench, before adding how he believed the Florida Supreme Court would agree.

"Looking through other cases," King told reporters, "the Florida Supreme Court regularly has upheld cases" with comparable aggravating factors.

For Emilia's mother, a woman who had worked hard all her life to give her kids the best she could, seeing Emilia on death row was, she said, this mother's "worst nightmare." She was "shocked" by the judge's ruling and needed some time to go home and process the road ahead.

Heather's family was nowhere in sight.

CHAPTER 96

JOSHUA FULGHAM WAS ready to face whatever fate had in store for him. He was thirty years old. He'd been behind bars now for almost three years. He had wanted to cut a deal with the SAO, but they still weren't offering. Ready and willing to accept a plea deal, the issue at hand for King was that the state had gotten a conviction in Emilia's case and she had been sentenced to death. The SAO couldn't roll over now and allow the mastermind, essentially, to take life.

"Brad King takes his responsibilities very seriously," said Terry Lenamon, Josh's lawyer. "He looks to the victim's family and proportionality on some levels. He had gotten a death sentence on Emilia, and because he believed that was an appropriate sentence, he didn't want to risk any appellate issues. . . ."

The idea was that if Josh was given a plea offer and took it, Emilia's attorneys could argue what is called "proportionality" in her appeal: What this means is that the "government and private actions should not be demonstrably excessive, relative to their moral and practical justifications."

What's good for one, in other words, has to be good for the other.

So Josh was now in a position to battle it out in court

against the SAO. To that end, Josh said later, holding little back, "The prosecutor in my case was a sick, obsessed fuck . . . and I hope he burns in hell."

There was certainly another way to put what was resentment for not cutting a deal, and maybe Josh's reaction was a good indication why the SA had not wanted to deal with him in the first place.

According to what Josh told me later, he had wanted to plead out mainly for the sake of *not* putting everyone through the rigorous, expensive, emotional roller-coaster ride of a capital murder trial all over again, adding, "So Heather could be put to rest."

As his trial approached, Josh was conducting a bit of a life review, especially regarding all the time he spent with Heather. Hindsight is always 20/20, especially as a man is about to face a noose on his way to the gallows. He begins to look at things differently.

But Josh said he didn't care what people thought about him, how genuine anyone believed he was or wasn't about his remorse. He was truly sorry for the things he had done to Heather throughout their lives. The bad behavior and the way he had treated Heather—this, despite murdering her!—had been weighing on his soul. He wanted now to do what was best for her memory by admitting to killing her and accepting a death sentence.

"Like I have said, over and over, since my arrest, I am not proud of any of this stuff and how I treated Heather. . . ."

Josh felt the prosecutor had a "grand slam" (though he probably meant slam dunk) with his case, "*only* because of my confession, which was done out of remorse for Heather."

In his heart, Josh said, he believed Brad King would have never "challenged the case," had Detective Buie been unable to get that final confession from Josh.

"They would never get a conviction if I didn't give them a confession, because Emilia was damn sure never going to talk until she found out I had."

Josh said he realized Emilia was going to "always blame" him and there were people who would "feed into her bullshit . . . but this shit happened and we went to jail."

Because they did not take his plea deal, Josh said, he was now resigned to fight. Why not? What did he have to lose?

His life.

Because if a jury in the same county had given a mother of four the death penalty, Josh knew his days were numbered if (and when) he was found guilty. So the state, he claimed, gave him no choice but to fight the charges, which he was now preparing to do with one of the top death penalty defense lawyers in the state representing him.

CHAPTER 97

ON APRIL 4, 2012, one minute after 9:00 A.M., SA Brad King took to the courtroom floor to give his opening statement. Right out of the gate, King stated that the state's burden was to follow the indictment charging Josh with the crimes of murder in the first degree and kidnapping. King called that indictment a "road map" that the state was bound by law to navigate through. He couldn't deviate from it, even if he wanted. His witnesses, he said, numbering in the twenty-person range, would walk in and testify to those facts supporting the indictment. Quite surprisingly, King noted a few moments into his opening, "I can tell you that for certainty before we ever start . . . you will *not* see Emilia Carr get on that witness stand and testify. It will *not* happen from my side."

Brad King gave no reason why.

After that, King talked about what the jury would hear. He said his witnesses were regular people "like y'all." Each one would walk into the courtroom, sit down and explain what they knew about this case as it pertained to the indictment. The state's focus would be on facts and evidence. In this case, unlike Emilia's, King mentioned, there was plenty of DNA and forensic evidence, not to mention a complete confession tying the defendant to the murder. And for a prosecutor, those three items amounted to a hat trick, or triple play, on the way toward a win.

The extra weapon the SAO had were the audio recordings of interviews with the defendant and his co-conspirator. Those would tell a story, King promised: a story of how two people lured an innocent woman into a trailer with the *intention* of taking her life, strapped that woman to a chair, scolded her, called her names, hit her in the head with a flashlight—and all *before* murdering her by asphyxiation.

And then King delivered, same as he had during Emilia's trial, a bit of dialogue that summed up his case and, by placing the relationship (or love triangle) at the center, the SA put a perfect little bow around his indictment package: "Now, not only was this relationship kind of tumultuous in the sense of people moving from person to person over time . . . through the years between these two in particular, [it] was a *violent* relationship. And you're going to hear, I believe, that on January the sixth, [nearly] two weeks *after* they get married, Heather Strong makes a complaint to the sheriff's office, which causes Joshua Fulgham to be arrested and taken to jail."

For Heather, King said, that was the death knell, the tolling bells in Joshua's head that became the beginning of the end of her life.

A murder plan was born.

Josh sat, staring at this man he utterly and angrily despised, a prosecutor he hated with fanatical passion. Josh's head was cleanly shaven, smooth as a bowling ball, shiny as a set of military shoes. He was dressed nicely in slacks, a striped dress shirt and a dark-colored tie.

As King got into talking about those phone calls between Emilia and Josh, while Josh was in jail on those trumped-up threatening charges, Terry Lenamon, a lawyer who had behind him some 120 jury trials and was considered one of Florida's most respected and skilled defense attorneys, especially when the death penalty was involved, objected repeatedly. Lenamon claimed those conversations had been discussed during a pretrial motion and not yet made open fodder to talk about in the courtroom.

Circuit judge Brian Lambert, however, overruled each objection.

So King continued.

If there was one advantage Terry Lenamon, who had handled more than eighty first-degree murder cases heading into representing Josh, had over Candace Hawthorne, who had arguably been in the same position with Emilia, it was that there was no need to focus on trying to get Josh off. Lenamon knew Josh was going to be found guilty. Anybody in that courtroom who might have believed otherwise was kidding himself or herself. The evidence was beyond overwhelming here. What Lenamon could instead channel his focus on was the death penalty phase of this trial and make sure that he saved Josh's life—and that began within the guilt/innocence stage of the trial.

The one piece of conversation jurors would hear that was going to bury Josh came out of his own mouth to Emilia' ears: *"I should have killed that bitch when I had the chance."* It was as good as an eyewitness account of this murder, maybe better, considering what happened weeks after Josh made that statement.

With some words, you speak them, and they cannot be taken back. This was one of those instances.

After spending about thirty minutes going through the same case he had during Emilia's trial, Brad King pulled it all together with some rather chilling final remarks, reminding jurors why they were in this courtroom and had been chosen to hear this case.

"[Heather is] put in a chair. . . . She's duct-taped to [it], and Joshua Fulgham . . . leans on her, and Emilia Carr was behind her, suffocating her to death. Then a bag was taped over her head and . . . she was killed. And that during that"—King paused briefly, not because he was so good at generating emotion within his pleadings to the seven male, seven female jury (there were two alternates present), but because he felt every word he was speaking personally— "she begged them *not* to kill her."

The images King was able to conjure up were alarming and chilling. Everyone in the courtroom could picture this crime having taken place, Josh and Emilia as the designers and executors.

King finally called the idea of Emilia and Josh luring Heather into the trailer exactly what it was: the "*intent* to terrorize or do bodily harm."

CHAPTER 98

TERRY LENAMON BEGAN addressing jurors at 11:00 A.M., not long after Brad King finished. Lenamon, who had never faced off against King before in a courtroom, presented the look of the man he was: an imposing figure. Lenamon was tall and heavyset, balding and flashy. He wore expensive suits and had a look of utter (and quite genuine) seriousness written all over his face. His voice carried with it the experience Lenamon had earned and the respect the man deserved. Beyond law school, Lenamon had graduated from famed attorney Gerry Spence's Trial Lawyers College and had become somewhat of an expert at case preparation and mitigation investigation—two aspects of defending the indefensible that would come in handy here. If there was a lawyer appointed to defend those who could not afford a credible defense, Terry Lenamon was that attorney. Joshua Fulgham could not have *hired* better counsel, even if he had a million dollars to do so. Lenamon had been known to call the death penalty "heinous, atrocious and cruel." He was prepared to fight for Josh's life, no matter how difficult the path, simply because he did not believe the government had the right to choose when someone lived or died.

Married to a prosecutor, Lenamon was one of only a

handful of lawyers statewide that met the qualifications to accept capital work. How he ended up with Josh's case was nothing short of a lucky break for Josh. The original lawyer appointed to the case had some problems with the state bar association, so the state called on local Ocala attorney Tania Alavi, who had worked with Lenamon on cases. She called Lenamon and he became lead counsel.

Lenamon believed unfalteringly that the government shouldn't "be in the business of killing people." He saw the death penalty as extremely "problematic when dealing with issues of race and minorities, social economics and other factors" that don't allow everyone to have a fair shake. What would help Josh tremendously in his case was that Lenamon lived by a quote that celebrated trial attorney Clarence Darrow stated long ago: "The only real lawyers are trial lawyers—and trial lawyers try cases to juries."

Terry Lenamon understood that he needed to focus his opening on that jury—reach each juror not by trying to make him or her believe Josh was somebody he wasn't, but by using the truth to humanize Josh, a man who had said repeatedly that he was sorry for what he had done. However, Lenamon knew from his years of addressing juries in such cases that this part of the job was a hell of a lot easier said than done. Many jurors had made up their minds, Lenamon knew, by the time they sat down. His job was to try and reach those who hadn't yet judged Josh, and change the minds of those who had. If there was one lawyer who could do this, it was Lenamon, who, as a member of Casey Anthony's legal "dream team," successfully argued against the state seeking the death penalty in the most-hated-mother-in-America trial of the century, thus persuading the state of Florida to seek life against Anthony, accused (and acquitted) of murdering her daughter, Caylee.

There was part of this case Lenamon was certain of: "That we were going to lose. There was no way we would prevail" with a not guilty verdict. In realizing that, Lenamon and his co-counsel, Tania Alavi, could focus on what Lenamon called an "integrated defense," whereby saving Josh's life depended upon them "maintaining credibility" with the jury even after Josh was found guilty of first-degree murder. "And then we could begin to flow right into our second phase."

Same as Brad King's time, the judge indicated that Lenamon had an hour to address the jury. Thus, Josh's lawyer began with his focus on the word "tragedy." He called what had happened to Heather the culmination and end of several tragic lives colliding with one another, finally blowing up in February 2009, when "my client, Joshua Fulgham, participated in the killing of his wife. . . ."

With that one admission, this jury knew Lenamon's client was taking full responsibility for his part in the murder of Heather Strong. "Remorse," Lenamon said later, "plays an important part in convincing a jury to vote for life." Anytime you had a client that was remorseful, Lenamon added, "you highlight that right away."

There was going to be no argument here by the defense regarding who did what to whom, as far as Josh's role. Yet, as quickly as he got started down that familiar road of what happened inside the trailer, Lenamon threw a curve (thus beginning his argument against the death penalty). Lenamon stated how Josh had not brought Heather to that trailer to murder her. Rather, his *intent,* Lenamon said, seemingly with a proverbial index-finger wag, was to get Heather into that trailer and make her sign that piece of paper giving him custody of the children, solely because he "feared" she would take his kids back to Mississippi and he would never see them again.

Once they got inside that trailer, meaning Josh, Heather *and* Emilia, "things went really bad and things happened very quickly," Lenamon explained. One thing led to another and Heather wound up dead. It wasn't a plan. There was no *intent.* It was something that took place during the course of an argument. Lenamon also believed Emilia "rubbed" the fact that Heather had slept with James Acome (and how Heather and Ben had set Josh up) "in his face," which turned Josh into a raging lunatic and he snapped. Although he knew it was going to be a tough sell, this was an important element of Lenamon's fight to save Josh's life. Take away the intent to kill. Take away the idea of Josh planning this. Take away the notion that Josh was a monster, lurking in the shadows, waiting for the right time to kill his wife. Take it all away and you turn him into a man who allowed an inferno of rage to take over after his pregnant girlfriend fed the flames. If Lenamon was able to do that, Josh just might be able to walk away with a life sentence—or better, a second-degree murder verdict and twenty years.

Lenamon talked about 295 calls, by his count, made from the prison by Josh to Emilia, Heather and Josh's mother, Judy Chandler. But "only five" of them were important in the scope of the murder.

"What I would suggest is the one call [Brad King] claims that was of real importance is the call where there was a threat—'I should have killed'—because he's angry about what had happened, him getting stuck in jail," Lenamon explained to jurors. He said jurors would "hear him tell the police that he never did what Miss Strong claims he did." He said she "lied [about] him in this situation." And though Josh had admitted to "a murder [plan] and being a participant in this murder," he believed he was "wrongly put in jail."

Lenamon then argued that it was not Josh who killed Heather, actually committing this atrocious act of murder.

"It was Miss Carr who killed her!" he shouted. Josh's part in this crime, Lenamon added, amounted to what he believed was, at best, "second-degree murder."

Emilia had been willing to do "anything she could," Lenamon explained later, "to manipulate the situation. Look at that whole ménage à trois situation the three of them were involved in." That, right there, Lenamon believed, proved "how far Emilia was willing to go" to please Josh and gain control over the relationship.

To jurors, Lenamon then sketched out the love triangle, which, after Ben McCollum became involved, was now a square, with four people involved. And in this instance Josh's chronic jealousy, the defense attorney said, drove him to a place he had never been.

In describing how Emilia fit into all of this, Lenamon chose an easy-to-digest narrative: He talked about how Josh was "in a relationship with Emilia Carr"—that this particular relationship was "kind of . . . convenient for Josh." However, as far as Emilia was concerned, she truly was "head over heels for Josh." And Josh, knowing this, "is kind of *using* Emilia Carr . . . because he really is *in love* with Heather Strong. Unfortunately, what you'll see is Emilia really is *in love* with Josh Fulgham." Thus, she was "so *in love* that her motive to kill" overtook everything else.

Emilia had been convicted and sentenced to death—she was the perfect scapegoat for Josh to pin intent and premeditation on. If there was the slightest doubt in any juror's mind that Josh was cajoled and pushed into this murder, he was going to walk away with twenty years or a life sentence.

As he began to merge into a discussion centered on minimizing the intent-to-kill charge and premeditation, Lenamon pointed out what he found to be a simple fact: The grave Heather ended up in had not been dug beforehand. Josh hadn't gone out there in the days before and excavated a piece of land to put her in, because he didn't know he was going to be involved in killing her. And while he talked about the nonexistence of intent and premeditation, Lenamon brought Emilia into this part of his narrative, portraying her as the driving force behind the actual murder, the master-mind and chief executor as things got under way inside the trailer.

"At that moment, Emilia Carr comes into the trailer and . . . strikes [Heather] with a flashlight, knocking her down." Then, he explained, Josh grabbed "her and sits her in the chair and is telling her to 'quiet down, quiet down.'" But it was Emilia Carr, the lawyer insisted, who pulled "out this duct tape, which Josh didn't know [she had] . . . and Josh does help her duct-tape [Heather] to the chair." He concluded the thought by stating how in "that moment . . . it's going to be clear. . . . There's no *plan* to kill."

From there, Lenamon said, it was Emilia who began arguing with Heather, not Josh, as had been stated previously. He said Emilia screamed at Heather, accusing her of sleeping with James Acome. And she did this, Lenamon suggested, to antagonize Josh and get him worked up into a violent frenzy. The way Lenamon painted this picture, it was Emilia who became enraged first. A shadow of cold washed over her as she scolded Heather, who was unable to move. Emilia even went so far, Lenamon suggested, as to tell Josh not three days after he was in jail, Heather had sex with James Acome on the couch in their living room.

"And Josh loses it. . . . He says, 'I don't care, let it happen.' And Heather starts saying, backpedaling, 'Listen, I'm sorry. I'm sorry. I'll leave you alone.' And Emilia's saying, 'You said you were going to leave us alone before.'"

At this point, it's too late. Emilia had pointed a gun (Josh as a weapon) in Heather's direction and, with her finger on the trigger (bringing up James Acome and sex on the couch), pulled it—this as Josh was already in borderline volcanic rage, red-faced and furious, ready and willing to act on his anger.

The word Lenamon used was "betrayal." That was all Josh saw. All he thought about. Heather had continuously betrayed him: James, Ben, the marriage, getting him locked up. It was all too much. Josh couldn't take it anymore. He had to act.

"I'm not asking you to make moral judgments here, or whether he was right or wrong," Lenamon said softly, ratcheting it down a notch, hoping to appeal to the jury's collective sense of right and wrong. "I'm asking you to think what his state of mind was. . . ."

Josh didn't commit this murder, set it up, plan it or make it happen. What he did, Lenamon argued, was *allow* it to happen, once Emilia started the process, and then cleaned it up afterward. And that—the fact that he did not plan or have *intent*—was not enough to put this man on death row. It was second-degree murder.

Concluding, Lenamon made sure the jury knew Josh was a pill-popping addict. Once Josh found himself behind bars, realizing the totality of what he had done, he tried committing suicide. Thus, Lenamon painted an image of a broken and remorseful man sitting in front of jurors, asking them to believe he had no intention of killing his wife on that day in February. Beyond that, however, Lenamon had a bombshell piece of information to drop, and yet he chose to keep it for the testimony portion of his case and not talk about it during the opening.

CHAPTER 99

BEFORE GOING INTO court that next morning, Josh approached Lenamon. The defendant pulled his attorney aside for a chat. Josh had only heard about Lenamon's track record and celebrity status shortly before Lenamon came on board. Josh was still having trust issues, wondering if his case was in the best hands possible.

"You sold me out," Josh accused Lenamon.

"Josh . . . what are you talking about?"

Josh explained that when he got back to his cell after the opening statements the previous evening, several guards had chastised Lenamon for telling jurors that Josh was a killer. Why did he do that? Why admit Josh was a killer when he didn't have to? Josh was now worried the jury would only see guilt written on his face when they looked at him.

"The guards," Josh explained, "they told me to watch out for you. They're saying things about you, man."

"Just trust me, Josh," Lenamon said. "That's all I ask. Look, we're on the same page here."

From that moment forward, Lenamon said, "Josh trusted me completely and allowed me to do my job."

The first day of the trial was a mirror image of Emilia's. The state called the same set of witnesses to talk about an unfolding missing person case that had begun with a phone call from Misty Strong: Brenda Smith, James Acome, Misty, Beth Billings, Ben McCollum and several MCSO deputies, all of whom explained how Heather was there one day, working, going about her life, having trouble with Josh and then—*poof!*—she was gone the next. And the more everyone thought about the circumstances of Heather's life, Josh Fulgham came to mind as the person most responsible for her disappearance.

As Detective Donald Buie testified, the jury viewed a videotape of Josh's confession. It was a profound testament in the entirety of the honesty presented. Here was Josh, broken and obviously feeling the weight of what he had done, explaining to investigators how he and Emilia lured his wife into that trailer, ganged up on her and, after chastising and beating her, placed a bag over her head and suffocated the mother of two to death. Josh had described horrible, gruesome images.

The confession Josh gave backed up what Lenamon had told jurors during his opening. If one viewed this interview/confession objectively, Josh clearly told the story of Emilia being the hammer, Josh the one holding it, waiting for the right moment to strike. There was even an exchange between Josh and his mother, Judy Chandler, at the end of the interview that had been recorded. After Josh gave it all up to Buie, the detective allowed him to call home. The conversation depicted a confused man taking full responsibility of his actions.

"I need to talk to you, Momma," Josh said.

"You need a lawyer?"

"No, I don't need to talk to a lawyer, Momma. I'm guilty. . . . I done it, Momma. I didn't do it by myself. . . . I just got sick of it, Momma. I wanted my babies. I don't expect you to take that responsibility of raising them, either."

"What?"

Josh was crying. "I said I don't *expect* you to take that responsibility of *raising* them. I just wanted them, Momma.

That's the only reason I did it. It wasn't even that, Momma. . . . You know . . . I told you she was leaving and going to Mississippi and I had you draw that paper up for me, but she wasn't leaving, Momma. I lied to you. She wasn't going nowhere."

"What?"

"I *lied* to you. . . . But it ain't going to matter, Momma. They got evidence and everything else, so it don't matter. I did it. I needed to get it off of me."

"I love you."

"I know you do, Momma. But I'm sorry. You didn't raise me to do shit like that. It's not your fault. . . . I didn't do it alone. . . ."

That conversation was something Lenamon seized upon: Josh's constant and consistent tale of not being the aggressor, but the muscle, was key here. Yes, he took part in the murder, but it was Emilia right there by his side, egging him on, facilitating it all. And now Josh was remorseful; he was sorry for what he had done.

As murder trials go, this one was brief—just a few days of testimony and both sides indicated they were done. Each witness had testified almost identically in both trials. There were no bombshells or surprises. Josh did not take the stand. Emilia wasn't called. The facts were presented, and each lawyer relied on his and her opening and closing remarks to send whatever message was necessary to jurors.

Once again, Rock Hooker delivered the closing for the state—a true masterpiece of composed style and elegance of presenting facts. Hooker began by stating one simplistic, utterly chilling detail that could not be denied or impeached: "He buried his wife in his pregnant girlfriend's backyard."

That one line painted Josh as a cold, callous killer, getting rid of a problem in the most horrendous way imaginable. One could almost hear the jurors thinking, as anybody in the gallery probably was, too: *Why not just divorce her and move on? Why did you have to* kill *her?*

Hooker, a true expert at taking the words of a defendant and using them against him in the most effective ways, quoted Josh from one of his confessions: "'I was still sitting on her and I could feel her getting weak and then she was gone.'"

The guy was talking about the mother of his children.

Hooker then focused on making sure the jurors were not persuaded by carefully chosen words, catchy turns of phrase or the twisting of the truth. The job they had in front of them was to "determine the facts," Hooker restated plainly.

Nothing more.

Nothing less.

Look at the facts.

And those facts, Hooker added, "have been proven beyond a reasonable doubt."

Quite heartfelt and emotional, Hooker reminded jurors why the trial was taking place to begin with: "Let me be clear, we're here because Heather Strong is dead and because she was murdered and buried in Emilia Carr's backyard. *That* is why we are here."

The one thing Hooker and King had relied on during both trials was the jury's intellect and common sense. In murder trials especially, juries share a common bond, an intense connection translating into them taking their jobs, collectively, very seriously. It's one of the reasons why each individual is chosen during that rigorous, often tedious voir dire process. It was that line of thought that Hooker tapped into when he said, "One thing the judge is going to tell you, and sometimes jurors chuckle when they hear this . . . the judge is going to tell you . . . that you're allowed to *use* your common sense."

Hooker pointed out that Josh, same as Emilia, had lied more often than not. Yet, there were certain fleeting moments within those lies for Josh that remained constant. When he finally admitted to the murder, he went back and corrected the record where he needed to.

The special prosecutor then went through a timeline of the case, before bringing up a PowerPoint presentation to explain the differences between first-degree and second-degree murder, and how Josh's case fit into the first-degree column. He talked about the "two ways in which a person may be convicted of murder in the first degree," saying one was "premeditated murder" and the other "felony murder."

"Heather Strong is dead. . . . There is a written agreement that the body found in the hole is actually Heather Strong . . . so that's proven. The second one was that the death was caused by a criminal act of Joshua Fulgham, or Heather Strong was killed by a person other than Joshua Fulgham, but both Joshua Fulgham and the person who killed Heather Strong were principals in the commission of first-degree premeditated murder."

Hooker explained what he meant: "Killing with premeditation is killing after consciously deciding to do so. Decision must be present in the mind at the time of the killing."

Simple logic: *I am going to kill you.*

The premeditation could take place seconds before the murder.

"The law does not affix the exact period of time that must pass between the formation of the premeditated intent to kill and the killing . . . ," Hooker made clear. "But it must be long enough to allow reflection by the defendant."

The other part, he explained, involved committing a felony in the due course of committing a murder. In this case, Hooker told jurors, "Heather Strong is dead. The death occurred as a consequence of and while Joshua Fulgham was engaged in the commission of kidnapping."

When placed into the context of such an honest, straightforward argument, well presented by a seasoned prosecutor, these charges seemed to fit Josh's case as though he'd written them himself.

Of particular interest, Hooker explained, was the fact that although Josh's case met the "elements of second-degree murder," it did not mean the state had not proven first-degree murder, too. When one looked at the evidence of Josh and Emilia talking on the phone, effectively planning and plotting to murder Heather, and then understood how the crime was carried out—lying to her and luring her into that trailer—one could only draw the conclusion (legally) that a first-degree murder had been committed.

"These people, they talked, they talked, and then they talked and then they *did* it. They did it. They *killed* her."

Hooker pointed jurors in the direction of that one call where Josh and Emilia discussed the woods in the back of her mother's house, the trailer and if Emilia's neighbor could see back there. He read from a transcript of the call.

Hearing this, jurors had to feel as though these two had been planning and plotting to murder Heather for weeks.

Concluding, Hooker asked jurors to recall that it was only nine days after Josh was released from jail that Heather wound up dead and buried in the backyard of Emilia's mother's house.

If there could be one criticism lodged against Hooker's closing, it was that it might have gone on a tad too long. He took the hour allotted to him. He didn't need it. His points were made concisely within the first fifteen minutes. By going long, a lawyer runs the risk of overselling. Hooker had stated some of the state's facts several times and jurors were clearly moved by a lot of what he had to say, but was it all enough to convince more than half of them that the state had proven first-degree murder?

CHAPTER 100

TERRY LENAMON LEFT the responsibility of closing the defense's case up to his more-than-qualified co-counsel, Tania Alavi, a strikingly attractive, dark-haired Ocala graduate from the University of Florida (1987), where she earned a Bachelor of Arts degree in criminal justice before going on to that same university's Levin College of Law, in 1991. Alavi had been involved in several death penalty cases on various levels. She had been recommended in 2010 for a judge's seat. Fundamentally, Alavi specialized in and understood family and federal law, both of which would help her here. Lenamon and Alavi made the perfect one-two punch working Josh's corner, because what Josh's case came down to—unlike many other capital murder trials (including Emilia's) where testimony was the more relevant issue at hand and general access to a verdict—was a shoot-out between lawyers. Josh was guilty—a fact they had decided and recognized going in. The question was, however: guilty of what?

As Alavi looked at her notes one last time before delivering her first closing thought, Lenamon looked around the courtroom and noticed several people in the gallery he hadn't seen before.

"It was kind of disheartening that [Brad King] had some people from his church"—which, Lenamon said, is one of those Bible Belt, conservative group of Christians, pro-death penalty—"sitting in the courtroom. You know, when something like that happens, you just shake your head and think, 'Oh, my, what's up with that?'"

Slim, tall and elegant, Tania Alavi had a soothing grace about the way she spoke and presented herself. It was clear that Alavi had thought long and hard about what to say, how to shape it into a narrative and what her focus should be. She had abandoned her original opening words, she said off the bat, because of how Rock Hooker had closed. Hooker had mentioned "conduct," Alavi told jurors as she began. But in providing jurors with an excerpt of an interview detectives conducted with Josh, Hooker had not allowed them to hear the entire context of what had been said. Effectively, Hooker had left some rather important words out of the excerpt, Alavi argued. And it was those *words,* Alavi said, that gave insight into who was the mastermind behind this crime and who had actually started this talk about luring Heather into the trailer.

Alavi quoted Josh from the interview as he talked about Emilia. Josh had said, "She told me right then, 'Josh, bring her back here later tonight. . . . We'll get rid of her.'" Alavi then explained how Josh and Emilia were "having a conversation" and Josh was telling her: "I'm getting back together with Heather. You need to get your stuff and get out of the house. . . ." Then she quoted Josh again from his final confession, which the state had acknowledged was the one uncontestable source in this case that they relied on. Josh said: "And right then, she came to me and she told me, 'Josh, bring her back here later tonight. Bring her back here late tonight. We'll get rid of her.' I said, 'Emilia, get out. Get your shit and get out. [Heather and I are] going to be together,' and she said, '*We're* going to be together. Bring her back here tonight and we'll do it.'"

From where Alavi viewed things, this was one of the most

important moments of the case for the defense: Long before Josh went to jail, back when Josh had left Emilia and moved back in with Heather, shortly before Heather and Josh were married, Emilia had fired up—within Josh's head—this idea of killing Heather.

The date was important, Alavi argued, because that conversation between Emilia and Josh had taken place long before February 15—a date, Alavi stated, that Rock Hooker had failed to clarify with jurors during his closing. "That was a conversation where Emilia was telling Josh in *December of 2008,* while she didn't get her stuff out of the house" that he was going back to Heather.

Quite smartly, Alavi used that theme of "words," which she'd started with, to get across several additional ideas relevant to the premise that there was one person—one mastermind behind this crime.

Emilia Lily Carr.

The one bell Alavi needed to stop ringing in jurors' ears was that *"I should have killed that bitch"* statement Josh had made to Emilia over the phone. That was fairly devastating to an argument of *"I just went along with Emilia."* It was something that needed to be addressed head-on—one of those statements jurors would retire to deliberations and focus on.

"There is a lot of smack talk going on between all of these people," Alavi explained, referring to the timeline wherein the statement had been made. She then mentioned how Emilia had even put a knife to Heather's neck, threatening her, yet Heather and Emilia had remained friends after that and saw each other on several occasions. In other words, don't take what the defendant said over the phone as gospel, or as some sort of sinister, well-thought-out plot, when all of the people in that circle talked "smack" in the same fashion, all the time.

Next Alavi talked about what she called a "diamond"

relationship—Ben, James, James's friend, Heather, Emilia and Josh each having his or her point on that diamond, all involved in a round-and-round association that was constantly in motion during this period in question.

"Now, what we also know [about] all these people [is that] Emilia's having sex," Alavi said, "with [James Acome], who is having sex with Heather also. She's having sex with Josh. She's been with Ben McCollum [and] you heard testimony that Emilia and Heather are even engaging in sexual activity together, having threesomes with either [another man] or with Josh."

It was one giant, convoluted, trashy mess of dysfunction. It was not your "typical" friendships and romantic relationships.

Josh's drug use came up next. Alavi talked about it at length, letting jurors know he was addicted to all sorts of pills and meth. Concluding that thought, she said: "And as jurors, you have to evaluate this case and the facts of this case in the *context* of where we are and who we are dealing with. Because these people, who, quite frankly, are leading dysfunctional lives, do *not* lead their lives the way the majority of people do."

It was a valid point in the scope of this case. Yet, most people did not commit ruthless murders, either.

From there, Alavi talked about how Josh and Heather and Emilia moved in and out of various trailers and houses; and Heather finally wound up with Ben McCollum, and Josh with Emilia. The idea that when Josh wasn't allowed bond after his first court appearance—at the time when he got on the phone with Emilia and said, "I should have killed that bitch"—wasn't evidence of premeditation, Alavi argued. Not at all. It was Josh thinking out loud, referring to how Heather had made up the charge that put him in jail to begin with. He felt tricked and ridiculed. Totally betrayed. He said those words out of anger, something he had said to Heather likely many times during arguments they'd had throughout their life together: *"I'll kill you, bitch."*

"Is that evidence?" Alvi asked, referring to the context in which she had placed Josh's comment. It sounded convincing, the way Alavi put it.

Only problem jurors might have with it was that Heather actually wound up dead this time. There was no changing that outcome.

One unequivocal fact, however, which had been backed up by testimony, was that Emilia solicited James Acome and his friend one day, dangling between five hundred and seven hundred dollars in front of them, hoping to lure Heather to a place so she could "snap her neck"—and she did that all on her own, without Josh.

During those nine days when Josh was out of jail, before Heather was murdered, Alavi told jurors, Josh had plenty of "nonconfrontational" contact with Heather. He had even brought over a packet of divorce papers for Heather to look at and sign. He saw James Acome driving his car one day, Alavi explained, and didn't confront him and become violent, but Josh, instead, called the cops and got his car back.

Was that the behavior of a man planning a murder?

Alavi didn't think so.

Throughout that entire time, Alavi speculated, Josh was likely thinking he was going to wind up with Heather in the end because that was how it always had turned out in the past. He was used to breaking up with her and getting back together. What made this breakup so different in that respect?

"[Detective] Buie even said himself during the course of the investigation," Alavi said, "it's one of the things he found out independently is that they *always* got back together."

The entire reason why Josh lured Heather to that trailer was to make her sign over custody of their kids because he feared she was preparing to take off for good. That was his only purpose. Yes, he might have been aggressive with her and spoke angrily; but his *intent* was never to kill her. That "idea" Josh had mentioned to Emilia over the phone: It was to get her into the trailer and make her sign that paper. The murder was all on Emilia—because Emilia knew, if nothing else, that Josh would one day wind up with Heather again. And what would she do then? She was pregnant with his child.

Alavi read from transcripts of the interviews Emilia gave and continuously put the onus of the plot and plan to murder Heather on Emilia, using her own words as ammo. It was a smart move. Some of the evidence backed up what Alavi argued.

As far as that dialogue between them on the phone about the wooded area around the trailer, who owned the land and if the neighbor could see the trailer from his house, Alavi clarified that by saying, "Remember . . . they *didn't* need to have this conversation when he went back to dig the hole. But what *was* the conversation? 'Where are we going to put her?'" Alavi paused, allowing jurors to think back for a moment to that jailhouse telephone call. Then she answered her own question, quite effectively: "Well, I thought that was already planned? Apparently not. The conversation is 'Where are we going to put her? The railroad tracks? Some cave?' He couldn't even get the door open and ended up putting her steps away from the trailer."

Alavi talked about the instructions jurors would be given by the judge and how they needed to follow the law, despite how they *felt* about the case. The main point she wanted to get across here was to remind jurors that they needed to figure out what Josh was thinking *before* the murder and what Josh *knew* before the murder?

Everything else, essentially, was conjecture.

"If you're thinking about [lots of] things and that is causing you to go back and forth in the slightest bit, they have not proven their case beyond reasonable doubt."

After about thirty minutes, Alavi indicated she was done. Confident she had said enough to raise concerns where first-degree murder was concerned, Alavi sat down.

Terry Lenamon looked over at his co-counsel and smiled respectfully. Lenamon realized he was working with one the best defense lawyers he had ever had the opportunity to share a courtroom with.

"She is incredible," Lenamon said later. "It was an honor to work with Tania."

Both sides presented rebuttals, which came across as a "he said/she said" type of playground argument between two kids. What became confusing during this portion of the closings was which interviews each attorney had been referring to. According to Josh's attorneys, there was only one interview jurors should take into account during deliberations: the final interview Josh gave to Buie when he admitted everything. All of those interviews that came before were a mixed bag of truths and lies.

Disregard.

Nonetheless, both sides finished by the end of the day and the judge gave the case to the jury, this after reading what were long-winded legal instructions both sides had been referring to during their closings.

CHAPTER 101

THE JURY WASN'T swayed by the defense's argument that Josh didn't know Heather was going to die when he lured her into that trailer. Within a few hours, Joshua Fulgham was found guilty of first-degree murder and kidnapping—the worst possible outcome for Josh at this stage of his trial.

Josh sat stunned. In a way, he, himself, had started to believe the defense's argument that Emilia planned the murder and he had just gone along for the ride as an innocent bystander. Yet, for the jury, it came down to those tapes of the prison calls and Josh's voice, so convincing and layered with anger: *"I should have killed that bitch. . . ."* You listen to Josh talk about a "plan" he had when he got out, one he didn't want to speak to Emilia about over the prison phone, and it is clear that he was not talking about scaring Heather or convincing her to sign a damn piece of paper turning over custody of the children to him.

"I knew this going in," Lenamon told me. "We pretty much decided that it was going to be fairly easy to prove intent, with all the evidence of Josh and Emilia talking. We knew this was going to be tough because of the way Heather was murdered. Anytime you have 'heinous, atrocious and cruel' as an aggravating factor, when the victim is clearly suffering and there is pending knowledge that death is coming, that's a huge, *huge* problem for a defense."

Although the ultimate punishment would rest in the hands of Judge Brian Lambert, the lawyers geared up to argue their cases for life and death in front of the jury during the penalty phase: Would the jury recommend, like it had in Emilia's case, death? Betting men would have probably put all of their money in favor of death in Josh's case. After Emilia's sentence, there likely wasn't anybody in that room—save for Josh's attorneys—who believed the jury would recommend any other sentence.

What the defense had going for it, however, was that the jury supposedly didn't know what Emilia's sentence had been. Both sides had gone through a long question-and-answer process—voir dire—with prospective jurors. So the jury was now going to hear Josh's argument for life without knowing that his co-conspirator was, at that time, sitting on death row.

Lenamon thought about it as the day closed and he began to process how he and Alavi would go about arguing for Josh's life.

His first thought was: *In the state's case, Josh was obviously the villain.*

The bad guy.

A walking volcano of rage that erupted inside that trailer.

"Betrayal," Lenamon said later, describing what was his second thought. "We focused on the idea that Josh was betrayed"—that and the notion of Josh not having the mental capacity, Lenamon further explained, to deal with said betrayal.

How, though, could Lenamon and Alavi turn a villain into a victim?

CHAPTER 102

APRIL 11, 2012, on this day, Josh was shuffled out of the courtroom after both sides finished delivering opening statements in the penalty phase of the *State of Florida* v. *Joshua Fulgham*. By now, the jury had to be rather exhausted from hearing lawyers talk. After all, they had just sat and heard closings from the lawyers during the guilt/innocent phase and here they were doing it all over again, just days later.

As they were making their way to the door, the bailiff said something to Josh regarding him mumbling under his breath. The bailiff wanted to know what, exactly, Josh had said.

"I said, 'If I get the death penalty out of this, I am going to kill you!'"

On April 12, the following morning, before the day's witnesses were summoned to testify, the judge asked Brad King—who had said he wasn't shocked by the statement when he later heard about it, calling the behavior "nothing new" from Josh—if he wanted Josh shackled for the remainder of the proceedings.

Before King could even answer, however, Judge Lambert said he wasn't so much in favor of doing it and would be hesitant to allow it, "absent" any serious "concern" from King's side.

"I'm fine," King said, looking over at Josh, who was calm and stoic.

"Okay," Judge Lambert said.

"I mean, I would hope that they're shaking him down before they let him come into the courtroom. . . ."

"Yes," Lambert verified.

Lenamon said he would speak to Josh about the incident, but this was an "emotional proceeding" and things might be taken out of context and blown out of proportion. The stakes were high. With regard to Josh actually saying what the bailiff had claimed, Lenamon offered, "Judge, for the record, [Josh] did not remember saying that."

All was forgotten and the penalty phase moved forward. As testimony got under way, Lenamon and Alavi called Josh's mother, Judy Chandler. Judy was tired and upset. She sat down and talked about a son suffering many traumas throughout his childhood; he then became a boy who caused her problems after he adopted a drug habit that spun out of control as quick as it got started. Throughout all of that, Judy said, Josh met the love of his life, Heather Strong, when they were just teenagers. From there, Josh's life got serious.

Babies.

Very little work—and no money.

Drugs.

More drugs.

Constant fighting with Heather.

Then a move to Florida.

As Judy talked about her own life, the jury was given some background and context into what was a dysfunctional cycle Josh had grown up in and then continued himself as he became a father. Judy had her own stories to tell of a fractured time living in Mississippi, a broken and wired jaw courtesy of an ex-spouse, along with many beatings that Josh, who had never really known his real father until he was an adult, had witnessed.

Judy's testimony was the perfect setup for the defense's

next witness, Dr. Heather Holmes, a clinical and forensic psychologist out of Miami. Holmes, who was about to drop a bombshell that many never saw coming, had done an extensive investigation into Josh's life.

"Truth," Lenamon said later. "That was what Gerry Spence taught me. You speak your truth in a court of law—always."

Alavi and Lenamon needed to convince the jury that Josh did not deserve death; his crimes were committed due to a lack of nurturing he had received as a child and his below-average intelligence, all of which were part of a foundation built on some rather shocking abuse allegations that emerged during that character and personal study Heather Holmes had launched into Josh's life.

Under questioning by Alavi, Holmes listed an impressive and vast list of credentials, before talking specifically about her expertise in forensics, "particularly intelligence testing," among many other subcategories within the forensic psychology fields.

Brad King listened closely as Holmes talked about her extensive experience testifying in death penalty cases—this as the words "mental retardation" kept coming up. One had to wonder while listening what Lenamon and Alavi had up their sleeve with this type of expert testifying on the stand? What claim were they planning to make? Holmes had some knowledge in dealing with "mentally retarded" adults and children, sure, but what did it have to do with Josh?

Holmes said she met with Josh on three separate occasions. Maybe more important than those meetings and interviews, however, Holmes had reviewed all of the notes in the case from, among several experts, a mitigation specialist Lenamon had hired. All of the specialists working for Lenamon had interviewed scores of people connected to Josh throughout his entire life. They had written a detailed, sweeping report, and Dr. Holmes said she spent long hours reviewing it. She also studied a report written by a neuropsychologist and a second report scribed by Dr. Steven Gold, a post-traumatic stress disorder (PTSD) specialist, each of whom had also been hired by Lenamon to interview and meet with Josh on several occasions.

The questioning then turned to whether Dr. Holmes had looked at any research related to Emilia Carr. Emilia's personal story was important to Josh's case. Lenamon and Alavi had to convince jurors that Emilia was much smarter than Josh, whom they painted as an uneducated "country boy," as Lenamon called him—a guy who had been totally taken in by her constant badgering and that "I'll take care of everything, you just leave it to me" talk during those prison calls.

In studying Emilia Carr, Dr. Holmes said, she focused on Emilia's IQ test scores. Emilia was certainly more intelligent than Josh, based on those test scores, but she was also smarter than the average person. In effect, Emilia came across as a rocket scientist compared to Josh, who had the intellect, many claimed, of a young adult.

A plan by the defense was obviously coming together: The supersmart woman had taken advantage of the stupid Neanderthal Southern boy/man, who would kill his own wife on demand, if plied with enough promises and sex, and was then pushed hard enough.

But there was more—plenty more.

Holmes said she had interviewed Judy, too. And that interview had opened up an entire new vein in Josh's childhood he hadn't talked about, giving the doctor some insight into why Josh had turned out the way he had.

Alavi asked if Holmes had come to any conclusion after that interview with Judy.

"Yes," the well-respected doctor testified. "I believe Josh suffers from post-traumatic stress disorder."

Holmes talked in general terms for a moment about people suffering from PTSD, mentioning Vietnam vets coming back from the war after experiencing "life-threatening" conditions abroad for a prolonged period of time. The other part of it, Holmes added, was how PTSD patients talked about witnessing "difficult things," having a front-row seat to violence, killing and abuse of all types—in a vet's case, torture and killing and those violent battlefield actions were on top of the list.

"How is it that you went about arriving at the conclusion that Josh suffers from [PTSD]?" Tania Alavi asked the doctor.

"It was based on the interviews, symptoms that he reported," she stated. But also "evaluations of the doctors who had—one of them who has a very specific specialty in this area."

"You talked about one of the ways you arrived at that conclusion was based on the *extreme* amount of trauma he suffered," Alavi asked. She took a moment. The attorney allowed the doctor to consider the first part of the question, and then she dropped that missile nobody saw coming: "Did that include *sexual* abuse?"

"The sexual abuse was *extreme,*" Holmes said slowly, bringing this up for the first time in the trial. "It. Was. *Significant.*"

They discussed various types of sexual abuse and how some forms of abuse can be "more significant" than other types, especially where long-term trauma had been studied.

This had come out of left field: Not once during his interviews with police, during the testimony portion of his trial or when speaking with Emilia (or me), had Josh ever mentioned being the victim of sexual abuse as a child. This revelation emerged during the investigation Dr. Holmes had undertaken. And when she explained the type of sexual abuse Josh had allegedly endured, it might explain why he would want to keep it hidden.

For Lenamon and Alavi, the sexual abuse Josh had supposedly suffered was now the focal point of their case. It was the main artery feeding all of Josh's later behaviors and psychological problems. The doctor said that because of the sexual trauma Josh had undergone as a young child, he'd had trouble all his life with sexual boundaries, in particular. It was the reason why he had become so enraged when Heather crossed those so-called boundaries and admittedly slept with James Acome just days after Josh had gone to jail.

"I mean, clearly they run the gamut," Holmes testified, referring to the various "types" of sexual abuse and how a victim can be affected. "You can be exposed to somebody who is an exhibitionist. It can go from a noncontact offense, such as viewing child pornography. It could go all the way up into penetration, intercourse, incest, repeated exposure. The extreme depends upon the actual age of the victim."

The key question in Josh's case, as in any case with such similarities, Holmes mentioned, was this: Did the abuse occur "before development of sexual identity or awareness of either what sex is"? In other words, did Josh understand sex before he was abused? If the abuse had been his *first experience with sex,* either as an act or hearing about it, his brain would have been wired totally different as it pertained to sex of any type.

"I believe it began between the ages of six and seven," Holmes testified, speaking of Josh's case and how, for Josh, it appeared to be doubly traumatic. "That . . . can be *very* damaging. The longer it goes on, the more frequently it occurs. . . ."

This was the type of expert testimony—as graphic as it would get, as they talked about the actual abuse—that had not been presented in Emilia's death penalty phase. For Lenamon and Alavi, they believed it would make the difference for Josh. The sexual abuse, Lenamon explained, was the driving force behind Josh's entire problem with females, especially his wife. Add physical abuse at home into that, sprinkle on a bit of Josh witnessing violence routinely—and there you have it: the perfect wiring for a future violent offender.

"What *about* the effects of that on Josh?" Alavi pressed Holmes. "Did you form any opinions about that?"

"Yes, I did. . . . He has a lot of difficulty with sexual boundaries, which is very common for somebody who's been abused. And he has a *lot* of difficulty in relationships with women. . . ."

According to these experts, the mind did not always work in mysterious ways, but pretty much in a direct manner: A kid is sexually abused early in childhood; then his or her entire sexual identity and understanding of sex becomes poisoned and unhealthy as it unwinds throughout his or her life. The wiring is crossed early on and, if not treated immediately and properly by a professional, will then dictate (and feed) who that person becomes later on, particularly as they begin to have romantic relationships.

Holmes went on to say she had corroborated the abuse with independent sources and interviews. So this was not Josh's word against everyone else's, or Josh coming up with an eleventh-hour surprise personal admission to try and save his life. For all intents and purposes, Josh had tried to hide this for as long as he could.

As Josh grew up, not knowing his real father, living in a household where, Judy herself had testified, abuse was a regular part of life, Josh had never learned what healthy relationships were. Throughout his adult life, Josh suffered from PTSD as a symptom of his childhood. He couldn't escape it. In addition, being a male, he did not want to address it in any way or share what happened with anyone because he believed that help in that manner showed weakness and took away from any masculinity he thought he had left.

Summing up her findings, Holmes said at one point, "You're talking sexual abuse, witnessing severe domestic violence, undergoing physical abuse, as well as, you know, exposure to *very* difficult things . . . witnessing other tragedies. It becomes more complex and it also becomes more infiltrating in how it affects your life because it's coming from various different locations."

Witnessing abuse, hearing about it or projecting inside his own head that it might happen to someone he knew (especially one of his own kids) became a trigger for Josh as he grew older. The idea that Josh believed there might be an abuser in his house near his kids (he presumed this about James Acome), or that Heather was going to take the kids back to Mississippi, where there might be a second abuser, was all too much for Josh's violated, childish, strained mind to handle. He did not know how to deal with this information or how to react to it. That internalized anger Josh had projected at his abusers all his life—explosive and ready to blow, pent up all those years—would run the risk of bursting. So when the opportunity presented itself that Josh could fix the problem by getting rid of its source (Heather), he seized upon that end and acted on impulse. Having Emilia there as chief instigator, pushing him along, just made it all that much easier for Josh to effectively snap and kill Heather in order to quash all the pain from childhood reemerging and retraumatizing him. The murder became a release.

"When you witness extreme domestic violence," Holmes told jurors, "and clearly [Mr. Fulgham's] mother testified she had her jaw broken and wired shut. . . . [And] when it starts becoming . . . a part of your daily life, you don't feel safe in the home." He dredged up the old cliché that it was akin to "walking on eggshells," adding that exposure "to extreme amounts of trauma, whether you're experiencing it or witnessing it as a child," research proved in case after case, "the effects" were detrimental on a child's "developing brain."

From the way Holmes described Josh's childhood, the

kid didn't have a chance of growing into a healthy adult or a productive member of society.

After being prompted, Holmes explained exactly what type of sexual abuse Josh had endured: "[His abuser, a female, would] . . . provide him with cigarettes and ask him to perform oral sex on her. He recalls her pressing his head down there and feeling very, *very* claustrophobic."

As the testimony continued, Holmes described a young man who, basically, would not and could never be normal. Over time, Josh even developed an internal problem with women in general. And as soon as Josh was old enough and strong enough to control females himself, he found he had no choice in the matter but to lash out and commit acts of violence against those females who crossed him in any way. As that narrative played out in his life with Heather, Emilia Carr came along, a woman with above-average intelligence—and the puppet had now met his puppet master. Holmes said Josh's IQ tests showed him scoring in the neighborhood of 80, thus putting a 40-plus-point difference between him and Emilia.

"Anything below seventy," Holmes clarified, putting Josh into an intellectual context, "is considered mental retardation."

The doctor then suggested that because Josh had been in a sexual relationship between the ages of six and twelve—which was, in reality, abuse—he was stuck there, emotionally and educationally. And because of this, Holmes reiterated, when he met Emilia and she began to manipulate him with what Josh himself described as "the best sex of his life," taking total control in the bedroom, well, Emilia had hit on the core weakness within Josh emotionally—one she was able to exploit any way she wanted.

It was a solid, well-studied, well-researched argument.

Brad King did not have much in the form of cross-examination for Dr. Holmes. He focused on the idea that

Josh's substance abuse and his personality disorders did not excuse first-degree murder.

Josh wasn't "mentally retarded," King seemed to get across under cross-examination questioning, as had been suggested by the defense. It was ridiculous and the absolute wrong message to share with jurors.

Beyond that, King argued the validity of the testing done of Emilia, trying to say she was not as smart as the doctor had assessed. Moreover, there had been testing done on Josh while he was in juvenile detention long ago and very little of it backed up Holmes's findings. In fact, Josh had never mentioned being sexually abused.

Over and over, Lenamon objected, hammering home one core issue, like any good defense attorney should: There were no grounds for King to be making such accusations as challenging the doctor's study and research. A lot of it was objective evidence, clinical.

Unimpeachable.

The objections alone wore Brad King down.

In the end, Dr. Heather Holmes presented a compelling argument that she was not about to back down from, no matter what Brad King tossed at her. King would have to bring in his own experts to criticize her work—which he wasn't prepared to do, of course.

During closing arguments a day later, the state contended the opposite of what Lenamon and Alavi had sold so well during the defense's penalty phase case. King and company told jurors not to be fooled by a carefully constructed defense narrative. The truth was, Joshua Fulgham actually had manipulated Emilia *and* Heather—and he did it solely because he wanted money to bail himself out of jail and hire a good lawyer. Josh made this clear, Hooker and King both said at times, not only during many of those prison calls to Emilia and Heather, but also when he spoke to his mother, Judy Chandler.

"'I'm gonna kiss Emilia's ass to get that money,'" the state quoted Josh as saying during one call to Judy. The money in question was Emilia's tax return. "'I need help. I need to work. I need to see my babies. I just got to get out.'"

Lenamon and Alavi staunchly objected to the admissibility of several recorded conversations before and after they were played by the state. The exchange between the lawyers was a bit emotional and nasty as they argued about it for more than an hour.

The main thrust of Lenamon and Alavi's objection during the state's closing was that Brad King and the state could not have it both ways. King could not argue *now* that Josh had manipulated Emilia when, during Emilia's trial, King had argued the exact opposite—that it was Emilia who manipulated Josh.

The state's positions in both trials contradicted each other. Lenamon would not stand by and allow King to do this.

The objections and counterarguments by King went nowhere. The jury, of course, could not *un*hear something it had heard from the SA, and Lenamon knew that.

Nonetheless, King finished his closing by telling jurors not to believe Josh Fulgham, an admitted murderer and liar.

Lenamon stuck to the same theme he had during the entire penalty phase: Josh had admitted guilt; he was remorseful; he only wanted the jury to understand that he was not in control of himself during those moments of terror for Heather inside that trailer because he had been severely abused and did not know how to handle rejection, betrayal or jealousy.

"That man there," Lenamon said, pointing to Josh, who sat with a glaze of demoralization on his face, staring straight ahead, with a look of abstract nothingness about him, "he *deserves* to die in prison."

It was a bold statement made by a seasoned defense attorney, and Lenamon let it hang in the courtroom for a brief period. He wanted jurors to take it in. He knew that in giving the jury "an out," a way to feel good about sentencing Josh to life, each juror could walk away satisfied that justice had been entirely served.

Concluding, Lenamon projected his ideal outcome to jurors: "He's going to die in prison, as opposed to being *killed* by the state of Florida."

Would everything Terry Lenamon and Tania Alavi had done, however, be enough to save Josh Fulgham's life?

CHAPTER 103

JOSH TOLD ME that the sexual abuse argument presented by his lawyers during the penalty phase was a total fabrication made up by someone in his extended family.

When me and my cousin were young, Josh wrote to me in a final letter between us, *we experimented and tryed [*sic*] some sexual things.*

That same cousin, Josh went on to proclaim, got into some trouble one day when she was young: *[She] took that little bullshit we were doing and made it out that [someone else in our family] was doing shit to us.*

Regarding his cousin, she wrote: *[She] lived that lye [*sic*] for so long and used it as a crutch for her fuck-ups and she has now convinced herself that it really all did happen.*

He never wanted any of it to "come up" during his trial, but his cousin had his "defense team convinced."

It was here, in that same letter, where I experienced the flip side of Joshua Fulgham: an explosive, angry man who could turn on a dime. Josh said he didn't "want any of it to come up" in this book, as if he had some sort of control over the content of my writing.

The sexual abuse allegation is beyond Josh's control. It was part of Josh's trial—a major argument on the part of his defense team. For him to now come forward and claim it was nonsense is noble and honest, but it doesn't change the outcome of what happened to Josh during the penalty phase of his case.

Further, Josh took the moment to show me that part of him I knew was always there, simmering underneath all his previous letters, just waiting to burst. In all of our correspondence, Josh had been rather cordial and open. He told me things that, after I researched, I found to be honest answers to my questions. I had promised Josh that I would tell his story how it was told to me by him; but, of course, I would also use the record and conduct my own interviews and investigation into the factual side of this story as uncovered by law enforcement. In my view, when a jury convicts, the record becomes "fact." I have found that most juries and investigating law enforcement agencies display integrity and conduct honest investigations for the greater good of the case. In that respect, I found nothing out of whack here in either Emilia's or Josh's cases. The truth is funny that way: As you wade through the research later, after all is said and done, an ultimate reality rises to the surface without much effort, and that truth becomes utterly and indelibly obvious—as long as you're willing to *accept* it.

Getting back to that last letter from Josh, he wrote about a "feeling" he'd had, whereby I had "trashed" him in my book "so bad that it really doesn't matter."

What proved to me then that there was another side of Josh was how he attacked Heather and her family in an extended rant. Up on his soapbox, Josh wrote, *[The] local media made it look like Heather was a loving caring mother and just left a PTA meeting.* However, he complained, they made him look like the "big bad mean abusive husband." He then lashed out furiously at Heather's family, calling them all by different, vulgar, disparaging names, accusing them of all sorts of personal shortcomings and the most egregious and morally deplorable crimes imaginable.

The tirade Josh went on in this letter lasted for three,

single-spaced pages, ending with a final page of Josh saying how he "thought" that being "honest" with me throughout our correspondence would have generated some sort of loyalty on my part. He felt that I would not take sides or bring up certain aspects of his case that the court and media, by his estimation, had made into a big deal.

After I saw what you had to say in this letter you sent it is likely not [going to happen], he added.

The letter I had sent Josh after learning of the supposed sexual abuse was fairly straightforward:

> *I have a few final questions for you.*
> *Sexual abuse mentioned during your trial? You never talked about that with me. Please tell me about it. It is very important to your overall story and my readers understanding who you are and how your life turned out the way it did.*

While I had his attention, I thought I'd ask several additional questions about Emilia to help me understand the relationship between them a bit better:

> *Emilia has a "Free Emilia" Facebook page— what are your thoughts on that?*
> *One final question: Did Emilia ever mention to you that her father and uncle sexually abused her? If so, what did she tell you?*

And then I concluded with a few final thoughts:

> *I wanted to thank you for your honesty. It really comes through in the book. You won't like everything written about you, but let me say that your voice is loud and clear and all over this book!*

It was that one combination of words: *You won't like everything written about you. . . .* That observation rattled Joshua Fulgham to his core. No doubt about it. I could picture his mind racing after reading it. He began right there to project and predict the future. He felt like I had betrayed him—and we know how Josh deals with feelings of betrayal.

Concluding his letter to me, Josh asked if I could send him a few more copies of my books (I had sent him several already after he requested). He also said he'd be happy to answer any more of my questions, even if I didn't send him the books.

I drafted a response to Josh, signed the letter, sealed it in an envelope, but then I never sent it. Picking the letter up, walking it over to my office mail slot, I thought: *You know, this guy, despite any remorse he's shown and how open and honest he actually was with me, is a vicious murderer who took the mother of his children away from them—and not only made Heather Strong's entire life a miserable hell all those years she stayed with him, but then made the final moments she spent on this planet even worse. All of that happened before he violently killed her in a most painful manner, in addition to having her romantic rival standing by and helping out. . . .*

I took that letter, walked it back over to my files on the case and slipped it into a folder, where it sits today. *This son of a bitch doesn't* deserve *a response from me!* I thought.

CHAPTER 104

REGARDLESS OF WHAT Josh later wrote to me years after the penalty phase of his case concluded, the jury bought it during his trial and spared his life. In a total contradiction to the outcome of Emilia's case, the jury believed Josh Fulgham deserved to live out the remainder of his days behind bars.

It was a shock to nearly everyone close to this case, with the exception of Lenamon and Alavi, who were, by and large, the reigning champs at saving people from death row in the state of Florida. And, to be clear, Lenamon and Alavi never knew that Josh's cousin—if we believe Josh—had made all of that up. They conducted an investigation and used the results of it to fight for their client's life.

As the verdict was read, "sighs of relief," reported one media source, could be heard inside the courtroom.

No doubt Judy Chandler was among those breathing a bit easier as she learned her son would not be placed on death row.

Josh bowed his head after the verdict echoed throughout the courtroom. It was a comforting feeling, more than sheer relief or victory. Josh was thankful it was all over, for one. Two, obviously, he wouldn't be executed. Josh couldn't say it enough: He was sorry for what he had done. To that end, should a remorseful man, who had admitted his role in a murder, be condemned to death? Josh had wanted death long ago. Now, though, he was thankful to be alive.

For Terry Lenamon, his record was now nine out of eleven times he was able to convince a jury to save a life. Those aren't bad numbers if you consider the alternative.

Something that had bothered Lenamon going in was the lack of willingness on the state's part to cut a deal for life without parole. The way Lenamon saw it, the state could have avoided the entire cost, both financially and emotionally, of another murder trial and penalty phase.

"But, on the other hand, I understood why Brad King went forward," Lenamon commented. "He had to."

The state wound up not arguing for the judge the "override" the jury's recommendation. Soon the judge affirmed the jury's verdict and Josh was sentenced to two consecutive life terms. There was no chance he would ever see the four walls and oak desk of the state parole board or a door leading to the outside world. Josh claimed he was happy with the sentence. He believed he deserved it.

Walking out of court, Brad King disappointed reporters when he said he was not going to make himself available for comment.

What life in prison did in Josh's case, however, was open up a host of questions surrounding Emilia's death sentence. Emilia's new lawyer, a guy who had once represented Aileen Wuornos, came out swinging after Josh's verdict. Volusia County public defender Christopher Quarles was happy to see a jury in basically the same case vote for life, especially after a jury had voted for death under the same set of mitigating circumstances and, presumably, less evidence. It would prove to be a great point of contention to argue in front of the Florida Supreme Court.

"I like this development," Quarles told the *Ocala Star-Banner* on April 23, 2012. "I'm just not sure what I'm going to do with it. I think it's relevant. I think I've got some good issues already, but you can never have too many. . . ."

Quarles had practiced law for over thirty years. It was the first time during any of those three decades inside a courtroom, he explained, that he had ever seen two defendants in the same case receive such categorically different sentences.

After Josh's verdict came in and his life had been spared, Terry Lenamon had some rather strong opinions regarding the outcome of Emilia's case and Emilia's former defense team: "I truly believe that her lawyers did a horrible job. Had I represented her, she would have gotten life."

There was a sense of compassion in Lenamon's tone. He wasn't gloating or ruffling his feathers. It wasn't about that for the experienced lawyer. In fact, Lenamon respected those lawyers who had represented Emilia. But he was seriously concerned regarding the way Emilia's case had been tried from the beginning, and more so where the state's desire to seek the death penalty was concerned.

"For one," Lenamon added, "you never, *ever* put your client on the stand. Never!" Furthermore, he said, how could a mother of four, whose codefendant played an equal role in the murder, be sentenced to death for that same crime? Both Josh and Emilia had been found guilty of the same charges: first-degree murder and kidnapping. It made no sense to Lenamon. And he hoped, he said, that the appellate court would see the problems with Emilia's case, especially during the penalty phase, and reject that decision to put her on death row.

"Emilia Carr was sexually abused," Lenamon said passionately. "Sexually abused!" It should have been a major part of Emilia's death penalty phase argument. Lenamon had proved in Josh's case that what had allegedly happened to Josh as a child made the difference. In addition, in Emilia's case, the abuse was a matter of public *and* court record. Yet the abuse was never put front and center and ardently argued as a mitigating factor leading to her committing the crimes.

The major problem for Emilia, of course, was that she was still saying she'd had nothing whatsoever to do with the planning of or murdering of Heather Strong.

Zero responsibility.

Zero remorse.

Zero empathy.

How could any lawyer defend that?

CHAPTER 105

IT TOOK TWO years before the Florida Supreme Court would find the time to hear Emilia Carr's case. Christopher Quarles stood and argued Emilia's appeal first thing Monday morning, February 3, 2014. At this time, the state supreme court was made up of seven justices: Ricky Polston, Barbara Pariente, Fred Lewis, Peggy Quince, Charles Canady, Jorge Labarga and James Perry. Quarles was allowed, as was the attorney general's office (AGO), a time limit of thirty minutes to present his case. Quarles and James Purdy, a Seventh Judicial Circuit Court public defender, had meticulously prepared (and filed) what was a 108-page brief on Emilia's behalf. They cited dozens of case histories throughout the country relating to Emilia's. The brief was full of factual detail consisting of specifics relating to Emilia and how the jury had reached a guilty verdict.

In that brief, Emilia's lawyers focused mainly on Emilia's testimony and her account of what happened, which she had not varied from or been swayed to change since her conviction and sentence. Emilia stood behind the story that yes, she had repeatedly lied to Detectives Buie and Spivey, but she had only done it out of fear of losing her children and the intimidation she felt in the need to come up with information that the two investigators pushed her to find out.

The fact of the matter was that she had no involvement in Heather Strong's demise, the brief stated in the first paragraph.

The lawyers went on to write that Emilia "did not even see" Josh Fulgham on that night in question and they "never discussed" having Heather Strong killed.

As to Spivey's report detailing the account Emilia gave about witnessing Heather in the chair dead and Emilia feeling for a pulse: *Emilia never saw Heather in the trailer either dead or alive. In fact, she did not even know who had actually killed Heather.*

The next argument presented in the brief was interesting. In total contrast to the state's "theory," Quarles and Purdy contended that Emilia had never attempted to "blame" James Acome's friend and James Acome for Heather's death: *Rather, Carr was attempting to blame Josh Fulgham and his mother.*

This was a new revelation—it had never come up before this brief.

So, then, why had Emilia mentioned James and his buddy, to begin with?

She only referred to Acome and [his friend] during her conversation with Michelle Gustafson in an attempt to persuade Gustafson that she was on Josh Fulgham's side, the lawyers wrote.

The brief described a narrative history of Emilia's life and her role in the Yera family as its golden child—and how she had been subjected to a childhood of absolute shame and shuffling around from one home to the next. For the first time, the sexual abuse inside the Yera home was outlined and explained in detail: *At the age of five, Emilia Carr was removed from her home by state authorities, due to her father and grandfather's sexual abuse of her sibling. . . . The family [without Emilia's sibling] . . . reunited after they moved to Boardman. . . .*

Emilia's sister, the girl taken from the home, lived nearby with her grandmother. Throughout those early years of childhood, Emilia's sister "was taken for visits" over to the Boardman home: *Each time, she was repeatedly exposed to her perpetrator. . . .*

The doctor brought in to explain this during the penalty phase of Emilia's trial: *[He] explained that Emilia's family situation affected Emilia's development as a person.*

Emilia was ultimately "molested by both her grandfather and father," the lawyers argued: *She had early memories of the grandfather fondling her genitals and asking her to perform certain sex acts in exchange for money. As she developed, her breasts were routinely fondled by her father. She remembered showering with her father and being forced to wash his penis. The abuse finally stopped when Emilia stepped up to protect her little sister.*

Essentially, Quarles and Purdy had learned something from Terry Lenamon's win and how Lenamon was able to get jurors to understand that abused children without sexual boundaries, if the condition is left untreated, grow into adults who view the world in an entirely different manner. Betrayal and jealously are not mere emotions that can be dealt with by working through them, as most healthy people do; they are controlling aspects of the abuse victim's life, leading to a host of emotional problems.

The overall arching theme of their argument, after setting the stage with a defendant growing up in a terribly unhealthy and abusive environment, became clear when the lawyers wrote that Emilia's trial, based on what they now knew, was "unfair."

Why?

[The] State successfully convinced the judge to exclude relevant, critical evidence relating to Josh Fulgham's relative culpability in the murder . . . [and] by stretching the rules of evidence, the jury was not given an accurate picture of Josh Fulgham's more important role in the murder of his own wife, the brief stated.

Josh had carefully planned and carried out this murder,

dragging Emilia, kicking and screaming, into that diabolical plot against her will.

Equally as compelling was Quarles and Purdy's explanation of why the supreme court should toss the entire verdict out and start over: Emilia and Josh should have been tried together. *[Because Emilia's] trial was severed from her codefendant, evidence of Fulgham's actions was improperly introduced by the State at the guilt phase.*

Furthermore, *[Emilia couldn't] confront that evidence, thus violating her constitutional right to confrontation.*

Facing the justices, Quarles said, "I think the evidence is very clear that Joshua Fulgham is more culpable. He had the motive, he hatched the plan, he brought the victim to the scene of the crime, and it's *very* unfair [that] . . . he is serving a life sentence when she is sentenced to death."

There could be no truer argument in the face of the law at this stage.

Justice Charles Canady spoke up at one point, making a comment about Emilia having an IQ of at least 125, as opposed to Josh being "intellectually challenged." Canady wanted to know what Emilia's lawyers thought about that.

They stood firm on the ground of that accusation never being proven or established with any professional validity.

Then the AGO spoke, sticking to the core foundation of the state's case against Emilia: "In the actual commission of the crime, Miss Carr was heavily involved in what was going on," Assistant Attorney General Sara Macks explained.

That fact had been substantiated not only by the evidence, and some of what Josh and Emilia had talked about on the phone, but by Emilia's own admissions to Michelle Gustafson.

Period.

Macks went on to say that there was no doubt a premeditated plan between Emilia and Josh to begin a life together, and the means to that end was getting rid of the source of their problems: Heather.

Each convicted murderer could now go back and claim, "Oh no, we weren't planning to kill her, but only scare her. And all the conversation about getting rid of *'that bitch,'* well, that was just 'smack talk.'" But the end result here, despite how Emilia and Josh wanted to portray their roles, was that Heather was murdered, and both Emilia and Josh had admitted to playing a part in that murder before and after it took place.

Bringing up a valid point, Justice Jorge Labarga asked why the judges in both cases did not get together and wait until both verdicts had been reached before sentencing them after receiving *both* jury's recommendations.

Macks said there was a delay for over a year in Josh's trial.

Quarles argued that Emilia's participation in the crimes and her murder trial should have never been "a death case," to begin with, and should never have been tried as such.

The justices said it would be some time before their ruling.

CHAPTER 106

ACCORDING TO JOSH, although he said he "tossed all of the letters away" out of anger and resentment, Emilia kept trying to contact him after they were both sentenced and incarcerated.

I wondered how this was possible, seeing that prison-to-prison correspondence between prisoners is not allowed.

But Josh insisted that Emilia used a friend as a third party to accept and then redistribute the letters. Nevertheless, Josh wrote, *It just shows you that Emilia still tryes [*sic*] to keep in contact with me, and yet she tells people it is me who writes to her.* He wrote that *[I] respond to her letters sometimes just for entertainment.*

In several of those letters, Josh claimed, Emilia asked him to write to the governor and tell him that there was a "mother of four on death row that is innocent."

Josh thought this request was funny, writing to me, *There might be a mother of four . . . on death row that is innocent, but it is* not *Emilia. . . .*

The media made a "big deal" out of a letter Josh was able to get to a man who had been sentenced to life in prison. Josh reached out to the man after hearing how upset he was by the sentence. In his letter to that man, Josh said how living life behind bars wasn't so bad, actually, because you could get *Playboy* magazines, watch TV and get an MP3 player and download music, he pointed out.

The press and the SAO had a field day with this, claiming Josh was spitting in the face of the justice system and laughing at his sentence, thus mocking those jurors and the judge who had spared his life. And rightly so, it certainly seemed, with the wording Josh chose in that letter, he was gloating.

Josh told me that his intention was never to delight in the fact that he had beaten the system and escaped a death sentence. He was simply trying, as an elder con of sorts, to explain to this guy that there were rules and "dos and don'ts" associated with now being a member of the "chain gang."

I wanted to encourage him, Josh wrote. *That's all.*

It was Brad King, according to Josh, who facilitated that onslaught of media coverage over the letter.

Josh went on to explain that he had no idea why his case was chosen to be what he called a "big story" in the media at the time it was tried. He didn't understand why he was turned into, again, by his account, a "superstar" criminal. But he suspected that for prosecutor Brad King: *I gave him a case wrapped in a gold box, so he makes it looks like he done all this hard work to put a murderer away.*

Brad King did his job as a public servant and law enforcement officer of the court.

In the end, contradicting an earlier statement, Josh Fulgham said the jury in his case got it right: *I am wrong for what I done and I will pay for my part. . . .*

Regarding Emilia: *If [she] was innocent, I would not have her sit on death row or even in prison at all. But Emilia is just as guilty as me, if not more.*

There is one everlasting truth in this story, a slice of reality that cannot be denied: Despite the problems she had throughout her life, what she did personally, how she interacted with her family, the men she chose to have in her home, Heather Strong was an innocent victim, viciously murdered by two people she somewhat trusted not to take things as far as they did. Heather will never get a chance to soar like the eagle she dreamed herself to become one day. She will never be allowed to change her life's path. She will never have the chance to hold her babies and smell that sweet, rosy, cherubic, baby powder aroma of childhood on their skin. She will never have the opportunity to love again. And maybe the worst fear Heather had all her life is now a reality: Her children are without a mother, a woman who loved them more than they will ever know.

That is the tragedy here.

EPILOGUE

THERE'S SOMETHING TO be said for remorse, at least when it pertains to a convicted murderer admitting his or her role in the crime and sharing genuine sorrow. Remorse, in this manner, can only be defined as a deep regret for one's actions. Yet, within that regret, one who is truly remorseful must also express some form of repentance for the wrong he or she has committed. There has to be a sense of guilt and an understanding that a great moral wrong took place, and he or she is sorry for it and is willing to take responsibility.

It's rare that a writer/researcher/crime expert hears an ounce of true remorse from a murderer. I've hardly ever experienced a convicted murderer sharing true remorse, in some twenty-five nonfiction crime books that I have written. I have interviewed dozens of criminals and murderers, even serial killers. This is why, for me, when I hear it from the mouth of a convicted, admitted murderer, it not only stands out, but I need to take a step back and evaluate the validity of that so-called remorse.

Thus, the question presents itself: Is Joshua Fulgham truly remorseful? (We cannot evaluate Emilia because she still claims no involvement.)

I think this case proves that remorse, when it is genuine,

can go a long way in the feelings of a community put in a position to judge innocence and guilt, life and death. You show a jury you're truly remorseful, absolutely sorry for what you did—and let's be clear, I don't feel Josh actually did that as well as he could or should have—and the jury will give you the benefit of the doubt. Rightly so, they won't let you off the hook, but they might just allow you to live because, in the end, most people, when given the opportunity, will forgive.

I DO NOT yet have a Florida Supreme Court decision in Emilia's case at the time of this writing—and I feel bad for that as a writer publishing a book about this case. In my humble opinion, sticking my neck out, I believe after reading and studying her case, reviewing all of the documents and conducting interviews with many of the people involved, the Supreme Court will likely rule in Emilia's favor and kick the case back to the lower courts, where she will either fight for another trial (which she shouldn't) or accept a life sentence (which she should).[3]

There is a "Free Emilia Carr" Facebook page, with 177 members (as of this writing). The photos on the page tell a story. In the various photos of Emilia wearing orange johnnies, we see a seemingly sad, lonely, innocent-looking young woman in prison. At times, she's standing behind a cartoonish background or a white wall, sometimes smiling, sometimes looking coyly (maybe even sexily) into the camera lens. Sometimes she's posing as if for a fashion shoot, but also, more sobering, at times looking through those looking back, as there seems to be a devilish gaze absolutely present in Emilia's stare.

[3]Please Google "Emilia Carr, supreme court decision" when you're finished reading this book for an update—which might just be available by then.

Those are the many faces of Emilia Carr. She is an enigma. In listening to all of the prison phone calls between Emilia and Josh, you truly get a sense of who this woman is. Her true character comes through without Emilia trying. In my opinion, Emilia wanted Heather out of the picture so she could be with Josh, a man who—truth be told—never loved her and never would. Emilia felt Josh would protect her. She needed that. She felt Josh would take care of her. She needed that, too. And also that Josh would provide for her, an important element of this story from Emilia's point of view. Emilia was kind of bouncing through life at the time, not really knowing what would come next. Josh was Emilia's savior. It was one of the reasons, I believe, she purposely got pregnant with his child. I say *one* of the reasons, because the other was to throw that pregnancy in Heather's face. Heather was a woman Emilia clearly viewed as her rival and someone whom Emilia hated with an intense passion.

The "Free Emilia Carr" Facebook page is filled with stories of DNA exonerating the innocent and tales of men who died on death row before being able to prove their innocence. It's also filled with foul language and nasty remarks pointed at Emilia that, as of this writing, the webmaster has been cleaning up and deleting, encouraging posters to keep the discourse clean and civil.

Emilia's sister Milagro posted a rather simple, yet revealing, message back on July 19, 2013: *Help free my sister.*

Within those four simple, sad words lies another characteristic at the heart of this story from Emilia's perspective: her family.

I reached out to Emilia's Facebook community and asked for comments, interviews, etc., posted my e-mail address and encouraged anyone, within reason, to become a voice in this book.

Not one person contacted me.

Likewise, Emilia sent me phone numbers of family and friends. I left messages—on those numbers that were actually active; many were not—but nobody ever called me back.

Emilia initially said she did not want to talk to me. She referred to me as part of the vast conspiracy of evil media out in the world that had judged her and made her life hell by publishing erroneous accusations about her. I have yet to correspond with a convicted murderer who has not made this same allegation. (Josh did it in the end, too!) Emilia specifically mentioned a television series that profiled her case and said the show painted her as a wicked, twisted murderer. She said she wouldn't be a part of me doing the same thing.

But there was something I felt in that first letter from her. I could tell she wanted to continue talking to me, but she just needed a little prodding.

So I explained in a second letter that I have never been part of "the media." I'm not a reporter. And she shouldn't confuse me with being a member of any news group or media outlet. I told her I was a book writer/investigative journalist doing my own thing—answering only to my editor—and that if she wanted to speak about her case without "the media" getting in her way, this was her chance. Probably her last chance. I had offered the same to Josh. (I offer the same to any convicted murderer I write about.) I told Emilia I would not censor her story or turn it into something it's not. I explained how I thought there was more to her story than what had been reported. I called it a "much bigger story" than anybody was likely aware of by simply reading news accounts or watching crime television. In her first letter to me, Emilia had mentioned several instances from her case—she referred to them as "what the hell" moments—that did not make sense. She did not elaborate.

In my second letter to her, I wrote:

> *If you and your supporters want to reach a large audience with your message, I am offering that*

*opportunity. But it's up to you. If there are a lot of
"what the hell?" [moments] in your case, as you
say, I need you to point them out and comment on
them in the book.*

Finally I concluded by telling Emilia to reach out to all of
her supporters and to have as many as she'd like contact me.
I wanted their input. I wanted Emilia's complete story from
friends and family. I should note that as I got deep into my
research, within Emilia's background, I could not find any
history of violence or odd behavior or anything resembling
a woman who would go on to commit a murder with another
person. Generally, when you unpack a murderer's life, there
are shimmering (and often shivering) moments of a person
who you later could see killing another human being. "Aha"
moments, for certain. I'm not talking psychopath stuff, like
with serial killers or mass murderers, spree killers and the
like: maiming and torturing animals, setting fires, bullying
kids to the point of violence, stockpiling weapons in their
bedroom closet, YouTube manifestos and so on. But there
are glimpses into that later behavior, such as perpetrating
child abuse, violent spats with significant others, assault
charges, not being able to hold down jobs, even theft and a
total disregard for any type of authority. We see a lot of this
in Josh's case. Yet, as I looked into Emilia's background and
squeezed out the details of her life, I could not come up with
anything even remotely resembling that of a twisted, evil
person who had the wiring that would lead ultimately to the
circuitry of a killer. It's not unheard of, of course. But it is
rare not to find anything of significance.

In that second letter, I ended by saying:

*If you're interested, start by telling me about
yourself: where you grew up, your life as a
child/teen/young adult, and how you met Joshua.*

Let's start there. . . . Love to have you on board. If
not, I am sorry you feel that way and I wish you all
the best.

What did Emilia have to lose in talking to me? After all,
she was sitting on death row.

She wrote me back a three-page letter beginning a dialogue about her life story (all of which I included in this
book). But I never heard from her again.

Part of this might be because of her being on death row.
All of her letters to me were clearly opened, read, repackaged
in the same envelope and sent on to me (as were many of
Josh's). Emilia also mentioned that it took weeks to receive
my letters.

In a final missive, which I wrote on March 25, 2014, I
included the following:

I got your letter. Thanks. I'm glad you decided to
start writing. Josh is writing to me, also, so it's good
to have both of your voices heard. That's balance.

Because it takes so long for you to get my letters,
I will suggest that you do the following. Send me a
long letter with everything you need to say, so if I
run out of time on my deadline . . . at least I'll have
something. . . .

I wrote out several questions. Among them:

Tell me about Josh in as much detail as you can.
Tell me about your life together. How you met . . .
Tell me about Heather? Your feelings [for] her? Tell
me what happened. In your words, go through what
happened that day. . . . Tell me about your dealings
with police. Tell me how you feel now. How does it
feel to be on death row? Why do you think you got a

death sentence? . . . Also, encourage relatives and
friends to send me (my e-mail address is below)
photos and letters and anything that can help
explain/show my readers who you are.

As the end of June approached, ninety days later, I still
had not heard from Emilia. Nor had I heard from anyone in
her family, her friends or her supporters. Everyone from
Emilia's side was entirely silent.

Josh, of course, wrote many letters describing his life,
from his point of view, in great detail, save for mentioning
that sexual abuse.

So I wrote back to him, asking about it—and we've already
seen what his response was.

Josh also said he hadn't spoken to Michelle, his sister,
since his arrest. And this troubled him. He asked me to reach
out to Michelle and tell her, "I love her and miss her very
much. . . ."

Emilia was convicted, I believe, on the conversation
Michelle courageously recorded inside her car on the afternoon Buie and Spivey sat nearby and listened. That was the
day the state's case was made and a potential life sentence
turned into a death sentence.

In the end, I hope Emilia is booted from death row and
placed in a maximum-security facility for women for the
remainder of her life. That would be, in my personal view, a
just sentence. I don't say this out of religious beliefs or
personal thoughts regarding the death penalty; I say this
because it is the only just sentence for Emilia. If any one of
the two deserved the death penalty in this case, my belief is
it should have been Josh. For my money, there was clear
intent and premeditation on Josh's part. I don't believe one
or the other played a more violent or bigger role in Heather's
murder. They were both equally responsible. I do think,
however, Josh had a plan while behind bars to pay Heather
back for what she and Ben did to him. That all being said, it

would still be hard for me to vote death, had I been on the jury, for a man (or woman) who had been abused sexually the way Josh (supposedly) and Emilia (definitely) had been. Once childhood sexual abuse enters the picture, accountability for later actions has to be viewed under an entirely different microscope.

What's interesting to me is that as soon as I mentioned to either Josh or Emilia that I was talking to the other, Emilia stopped corresponding with me and Josh snapped. That alone says a lot about them.

I WOULD LIKE to end by sharing some words about Heather Strong. Here was a woman who worked her ass off as a waitress to take care of her children. Unfortunately, she had a shithead for a boyfriend/husband, a man who knew the difference between being responsible for his family, taking care of them, and just being a deadbeat drug abuser who blamed society for the shit life he *created* for himself and everyone around him. Heather kept trying to dig out from underneath the dysfunction she often found herself facing, day in and day out, when she was with Josh. When she finally found a good, honest man—Ben McCollum— who loved her and her kids, a man who wanted to take care of her and give her and the kids a normal, healthy life, Heather was emotionally ill-equipped to deal with that sort of love. As a result, she did what she always did and went back to Josh, where, as unhealthy and dysfunctional as that relationship always was, it provided that all-too-familiar (and tragic) codependency of comfort that kept Heather returning—in order to feel normal. True, honest love, like that which she shared with Ben, was not something Heather was used to or could handle. It was uncomfortable. She had no idea how to deal with it, accept it or enjoy it. Her life was a loud roller-coaster ride with Josh. When she met up with the quiet comfort Ben gave her, it was too overwhelming.

That is the lesson here for any female reading this book and realizing she might be in a similar situation. Please, I beg of you: Don't allow Heather's murder to have taken place in vain—learn from it. Get out of that unhealthy, dangerous and violent relationship and stay the hell out! Run as far away as possible. Remember, if he has ever shown you who he truly is, please believe him—because that's who he is. He will not change, despite what he promises.

ACKNOWLEDGMENTS

THE MOST GRATITUDE I can ever extend, perpetually there alongside my heartfelt appreciation, has to go to my readers. You continue to support my work and I am humbled by your continued presence every time a new book is published. I say this in every book, but I am forever at a loss for words when trying to say thank you, because nothing I can say is, in my opinion, enough. My readers are the most important part of what I do.

I also want to extend a big thanks to the fans of *Dark Minds* on Investigation Discovery: I am honored by your dedication and willingness to watch the series and support it. That work behind the series takes so much out of me emotionally, to have such a large and dedicated audience, week after week, makes me believe the message is being heard.

My publisher, Laurie Parkin (who retired in 2014 after forty years in the biz!), and the entire team at Kensington Publishing Corp. deserve my utmost respect and gratitude for the passion and confidence each one of them puts into the books I write. These are great people who love what they do. To be part of Kensington's continued success as an independent publisher is a blessing. I am lucky. I tell myself this every morning as I awake and get to work.

As I was finishing work on this book, I met Norma Perez-Hernandez, my editor's personal assistant, at a publishing event in New York City one early spring evening in 2014. Norma and I had a nice conversation and she enthusiastically praised my work, which I was greatly humbled by. I wanted to say thank you to Norma for not only being so excited about books in general, but for taking the time to stop and talk about my work and build so much excitement about it around the Kensington offices. I'm grateful for having a cheerleader like Norma in the business, excited about my books, championing them within the day-to-day grind of the publishing industry—but I feel blessed that I was able to meet Norma and say thanks for the encouragement and support!

I would like also to give my sincere appreciation to everyone at Investigation Discovery and Beyond Productions involved in making *Dark Minds,* the best (nonfiction) crime show on television. I've said this before many times, but it also needs repeating: It takes an army of devoted people to produce a television series. Among those I want to personally thank: *Dark Minds* show runner and series producer, by far the best in the biz at what he does, Andrew "Fazz" Farrell, who has been a mentor and blessing in my life. Likewise, each of the following, in his or her own way, has taught me everything I know about making quality-grade, great nonfiction television: Alex Barry, Colette "Coco" Sandstedt, John Mavety, Peter Heap, Mark Middis, Toby Prior, Peter Coleman, Derek Ichilcik, Jared "Jars" Transfield, Jo Telfer, Claire Westerman, Milena Gozzo, Cameron Power, Katie Ryerson, Inneke Smit, Pele Hehea, Jeremy Peek, Jeremy Adair, Geri Berman, Nadine Terens, Samantha Hertz, Lale Teoman, Hayden Anderson, Savino (from Onyx Sound Lab in Manchester, Connecticut), David O'Brien, Ra-ey Saleh, Nathan Brand, Rebecca Clare, Anthony Toy, Mark Wheeler, Mandy Chapman, Jenny O'Shea, Jen Longhurst, Anita Bezjak, Geoff Fitzpatrick, John Luscombe, Debbie Gottschalk,

Eugenie "Jeannie" Vink, Sucheta Sachdev, Sara Kozak, Kevin Bennett, Jane Latman and Henry Schleiff.

For my entertainment lawyer/business manager, Matthew Valentinas, a warm thank-you for embarking on this journey with me. I believe Matthew and I were destined to meet and connect. I appreciate Matthew's passion for this business, inherent knowledge of television and film, and desire to see me succeed.

I would also like to thank Deb Allen and everyone at Jupiter Entertainment for helping me with the Carr/Fulgham case, encouraging me to look deeper into it, and providing me with documents and photos.

Terry Lenamon, Johnny Strong, Donald Buie, Brian Spivey, Staci Winston, Kae Charman, Patricia Ardovino, Captain Linda Vyse, Ben McCollum, and all of my anonymous sources, I appreciate the time and attention you gave to me while I worked on this important project. There are so many others, who asked me not to mention their names. I will respect that request and just give an overall thanks to them all.

I also want to mention that on June 9, 2014, Ben McCollum died in a "one-vehicle accident in Orange Lake." Ben was thirty-seven years old. His obituary said he was "talented, outgoing, helpful to those in need and a good friend." This news was shocking. I had been talking to Ben about creating a reality series based on his garage and his life. We lost touch. All indications, as the sections of this book about Ben implied, prove that Ben McCollum was a wonderful person and respected member of his community—I am sure he is and will be greatly missed. This news made me sad. I want to express my deepest condolences to anyone that knew and loved Ben, especially his family.

I cannot thank either Josh or Emilia for their participation because they murdered a human being and I detest that crime (and them) at the highest level.

We all need to thank Heather Strong for her courage to stay with this jackass as long as she did for the sake of her children. My only regret in looking at this case was that she didn't leave long before he killed her. Going back and looking at the trajectory of their lives and how it played out, I could almost see murder coming down the road. It was inevitable. I am sorry Heather never saw it herself—though, part of me thinks she probably did.

Lastly, my family: Mathew, Jordon, Regina and April, whose dedication to her schoolwork and sports continues to be a true inspiration. I am lucky to have such wonderful people in my life. I never take this blessing for granted.

Don't miss the next exciting real-life thriller by
M. William Phelps

ONE BREATH AWAY

Coming from Kensington Publishing Corp. in 2016!

Keep reading for a preview excerpt . . .

CHAPTER 1

IT WAS ONE of those telephone calls in the middle of the night we all fear. The kind that jolts your heart, puts a pit in your gut, startling you awake. Adrenaline pumps through you the moment you open your eyes.

Somebody has died!

Quickly roused from REM sleep by that familiar ring, she had no idea that everything, as she knew it, was about to change. Nor would their lives ever be the same again, once she got out of bed and put the phone to her ear.

"Hello? What is it?" She could barely get the words out.

That time of night, hell, you'd *expect* bad news on the other end of the line.

The day preceding the telephone call, however, had started out like any other Sunday in forty-year-old Rachel Robidoux's life. Rachel woke up at her usual five in the morning to get ready for work. It was October 24, 2010, the weather rather balmy for this time of the year in St. Petersburg, Florida. As Rachel opened the door to leave, a wall of humid, tropical, almost wet, 75-degree morning air hit her in the face.

Within Pinellas County, St. Petersburg is a rather large city, a population of about a quarter million, give or take. With Tropicana Field downtown, home to Major League

Baseball's Tampa Bay Rays, St. Pete, as locals call it, still holds on to that resort-town feel its founder had intended back in 1875 when the city was born.

Rachel Robidoux worked at Denny's on Thirty-Fourth Street, North, downtown. She'd been there for well over a decade. Normally, on Sundays, Rachel worked the day shift: seven to four. To this mother of five, although she'd gotten used to it by now, St. Pete might as well have been New York City, Rachel herself having been born and raised (mostly) in a one-stop-sign, one-intersection, everybody-knows-everybody, small New England town.

As the end of her shift on that Sunday approached, Rachel took a call from one of her five daughters, Ashley McCauley, who had turned seventeen that past April.

"You want to go to Crescent Lake Park with Grandma after you get out?"

This sounded like a good time, Rachel thought. "I'll pick you two up soon," she said.

Crescent Lake Park is in an area of St. Pete where families and lovers and kids hang out on those seemingly endless, perfect Florida days, with skies that warm robin's-egg blue color. People flock there and enjoy the ducks and geese and swans, as well as the company they keep. Rachel needed this comforting space in her life. Not that things had been chaotic or all that difficult lately, having been through some rather extremely tough times in her life, same as just about every working-class family in the country. However, she'd had some issues over the past few years with her oldest daughter, Jennifer "Jen" Mee. Jen had turned nineteen in July, and her life, as Rachel later put it, had not gone along a trajectory Rachel and her husband, Chris, Jennifer's stepfather, would have liked. Jen was Rachel's firstborn, a child from a failed relationship when Rachel was twenty-one. In fact, Jen was just eighteen months old when Rachel met Chris, Ashley three months old—their other children, Kayla, Destiny and McKenzie, Rachel and Chris had together.

As far as the oldest girls were concerned, however, Chris Robidoux had always considered himself their father.

A little over a year ago, Jennifer had moved out of the house and on her own some weeks before her eighteenth birthday. Before that, she had one foot out, anyway, often staying with one friend for a month, or babysitting and staying with other friends for a few weeks here and there, maybe sleeping at a motel or on a park bench. All this happened after Jennifer had garnered international fame in the days surrounding January 23, 2007, for experiencing a bout with the hiccups that lasted for about five weeks. Still, with Jennifer moving out and "changing," as Rachel liked to say, it wasn't the major problem between Rachel and her daughter. For Rachel, it was more of the people who flocked to Jennifer after her star rose, on top of the guys Jennifer had been dating now for what was about four years.

"Thugs," Rachel called them.

Although Rachel and Jennifer spoke as much as two to three times per week, their conversations weren't like they used to be. Definitely not the personal talk mothers and daughters have. These days, Rachel understood (though she later admitted some denial on her part), Jennifer was shielding parts of herself and her chosen lifestyle. Just a look at Jennifer's Myspace page, back when that gulf between the mom and her daughter began to grow, had given Rachel and Chris an idea of where Jen was headed.

My love is nt a game im real n dnt wnt a fake lien cheaten azz nigga.

"I guess I should have known with the signs," Rachel recalled, "but I didn't. Jen was into some 'activities' and later she [said she] was ashamed of it all."

Rachel had no idea the extent to which Jen was involved in that street life, ripping and running with a group of hard-boiled, seasoned ruffians and tough street kids her own age. Jen had become somebody she had actually once said she despised. Maybe some naiveté existed on Rachel's part, or just a mother struggling to keep up with a middle-class lifestyle and still having three young kids at home, but Rachel lost that close touch with Jen. As they drifted, she felt her daughter was old enough to begin carving out her own life, make her own mistakes and take responsibility. Besides that, Chris and Jen had been at odds for a long time now, butting heads like rams. Both Rachel and Chris knew they couldn't change Jennifer, or tell her how to live. They had been through so much during Jen's hiccup period—both parents were tired, frustrated and ready to move on.

CHAPTER 2

DOWN AT CRESCENT Lake Park, after Rachel had stopped and picked up her mother and Ashley, they sat and enjoyed the early evening. They fed the ducks, talked and caught up on each other's lives. That early-morning humidity and warmth had turned into a scorching afternoon sun. During the week, Rachel lived at her mother's house just outside downtown St. Pete. Rachel and Chris and the kids had a house about ninety minutes out of town in the north, so it was more feasible and less expensive if Rachel stayed with her mother and father during the workweek. Chris collected disability—a stay-at-home dad, watching the kids, tending to the household chores. He had suffered several ailments—some psychological, others medical. The situation of Chris being home with the kids had been by design in some ways, Rachel said. The decision was made after an incident some years back that greatly disturbed the entire family's trust in anyone else being around their children.

Throughout that afternoon, Rachel had called Jennifer several times. She hadn't been able to reach her. Rachel, of course, wanted Jen to join them at the park. But for some reason, Jen wasn't responding to her phone calls, texts, or voice mails. And although Jen had changed and lived what Rachel and Chris saw as an unhealthy and dangerous lifestyle, they were not estranged. They disagreed about things, but they always talked and saw each other when they could. Not answering her phone and not calling back was out of Jen's character.

"I was actually upset that I couldn't get hold of Jennifer on that day," Rachel remembered.

Where the heck is she?

Something happened during Rachel's break at work earlier that morning that had upset Rachel, especially now as she thought back on it later in the day.

Jennifer had called. "Mom?"

"Yeah? Jennifer, hi. How are you?"

Jennifer knew her mother had had surgery for a recurring cist a few weeks prior and had been in a lot of pain. She was taking powerful pain medication for it.

"Do you have any pain pills left from your operation?" Jennifer asked.

Rachel was alarmed. "Pain pills? Why would you need *pain* pills, Jennifer?"

"Mom, listen . . . Lamont got hurt. He's in a lot of pain." Lamont Newton was Jennifer's most recent boyfriend; she had been dating the twenty-two-year-old St. Pete native for the past several months. Lamont seemed like a "nice guy," Rachel said. He was five feet nine inches tall, in great physical shape at 165 pounds. Lamont sported Bob Marley–type dreads down across his shoulders, bushy eyebrows and clean-shaven facial skin. He generally had a calm disposition; he was polite. As Rachel saw it, Lamont was an excellent alternative and the polar opposite to Jen's previous boyfriend—a pants-down-to-his-knees, boxer-shorts-showing, ball cap tipped to one side, "yo" this, "yo" that, spot-on "thug" and violent abuser—a man who had beaten Jen on more than one occasion. In contrast, at least on the surface, Lamont came across as a guy who was entirely into Jennifer as a partner—not after what he could get from her.

"We wanted her to date within her own race," Rachel

explained at the risk of coming across as bigoted, claiming she and her husband were anything but racists. "Yet, Jen said she had chosen colored men to date because she had lost faith in—and wanted nothing to do with—white men altogether." Her decision had stemmed specifically from a very difficult period in her life when Jen was a child.

"No," Rachel said to the request for pain pills. "Tell him to go to the hospital, Jennifer. I need my medication."

Jennifer didn't sound frantic or fazed. However, Rachel was quick to point out: "She didn't sound normal, either. More anxious—I felt like something was wrong, but I was clueless."

That request had come from Jen as though she was simply calling and asking her mother for some pain meds to help her boyfriend work through a back issue. And when she couldn't get the pills, well, that was it. They said their good-byes to one another—will talk to you later—and hung up.

But something was indeed wrong with Jennifer. Rachel had no idea that within a few hours after that phone call, their lives would take a turn none of them ever saw coming.